ARTS AND CRAFTS ARCHITECTURE ACROSS AMERICA

ARTS AND CRAFTS ARCHITECTURE ACROSS AMERICA

Maureen Meister

Yale University Press New Haven and London

Publication of this book has been aided by a grant from the Wyeth Foundation for American Art Publication Fund of CAA.

Published with support from the Fund established in memory of Oliver Baty Cunningham, a distinguished graduate of the Class of 1917, Yale College, Captain, 15th United States Field Artillery, born in Chicago September 17, 1894, and killed while on active duty near Thiaucourt, France, September 17, 1918, the twenty-fourth anniversary of his birth.

yalebooks.com/art

Designed by Leslie Fitch; with additional design by Tina Henderson, Miko McGinty Inc.
Jacket designed by Rita Jules, Miko McGinty Inc.
Set in Minion and Freight Sans by Tina Henderson, Miko McGinty Inc.
The typeface used for the book title, chapter titles, and author byline is LTC Kennerley, which was designed by Frederic W. Goudy in 1911.
Printed in China by Regent Publishing Services Limited

Library of Congress Control Number: 2025930618
Authorized Representative in the EU Details: Easy Access System Europe, Mustamäe tee 50, 10621 Tallinn, Estonia, gpsr.requests@easproject.com
ISBN 978-0-300-28102-6

A catalogue record for this book is available from the British Library.

10 9 8 7 6 5 4 3 2 1

Jacket illustrations: (*front*) Leila Ross Wilburn, Carr House, Atlanta, 1919, image provided by Atlanta Fine Homes, Sotheby's International Realty, photograph by Henry R. Hibbert; (*back*) top image: Ralph Radcliffe Whitehead and Bolton Brown, White Pines, Byrdcliffe, Woodstock, New York, 1903, photograph by David Feigenbaum; middle image: Marion Mahony, Adolph Mueller House, Decatur, Illinois, 1910–11, photograph by Randy von Liski; bottom image: Mary and Ernest Blumenschein House (Blumenschein Museum), Taos, New Mexico, 1919–20 and 1931, photograph by Jamie Zucek, from FLICKR.
Frontispiece: Detail of figure 5.5.

Contents

Preface

Time and again when I was working on this book, *Arts and Crafts Architecture across America,* I was thinking about you, the person who would be reading it, and thinking about the ideas I want to share. You're the person I have cared about most in undertaking this ambitious endeavor. I have envisioned you as a college student, maybe nineteen years old, enrolled in a course on the history of American architecture. Or perhaps you're an architect who picked up this book for evening reading. Or maybe you're a traveler, and you recently visited Buffalo or Minneapolis or Pasadena, where you toured a historic house museum, heard about the Arts and Crafts movement, and want to know more about it. Or maybe you're an architectural historian, a specialist on some aspect of my subject. Whoever you are, the fact that you have decided to start reading these pages says something meaningful about you. You're the kind of person who is curious about architecture and curious about history. In all likelihood, you're also curious about the architecture and history of the community where you live. Welcome! I'm one of those people, too.

Writing this book has been a culminating experience for me, one that began many years ago when my husband and I moved to Winchester, Massachusetts, a commuter rail suburb near Boston. Shortly after I embarked upon a career as an art and architectural history professor, I became a member of my town's historical commission, which led to my research into local buildings. At one point, I was tracking down information about an architect who had lived in town early in the twentieth century, and I discovered that he had been a business partner with a man who was an architect of more than local significance. This man was H. Langford Warren, a resident of Cambridge who attained prominence during the late nineteenth century for founding and developing the architecture program at Harvard. In 1897 he helped establish Boston's Society of Arts and Crafts and would serve as its longtime president. I turned my attention to Warren and published a monograph on him in 2003.

A few years later, I widened my view to investigate the careers of several Boston architects who promoted an Arts and Crafts ethos in New England during the first decades of the twentieth century. They were close colleagues with the movement's proponents in England and understood the movement's principles, which encouraged designing buildings based on vernacular traditions, using native materials, and collaborating with artisans to enhance architectural works. Significantly, the architects in Boston interpreted Arts and Crafts ideas in their projects in styles that were altogether different from the Craftsman bungalows and Prairie School houses that historians have long associated with the American Arts and Crafts movement. Oriented toward England, the Boston architects promoted the view that the styles that were most appropriate for New England were English Gothic Revival, Anglo-Colonial Revival, and an English Arts and Crafts style that's derivative of medieval architecture yet quite abstract. The buildings are beautiful—simple and restrained, with picturesque rooflines, richly textured and colored natural materials, and exquisite ornament. In 2014 I published *Arts and Crafts Architecture: History and Heritage in New England,* and after that, I shifted my attention to a different topic entirely.

Just as I was getting started, I was invited to prepare an annotated bibliography on architecture and the Arts and

Crafts movement for *Oxford Bibliographies in Architecture, Planning, and Preservation.* The offer was intriguing, and I reshuffled my priorities to make the commitment. This digital resource, edited by Kevin D. Murphy, came out in 2020. Although I was familiar with a great number of the works that I ultimately included, I found that preparing the bibliography was illuminating and emboldening. No one had written a scholarly book on the influence of the Arts and Crafts movement on American architecture, and I could see how I might paint the big picture. I thus set my sights on writing this volume.

My hope for the book is to make the case that an Arts and Crafts outlook was pervasive in the United States at the turn of the twentieth century, resulting in buildings that vary stylistically yet are united by the philosophy that gave rise to them. The architects who designed the buildings I discuss valued regional cultural and architectural traditions; a love of nature, including local landscapes and building materials; and fine craftsmanship. These buildings display a range of styles, from Tudor Revival to Prairie School to Spanish Revival. Conversant with the English theorists, many of the architects expressed a moral concern for the condition of the worker in the face of industrialization. They also held strong opinions about how Americans should live—which meant how Americans built houses, churches, and educational buildings. The architects' moralizing and assertions, certainties and inconsistencies, sometimes made me cringe and sometimes made me laugh. They weren't timid about their views.

When organizing my material, I might have structured it around a sampling of well-known architects. Alternatively, I might have framed it around important centers of the American Arts and Crafts movement, which would have included Boston, Chicago, and San Francisco. Instead I elected to write chapters about the country's major regions, allowing me to show how architects responded to the Arts and Crafts respect for regional history, vernacular building traditions, and natural landscapes. I delved into ways by which the American states have been grouped and named as regions due to their similar geographic characteristics, cultural history, and political history. Some groupings that I settled upon are pretty standard, such as New England and the Pacific Northwest. On the other hand, I concluded that states such as New York, Illinois, and California warranted chapters of their own, given that the Arts and Crafts movement had a tremendous influence on the people and places within their borders. The book begins in New England, where leading proponents of Arts and Crafts principles formed close relationships with leaders in England. The next chapters move south, followed by chapters on the Midwest and Southwest, to end on the Pacific coast. I have made a point of connecting the chapters to each other by calling attention to recurring themes and by highlighting the people whose impact extended beyond their home regions. At the same time, I realize that the book will interest readers who peruse just a single chapter, and therefore, I have written each chapter to stand on its own.

As my research moved forward, I kept an eye out for historical developments in the United States that intersected with Arts and Crafts concerns that began in England, were transferred to this country, and influenced American buildings. One of the most significant developments, frequently related to the American Arts and Crafts movement, was the massive influx of immigrants into the nation's largest cities, leading to widespread poverty. Another development was the struggle of laboring men and women that accompanied the growth of factories. I also could see how the emergence of national parks in this country would pertain to my subject. I knew early on that I would write about all of these topics.

My research revealed some aspects of the period to which I hadn't given prior thought but that turned out to be relevant to my project. For example, I hadn't expected to read so often about tuberculosis, its impact on the architects and clients I would discuss, and the construction of retreats where Americans sought to recover from it. I also hadn't expected to encounter so many women as clients, adding to the presence of a few women who were architects and building designers. Above all, while I realized that the country's rail systems were expanding rapidly, I was impressed by how much the new links influenced the architects, not only by providing them with opportunities to build, but also by enabling them to meet their colleagues in person. I frequently noted how well the architects kept up with each other.

By the time I began writing the chapter about California, I felt as if I really had traversed the North American continent. Childhood memories of my family driving across the country came back to me. Augmenting these recollections were the hours I spent online looking at satellite views, passing over rivers, plains, and mountains. After peering down on a subject, I scrutinized street views to clarify my understanding of a building's physical context. I also watched more than a few online videos posted by historic sites, museums, and churches.

There was a social aspect to my investigation as well. Much as I have enjoyed becoming acquainted with the long-gone characters in this story, I have been delighted by conversations and email exchanges with some very-much-alive people from all parts of the country, people who have made this book possible. Too often, they labor without much glory. These special people, both professionals and volunteers, research and document the buildings and histories of their communities. They love to study local architecture, speak and write about it, and vigorously defend it. They are employees and volunteer members of historical societies, educational institutions, churches, and government agencies who share your curiosity and mine.

Librarians have been indispensable for my work, and I relied especially on the staff at the Boston Athenaeum and the Winchester Public Library. Their patience and good cheer have carried me forward. I also want to recognize the help I received from employees at the Wellesley College Art Library. Sometimes, when I was stuck, I received exactly the information that I needed from them. I'm grateful to all of these individuals.

I also wish to express my appreciation to the scholarly and specialized societies that have been invaluable to me in my career. They include the Society of Architectural Historians (SAH), the College Art Association, the Victorian Society in America, and the William Morris Society in the United States. Through the SAH, it has been my privilege to meet and befriend scholars whose publications and conference tours have laid the groundwork for my writing this book. These authorities include Theodore (Ted) Bosley, Beverly K. Brandt, Mark Alan Hewitt, Richard Longstreth, Jeffrey Karl Ochsner, James F. O'Gorman, and Jack Quinan. At SAH programs, I met the late Jean France, David and Patricia Gebhard, and Robert Winter. I wish I could speak to them now. Anne Bird, serving the membership of the SAH, has graciously assisted me over the years, and I was deeply touched when she jumped in when I needed contacts for a building in the book. My membership in the New England chapter of the SAH led to my meeting the late Cheryl Robertson, another Arts and Crafts scholar. And through the SAH chapter, I met Roger G. Reed, a valued colleague.

My particular interest in the Arts and Crafts movement was reinforced by my experience in serving on the board of directors of the William Morris Society in the United States. This small but mighty organization has introduced me to inspirational colleagues including Florence Boos, Jane Carlin, Morna O'Neill, Michael Robertson, and Anna Wager.

In the past year, my thoughts about this project have been stimulated by discussions with Elizabeth Macaulay, a scholar of the ancient world who has written about the interpretation of ancient architecture in New York City. Reading her draft manuscript about the revival of ancient architecture at American world's fairs, from the 1890s through 1915, provoked me to challenge myself and think hard about my subject, a complement of hers.

For a volume of this sort, the photographers are key contributors, and many of them took photographs specifically for this publication. Their willingness to respond to my requests has been extraordinary. I want to mention James Russiello in particular, who went far out of his way to help me. To all of the photographers, I offer my thanks.

Several people can claim this book as theirs. I have been grateful for the enthusiasm and ongoing effort of Katherine Boller, editorial director for the Art and Architecture division at Yale University Press. I've also benefited from the support of Elizabeth Searcy, editorial and production assistant at the press. Turning a manuscript into a book is no mean feat, and to accomplish that, I was delighted to work with Alison Hagge and Sarah Henry. For their contributions to the book, I also thank Leslie Fitch, Tina Henderson, Laura Hensley, Rita Jules, Dave Luljak, and Kati Woock. I also wish to acknowledge the scholars who read my manuscript and commented on it in peer reviews.

Finally, like most authors, I relied on my family for encouragement through the course of this project. My younger son, Stephen, good-naturedly engaged in conversations about my discoveries, even though the subject of my passion is not his. My older son, Peter, also asked about my progress, and when I asked him to take photographs for "the book," he promptly agreed. Little did he know then that he would need to make several trips in order to capture some of the more challenging images.

My most heartfelt thanks go to my husband, David Feigenbaum, the person who lived with this book over five years, heard about my work nightly, and never tired of my reports. A talented photographer himself, he took the New England photographs for me. Then, when I asked him if he could help me obtain the remaining photographs—no small task—he said yes without hesitation. When he started to realize the huge commitment he had made, he cheerfully kept moving forward. When he contacted photographers, he was pleased to encounter people who shared our fascination with buildings. David is curious about architecture and curious about history—like me and, I imagine, like you.

Introduction

Early Light

After the final stretch of track was laid, the president of the Southern Pacific Railroad stepped forward and the crowd let out a cheer. Tightening his grip on a shiny silver hammer, Charles Crocker struck a golden spike to secure the last rail, establishing train travel between Los Angeles and San Francisco, connecting Southern California to the rest of the United States. The celebration occurred in Lang, near the Santa Clara River, on September 5, 1876, seven years after the more famous ceremony at Promontory Summit, Utah, marking the completion of the nation's first transcontinental railroad.[1]

In the aftermath of the Civil War, Americans were on the move. Many were seeking work and business opportunities, some were pursuing sunshine and better health, and others were escaping the hectic pace of office jobs and city life. As the construction of rail lines continued and travel became easier, the bonds of the nation were strengthened, in reality and in the minds of the people.

During the closing years of the nineteenth century, the United States was experiencing dramatic growth by many measures. Millions of impoverished immigrants arrived on American soil to become new citizens at a time when the ranks of the middle and upper-middle classes were expanding. Factories multiplied, as did tall office buildings. Tenements multiplied, too, while villages and towns near cities evolved into suburbs. Against this background, the Arts and Crafts movement gathered momentum, its ideas about architecture and the allied arts spread by architects, artisans, and writers.

ARRIVAL IN THE UNITED STATES

Mid-nineteenth-century England was where the Arts and Crafts movement began, and its tenets reached the United States almost immediately. By the 1870s, Arts and Crafts concepts were attracting a following, and by the end of the century, formally organized groups were promoting the movement's ideals. As in England, architects joined craft workers to found membership societies. Boston, Chicago, and San Francisco became the country's earliest and most important centers of advocacy, while significant Arts and Crafts activities took place in Philadelphia, Detroit, and Minneapolis. Also like the English, American visionaries built small communities where residents pursued the arts and craftsmanship. Although such places never became common, Roycroft in western New York and Rose Valley near Philadelphia

FIGURE 0.1. Philip Webb, Red House, Bexleyheath, Kent, England, 1859–61.

REFORM-MINDED ARCHITECTS

Through the latter half of the nineteenth century, England's medieval past stimulated the imaginations of reform-minded architects.[11] Webb pursued the direction that he began at Red House, building country houses that were large but unpretentious, designed with gables and towers. He advised his clients on decorating with Morris products, as at Clouds House (1877–86) in East Knoyle, Wiltshire.[12] Richard Norman Shaw (1831–1912) aimed for unpretentiousness, too. Like Morris and Webb, he spent time in Street's office. After embarking upon a study of vernacular houses, Shaw developed an Old English style, including tall chimneys, half-timbering, and banks of leaded glass windows in his residential work, notably at Leyswood (1867–69) in Groombridge, Sussex. He also brought Morris's firm on board for interior decoration.[13] Yet another member of the early generation of architects linked with Morris was George F. Bodley (1827–1907). His church of St. Michael and All Angels (1860–61), Brighton, provided Morris's company with its first commission—a request for stained glass. In his subsequent church projects, Bodley became known for using bold massing based on Perpendicular sources.[14]

Several progressive architects and craft workers formed guilds and societies, taking their cues from Morris and notions about medieval shops that were more than a little idealized. In 1884 pupils in Shaw's office, including William R. Lethaby (1857–1931), established the Art Workers' Guild to encourage collaboration between architects and artisans.[15] Morris soon joined them. Promoting the creations of the craft worker was a guild priority, leading members to found the Arts and Crafts Exhibition Society in 1887. A year later, they sponsored their first show, held in London, which introduced the term *Arts and Crafts* as the name of the emerging movement. Another progressive thinker was C. R. Ashbee (1863–1942), who lived at Toynbee Hall, a London settlement house, while he was apprenticing with Bodley. In the course of serving poor East End residents, Ashbee directed a Ruskin reading group, and in 1888 he started a school and organization that became the Guild of Handicraft. Under his leadership, workers were trained in craft production, and their wares were sold at a London outlet. Eventually Ashbee led the group to the village of Chipping Campden in the Cotswolds, where the community struggled until the guild dissolved in 1908.[16]

The high regard for England's Gothic past, the emphasis on craftsmanship, and a respect for simplicity continued to shape the country's domestic architecture at the turn of the twentieth century. At the same time, Arts and Crafts designs became increasingly abstracted, with just a little half-timbering or an overhanging second story hinting at a building's medieval ancestry. C. F. A. Voysey (1857–1941) took this reductive approach, as at The Orchard (1899), Chorleywood, Hertfordshire, distinguished by two austere, front-facing gables (fig. 0.2). A member of the Art Workers' Guild, he designed furniture, wallpaper, and carpets.[17] M. H. Baillie Scott was another architect who created houses in a freestyle manner and, like Voysey, designed furnishings and decoration.[18]

By the close of the century, classicism had become irresistible, even for architects committed to Arts and Crafts principles. Neo-Georgians, including Ernest Newton (1856–1922), determined that England's vernacular architecture of the eighteenth century was sufficiently native for them to refer to it in their projects.[19] Having been a founder of the Art Workers' Guild, Newton remained devoted to fine craftsmanship. He also produced residential designs marked by simplicity and a lack of pretension. For Luckley (1907), a house in Wokingham, Berkshire, Newton evoked domesticity and charm with features such as a small front door and casement windows.[20] While the Neo-Georgian strain of classicism managed to work its way into England's Arts and Crafts movement, other classical styles of the period remained far removed from its tenets. Most importantly, the classicism taught at the École des Beaux-Arts in Paris was antithetical to Arts and Crafts thinking. It was too florid and altogether foreign. At its essence, England's Arts and Crafts architecture was modest and mindful of English tradition.

WHICH AMERICAN ARCHITECTS AND DESIGNERS?

As we investigate the Arts and Crafts architecture of the United States, the question arises about which architects and designers to consider so that we may comprehend the American response to the English movement. Who were the individuals who stood at the trend's forefront, and who else might be representative? We can begin by identifying architects and designers who championed the movement through their involvement with Arts and Crafts organizations, exhibitions, and communities. When focusing on these individuals, we include architects such as H. Langford Warren of Boston, Robert C. Spencer, Jr., of Chicago, and Willis J. Polk of San Francisco, all of whom participated in the country's earliest societies. Gustav Stickley, a designer whose career took off in Syracuse, New York, also holds a place in this tier due to his explicit advocacy of the movement through his *Craftsman* magazine.

Widening the circle, we can add architects who encountered Arts and Crafts ideas during their education or employment and adopted many of the beliefs, including Santa Barbara's George Washington Smith, who studied with Warren at Harvard, and Pasadena's Charles Sumner Greene, who worked in Warren's office. When architects published articles in periodicals or discussed their buildings with other writers, they often chose words that signaled their allegiance to the movement. They might allude to Ruskin's reverence for nature, history, honesty, and truth or paraphrase Morris's call for people to purge their houses of excess, to retain only the useful or beautiful.

A study of the Arts and Crafts architecture across the United States also should examine buildings that served the people and organizations most closely aligned with the movement. Making selections in this way leads us to include Pond and Pond's Hull-House in Chicago, Rathbone DeBuys's Newcomb Pottery Building (1902) in New Orleans, William B. Stratton's Pewabic Pottery (1906–7) in Detroit, and William Channing Whitney's Handicraft Guild Building (1906–7) in Minneapolis (see figs. 4.9, 6.1, and 6.15).

Recognizing the emergence of women and minorities as designers at this time, we look for individuals who were attuned to Arts and Crafts architectural features and building types and employed them in their work. This strategy allows us to consider Chicago's Marion Mahony, who designed sophisticated Prairie School houses; Cora Cadwallader Tuttle, who designed little bungalows in Madison, Wisconsin; and African American architect Paul R. Williams, who designed Tudor Revival houses—some large, some small—in Los Angeles.

Finally, certain buildings warrant our attention because they incorporate outstanding work by artists and artisans who were most closely committed to the Arts and Crafts movement. One of them is the Cathedral of Learning at the University of Pittsburgh (1924–37),

FIGURE 0.2. C. F. A. Voysey, The Orchard, Chorleywood, Hertfordshire, England, 1899.

designed by Charles Z. Klauder, where Samuel Yellin and his shop crafted imposing iron gates (see fig. 3.19). At the Dana House (1902–4) in Springfield, Illinois, designed by Frank Lloyd Wright, the artwork includes a female figure sculpted by artist Richard Bock (see fig. 5.6). At Paradise Inn (1916–17), designed by Heath and Gove for Washington's Mount Rainier National Park, guests are delighted by the craftsmanship and imagination of Hans Fraehnke, who encased a piano in small logs (see fig. 9.7).

THE CLASSICAL TRADITION

Diverse as the architecture of the American Arts and Crafts movement was stylistically, it differed in its forms and spirit from the classical architecture that appeared at the turn of the twentieth century.[21] Buildings based on the classical tradition were inspired by Greek, Roman, Renaissance, and Baroque sources, known through books and travel. Architects combined and recombined classical columns, pediments, arches, and domes in familiar yet novel ways. Front elevations were usually symmetrically composed, and building components were rigidly repeated. The result was formal and stern. Depending on the context, a viewer might admire a classical design or consider it intimidating.

In the United States, classical bank and insurance company buildings conveyed a message of trustworthiness through columned entrances and coffered halls. Train stations and museums, monumental and classically designed, replaced Victorian train stations and museums that were picturesque and Gothic. Wealthy clients at the turn of the century also signed on with architects who knew their classical architecture, hiring them to build mansions in the country or at the seaside. The better-trained architects could provide a building in the ornate manner taught at the École des Beaux-Arts, weighting its walls with sculpted garlands and chubby toddlers in flight. Indeed, through the early decades of the twentieth century, the nation embraced classicism. In 1893, when Americans flocked to the World's Columbian Exposition in Chicago, they were awed by its classical grandeur. The wonder that was Chicago led to City Beautiful plans in which urban leaders erected complexes of white civic buildings that were classical expressions of governmental authority.

As might be expected, most American architects could design buildings in a range of the period's popular styles. At a time when increasing numbers of Americans studied in architectural programs, subscribed to architectural periodicals, and joined architectural clubs or associations, they delivered drawings in whatever idiom the client preferred. To complicate matters, even an architect who was fully committed to the Arts and Crafts movement might occasionally decide to use a row of classical columns. This was true of Boston's C. Howard Walker. Yet when we analyze such an example, his William Fogg Library (1906–7) in Eliot, Maine, we see that the building walls of local fieldstone give it an informality and tie it to the land, imbuing it with an Arts and Crafts air (see fig. 1.15).

WRITING ABOUT THE AMERICAN MOVEMENT

Over the past fifty years, scholars have been writing about the Arts and Crafts movement in the United States. In books and exhibition catalogues on the subject, authors have consistently acknowledged the role of American architects; however, this book is the first to examine the nation's architects and their buildings in an extended and coherent way. An important early contribution to the literature is *The Arts and Crafts Movement in America, 1876–1916*, an exhibition catalogue edited by Robert Judson Clark, from 1972.[22] Eight years later, Peter Davey published *Arts and Crafts Architecture: The Search for Earthly Paradise*, by and large a study of British architects and their work, with a few pages devoted to American buildings in the Midwest and California.[23] Richard Guy Wilson offered a broader survey of buildings in this country in his essay for the 1987 exhibition catalogue titled *"The Art That Is Life": The Arts and Crafts Movement in America, 1875–1920*.[24] Four years later, Wendy Kaplan contributed a chapter on Arts and Crafts architecture in the United States to *The Arts and Crafts Movement*.[25] Both Wilson and Kaplan appreciated the diversity of the nation's response to the English Arts and Crafts movement and discussed regional developments. To meet a growing interest in buildings and places associated with Arts and Crafts ideas, James Massey and Shirley Maxwell assembled a well-illustrated state-by-state guidebook, issued in 1998.[26] Meanwhile, scholars and enthusiasts have written extensively about specific architects and parts of the country, relating them to Arts and Crafts interests.

In the ten chapters that follow, we'll consider how Arts and Crafts concepts entered the United States and were quickly disseminated. By framing the book around the country's major geographic areas, the pages will identify unifying interests in a given region's architecture based on its cultural heritage and natural features. We'll find that the well-traveled men and women living in the Northeast, Chicago, and San Francisco were the first to establish contact with the movement's English theorists and take action. Then, in just a few short years, Arts and Crafts principles reached more remote corners of the country, some of which have been little studied until now. The chapters will highlight and return to many of the period's most important American architects—influential figures who encouraged an Arts and Crafts outlook by way of societies, publications, and exhibitions. Through this investigation of these advocates and their work, we will trace the intertwining relationships among them and views that they shared.

At the turn of the twentieth century, these leaders were on the move. They were meeting regularly with fellow professionals, artisans, and supporters who advanced an Arts and Crafts ethos. Fascinated by regional history and landscapes, they were boarding trains and crisscrossing the nation, their journeys enabled by the newly laid networks of rails.

1 English in New England

At the very time when Arts and Crafts ideas were coalescing in nineteenth-century England, Bostonians were there, observing, hearing, and meeting the English movement's future theorists and practitioners. All involved were in their youth, and the friendships that formed between the Bostonians and their English counterparts would continue through the decades. By the end of the century, architects in Boston would take a distinctively English approach to the Arts and Crafts buildings that they erected throughout New England. Most of the architects descended from English stock, and knowledge of their family backgrounds encouraged them to look toward England for inspiration about design. Reinforcing this inclination was the fact that for Bostonians, the voyage by steamship to England was shorter than for other Americans, and the trip was relatively affordable. Moreover, Boston-based architects, even those of humble origin, easily obtained letters of introduction to meet England's rising stars, facilitated by extensive social connections on both sides of the Atlantic.[1]

The individual who paved the way for the Arts and Crafts movement in New England was not an architect, artist, or craft worker, but an art history professor. This was Charles Eliot Norton (1827–1908).[2] During the 1850s, as a young man in his twenties, he met John Ruskin, and after a chance encounter in 1856 at Lake Geneva, they began a close friendship. From then on, when Norton was in Europe, he visited Ruskin, and they maintained a regular correspondence. During the same period, Norton befriended the English artists Dante Gabriel Rossetti and Edward Burne-Jones. Like Ruskin, Norton admired medieval Italian architecture, and in 1859 he published *Notes of Travel and Study in Italy.*[3] Writing about St. Mark's Cathedral in Venice, he expressed preferences that would become more pronounced as he grew older. He explained how the church's thirteenth-century mosaics were superior to those of the sixteenth century, asserting that the earlier mosaics reflected an age of faith, of "comparative simplicity and self-forgetfulness."[4] Ruskinian values, including an admiration of the simple and the modest, guided him and would be adopted in future years by Boston's Arts and Crafts leaders. In 1856 Norton met and befriended William Morris; however, Norton's kinship with Ruskin was stronger. Ruskin, appointed the Slade Professor of Fine Art at the University of Oxford in 1869, was a model and mentor to Norton when he began teaching art history at Harvard in 1874.[5] In this new position, Norton found a calling, and he is recognized today as one of the university's legendary professors. His lectures presented a history of art and architecture in moral terms that were grounded in the English Arts and Crafts movement. When Bostonians founded a Society of Arts and Crafts in 1897, they elected Norton as their first president.

By the 1880s, architects in the city had become well aware of Morris and sought him out when they were abroad. Boston's most acclaimed architect, Henry Hobson Richardson (1838–1886), visited Morris in 1882 and subsequently corresponded with him.[6] In the mid-1890s, the architect George E. Barton (1871–1923) met Morris, an encounter that aroused the young man's interest in "sociological study."[7] When Barton participated in organizing the Society of Arts and Crafts, he hoped to improve the lives of working men and women. In the spring of 1896, Bertram Grosvenor Goodhue (1869–1924), another Boston architect, paid a visit to Morris at Kelmscott House, probably to discuss fine art printing.[8] Goodhue would become a longtime member of the Society of Arts and Crafts.[9]

Several Boston architects trained in the offices of English architects, and their personal experiences contributed to the depth of understanding in the Bay State capital about trends in England. In 1869, with a letter of endorsement in hand, Robert Swain Peabody (1845–1917) called on Alfred Waterhouse in London and was promptly put to work.[10] The office was busy building Manchester Town Hall (1868–77); however, Peabody was eager for experience in designing country houses, and he received the opportunity. One project to which he was assigned was Blackmoor House (1869), an Elizabethan Revival mansion in Liss, Hampshire, that would be enhanced with carved wood, sculpture, and stained glass. Exposure to such craftsmanship would inform Peabody's work when he returned home.

Two Boston architects who would serve as presidents of the Society of Arts and Crafts also trained in England. They were H. Langford Warren (1857–1917) and R. Clipston Sturgis (1860–1951). Warren, half English and half American, was born and raised in England, and in 1875 he started working as a draftsman for Manchester architect William Dawes.[11] Two years earlier, Dawes was hired to restore Manchester Cathedral (begun in 1421), a project that would have interested Warren.[12] As in England, the architects leading Boston's Arts and Crafts movement encouraged the preservation of New England's historic buildings and were commissioned to restore and rebuild them. Sturgis first trained under his uncle, Boston architect John Hubbard Sturgis (1834–1888), and then left for London in 1883 to enter the office of Robert W. Edis, where he stayed until the end of 1884.[13] Edis had just published a book on interior decoration including illustrations of Morris chairs and rooms that reflected the preferences of the Arts and Crafts tastemaker.[14] While working for Edis, young Sturgis absorbed ideas about uniting architecture with the decorative arts.

Just as Ruskin and Morris held an enduring love for their English heritage, members of Boston's upper echelon revered their own Yankee past. This reverence was a century in the making. In 1791 their esteem for the new nation's history led to the founding of the Massachusetts Historical Society, the first such organization in the United States. Beginning in the 1860s, Bostonians engaged in battles to save notable colonial buildings such as the 1737 Hancock House. John Hubbard Sturgis measured and documented it before the campaign was lost and the house demolished in 1863. Thirty years later, when the Massachusetts State House (1795–98), designed by the great federal architect Charles Bulfinch, was threatened with demolition, Boston architects took up the defense. Their crusade culminated in a narrow but successful vote by the state legislature and ended with the restoration of the building, completed in 1898.[15]

The presence of multiple programs offering arts education in Boston contributed to an environment that nurtured an Arts and Crafts movement. Institutions of higher education offered formal instruction to train architects, artists, and design professionals. In the view of New York City's Candace Wheeler, the Boston area was the country's "best nucleus for industrial art work."[16] Those who wanted to study art and design could enroll in the architecture program at the Massachusetts Institute of Technology, which opened in 1868; the Massachusetts Normal Art School, founded in 1873; Norton's fine arts courses at Harvard, from 1874; the school of the Museum of Fine Arts, Boston, established in 1876; and Warren's architecture program at Harvard, launched in 1893.

AN ARTS AND CRAFTS EXHIBITION AND A SOCIETY

By the end of the nineteenth century, Boston had become home to a flourishing community of men and women engaged in artistic disciplines. They were well-prepared to back the nation's first major Arts and Crafts exhibition, which opened to the public on April 5, 1897.[17] Thirty-seven Bostonians endorsed the endeavor, organized by a printer, Henry Lewis Johnson. Nine in the group were architects. Through the duration of the show, the Boston Architectural Club sponsored an accompanying exhibition on architecture. From the beginning, the city's architects were allied with craft workers. Just as architects were central to the Arts and Crafts movement unfolding in England, architects in Boston were the driving force for the movement in New England. They readily moved into this role. Close collegial relationships among them had been fostered through the Boston Society of Architects, established in 1867, and the Boston Architectural Club, dating from 1889. A year after the founding of the club, its members began holding exhibitions, setting a precedent for the Arts and Crafts show.

After the exhibition closed, architects, craft workers, and supporters continued to gather, energized by their success. In June 1897 they chartered the Society of Arts and Crafts. Norton, the first president, wrote their mission statement, proclaiming the members' commitment to bringing designers and workmen into "mutually helpful relations."[18] His words echoed those of Morris, published in 1882, calling for a "mutually helpful" union of the arts.[19] Architecture, to Morris and Norton, was the vehicle that would hold the movement together.

For two years, Norton led the Society of Arts and Crafts and then was succeeded by Arthur Astor Carey, a philanthropist sympathetic to Morris's socialism.[20] Eager to convince the society to take up labor issues, he was thwarted and resigned in November 1903. Warren, now heading the architecture program at Harvard, stepped in as the society's third president. He would remain in the position until he died in 1917. As an architect with a business mentality, Warren was pragmatic in steering the society, encouraging training and sales opportunities for the craft workers. The organization held classes and exhibitions, published a magazine, and opened a juried shop. While influenced by the ideas of Ruskin and Morris, the group's leaders also drew upon the lectures and writings of Ralph Waldo Emerson.[21] They endorsed the Massachusetts native's adherence to individualism, advocacy for self-culture, and respect for the plain Yankee. In applying Emersonian views to their work, the architects designed sober buildings, at first advancing the English Gothic Revival, and then the Anglo-Colonial Revival. Their great achievement came through bringing architects and artisans together. When the English architect C. R. Ashbee penned a letter on behalf of a countryman traveling to Boston in 1910, he urged his contact at the society to show the visitor projects in which "the craftsmen actually work *for* and *with* the architects."[22]

An early example of such a relationship was demonstrated at Trinity Church (1872–77), erected in Boston's developing Back Bay neighborhood and designed by Richardson. The architect had already collaborated with a talented sculptor, John Evans (1847–1923), and they worked together at Trinity and later projects.[23] Significantly, Evans would become a founding member of the Society of Arts and Crafts. To decorate the church interior, Richardson turned to the artist John La Farge (1835–1910), who provided murals and designs for stained glass. The heavy, lithic, Romanesque-inspired style that Richardson initiated was soon widely imitated across New England and the nation, but it would prove to be short-lived, lasting only through the 1880s. On the other hand, his close relationship with artists and craft workers would be admired and emulated by the generation of Boston architects who succeeded him.

PRECURSORS OF AN ARTS AND CRAFTS ARCHITECTURE

Through the 1880s, architects working in New England could observe precursors that foreshadowed a new Arts and Crafts approach to architecture. Examples of craftsmanship that originated in England drew their attention. The wealthy and well-traveled, too, shared this interest. Just a few years after Boston's Trinity Church was dedicated, donors commissioned stained glass windows that were designed by Edward Burne-Jones (1833–1898) and supplied by Morris's firm, three in 1880 and a fourth in 1882 (fig. 1.1). Morris and his associates executed a more extensive project at a large seaside cottage in Newport, Rhode Island, called Vinland (1882), built by Peabody and his partner, John Goddard Stearns, Jr. Stained glass windows by Burne-Jones illuminated the main hall, while windows by Walter Crane were installed in the library. Crane also produced a frieze for the dining room.[24]

During the 1880s, Peabody was clearly dreaming of England when he received commissions to erect several sizable houses. Reflecting his familiarity with the Old English work of Richard Norman Shaw, Peabody included

FIGURE 1.1. Edward Burne-Jones for Morris & Co., *Visit of the Magi*, stained glass, 1880, Trinity Church, Boston.

Tudor half-timbering in dwellings of stone and shingles. A country house at Moraine Farm (1880–82), constructed for John Charles Phillips in the Massachusetts North Shore town of Beverly, was precocious (fig. 1.2).[25] It was unlike the conventional Queen Anne houses of the era that were massed with multiple towers and gables and finished with elaborate ornament. The forward-looking residential designs, including examples by Peabody, were more tautly massed and sparingly detailed, later to be identified as Shingle style.[26] The Phillips House in Beverly fit in with the Shingle style, but it had a novel feature: a half-timbered pavilion that boldly projected over the main entry, supported by hefty wood braces on either side of the front door. Richardson and a handful of others were moving in the same direction, incorporating half-timbering into their residential work, but Peabody followed English examples most closely.

The architects who would lead the Arts and Crafts movement in New England quickly embraced this Romantic style for country and suburban houses. In 1886 a full-blown Tudor Revival country house was built in Lancaster, Massachusetts, designed by John Hubbard Sturgis and completed by his nephew (fig. 1.3). Not shingled at all, the John E. Thayer House was stone on the first story and entirely half-timbered on the upper story-and-a-half.[27] It was decidedly English and recognized as such. Around the same time, an imposing Tudor Revival house was designed by C. Howard Walker (1857–1936), a charter member of the Society of Arts and Crafts and president from 1922 to 1925 and 1930 to 1933. Located on Boston's North Shore in Manchester, Massachusetts, the two-and-a-half-story house from 1887 was entirely half-timbered, from the main level to the dormers.[28] Walker had trained under John Hubbard Sturgis and must have studied the Thayer House closely. The house that Walker designed was built for Edward Robinson, a curator at the Museum of Fine Arts, Boston, who would become its director and then director of the Metropolitan Museum of Art in New York.[29] In 1891 Ralph Adams Cram (1863–1942) designed a Tudor Revival house in Brookline that was brick on the first story and half-timbered above.[30] Like Shaw's Old English houses, the Eugene Fellner House had groups of banked windows filled with small panes. After the Society of Arts and Crafts was organized, Cram would serve as an active member and sit on its governing council.

In addition to the Tudor Revival dwellings, Elizabethan and Jacobean mansions appeared in New

FIGURE 1.2. Robert Swain Peabody, Moraine Farm, Beverly, Massachusetts, 1880–82.

FIGURE 1.3. John Hubbard Sturgis and R. Clipston Sturgis, Thayer House, Lancaster, Massachusetts, 1886.

England during the 1880s, further demonstrating the region's close relationship with English architects and architectural trends. Two of the grandest houses were in Newport. One was Wakehurst, the James Van Alen House, based closely on an Elizabethan manor house in Sussex from 1570 (fig. 1.4). Its conceptual design was developed in 1882 by Charles Eamer Kempe (1837–1907), an Englishman who became known for his stained glass, and construction took place from 1884 to 1887.[31] Peabody and Stearns made their mark as innovators again with Rough Point, an early revival of a Jacobean country house, built for Frederick W. Vanderbilt between 1889 and 1890.[32] Both of these massive stone houses, with high walls and parapet gables, exuded a commanding presence that differed from the kindly informality of the half-timbered Tudors. As time went on, the Tudor Revival would prove to be the most popular domestic style among the architects associated with the Arts and Crafts movement.

The church-building that appealed to England's Arts and Crafts architects also interested the Boston-based architects, and by the early 1890s, they pivoted away from Richardson's Romanesque and toward a revival of the English Gothic churches of the fifteenth century. Years later, Cram would attribute the shift to the architect Henry Vaughan (1845–1917), crediting him as "the apostle of the new dispensation."[33] Vaughan was English and had worked for George F. Bodley before coming to Boston in 1881. Within a few years, Vaughan was commissioned to design a chapel for St. Paul's School (1886–94) in Concord, New Hampshire (fig. 1.5).[34] Conceived as a parish church in the English Perpendicular style, its nave walls are buttressed, while a square tower with pinnacles dominates the end where the entrance is located. By the early twentieth century, Perpendicular churches had become common in towns throughout New England.

Ecclesiastic projects afforded many opportunities for architects to promote their colleagues in the allied arts, and the vision of medieval builders and craft guilds working together was inspirational. In an early demonstration of Arts and Crafts collaboration, in 1891 Cram and Goodhue, as partners in Cram, Wentworth, and Goodhue, took on the design and decoration of All Saints, Ashmont, in Dorchester, a section of Boston (fig. 1.6).[35] Modeled after England's Perpendicular parish churches, the building opened in 1893, and construction went on through the early twentieth century. Conveying an air of power, it has an enormous tower that is one with the

FIGURE 1.4. Charles Eamer Kempe, Wakehurst (Gerety Hall, Salve Regina University), Newport, Rhode Island, 1882–87.

FIGURE 1.5. Henry Vaughan, St. Paul's School chapel, Concord, New Hampshire, 1886–94.

entire west front. Weighty buttresses rise at the tower corners, with the entire tower mass capped by a parapet that is battlemented. The building is constructed of seam-faced granite, variegated in color, including rusty browns and yellow ochers. Quarried in the south of Boston, the stone reflects the Arts and Crafts preference for native materials.

Once inside, the visitor encounters an exposed timber roof that covers a long nave with a processional center aisle, the worship space receding into a deep chancel. Stained glass windows were added over the years. The first was made in 1896 by Harry Goodhue (1873–1918), Bertram's brother and a future member of the Society of Arts and Crafts. Unlike the pictorial windows of John La Farge and Louis Comfort Tiffany, Harry Goodhue's window resembles medieval examples, with a Madonna and Child posed frontally. Another window came from England, created by Christopher Whall, an influential stained glass maker who had worked with architects John D. Sedding, Edward S. Prior, and William R. Lethaby. Several windows were installed later, the work of Charles J. Connick (1875–1945), a future president of the Society of Arts and Crafts. The most prominent decoration of the church is the large stone reredos, from 1898, carved in the shop of John Evans, with an altarpiece painted by George Hallowell. Stained oak paneling around the chancel includes a frieze of biblical scenes carved by Johannes Kirchmayer (1860–1930). The artisans were all members of the society, and they produced a tour de force of Boston's Arts and Crafts movement.

Just as England's architects and writers of the early to mid-nineteenth century extolled their country's medieval architecture, opening the door to the Gothic Revival, so too did the Boston architects follow the same logic, becoming champions of New England's colonial and early federal survivors. This development led to Anglo-Colonial Revival designs that should be recognized as reflecting an Arts and Crafts mentality. Among the architects who contributed to this interest were John Hubbard Sturgis, Richardson, Peabody, and Charles McKim.[36] During the 1870s and 1880s, architects selected discrete features of New England's eighteenth- and early nineteenth-century houses and applied them to what were still essentially Queen Anne designs. Starting in the late 1880s, however, a few architects began imitating historic originals more closely. The architects also concluded that the Colonial Revival was a suitable choice for civic buildings.

FIGURE 1.6. Cram, Wentworth, and Goodhue, All Saints Church, Ashmont, Boston, Massachusetts, initial phase, 1891–94.

FIGURE 1.7. Alexander Wadsworth Longfellow, Jr., Thorp House, Cambridge, Massachusetts, 1886–87.

FIGURE 1.8. R. Clipston Sturgis, Schwab House, New Haven, Connecticut, 1895–96.

High style colonial and federal domestic architecture inspired the Cambridge, Massachusetts, home designed by Alexander Wadsworth Longfellow, Jr. (1854–1934) for his cousin Annie Longfellow Thorp, daughter of the poet, and her husband Joseph, built between 1886 and 1887 (fig. 1.7).[37] Massed like a Georgian house under a gambrel roof, it has delicate swags on the portico frieze and attenuated columns that capture the spirit of the Federal Style. The main staircase has carved twisted balusters and newel posts based on Georgian examples, while an elliptical ceiling is derived from federal period sources, in particular a design by Bulfinch. Longfellow's blending of features from colonial and federal period examples would become a standard approach of the Anglo-Colonial Revival that soon followed.

MEDIEVAL AS ARTS AND CRAFTS

The architecture of England's late Middle Ages offered seemingly endless possibilities for architects and their clients in New England at the end of the nineteenth century, and the enthusiasm continued, lasting well into the 1920s. In addition to designing Tudor houses and Perpendicular churches, the architects determined that they could apply the same vocabulary to new types of projects that were in demand: apartments and campus buildings. The architects considered themselves forward-looking.

By the mid-1890s, Boston architects vigorously promoted durable materials and quality craftsmanship, and their Tudor houses met this standard. R. Clipston Sturgis received a commission to design a substantial house in New Haven, Connecticut, for Yale professor John C. Schwab, erected between 1895 and 1896 (fig. 1.8).[38] Granite walls anchor the first story, while the upper story-and-a-half is half-timbered and stuccoed. Sturgis was no fan of the less durable wood-clad houses that were being constructed at the time, and he made a case against them in a paper he presented in 1897 to the Boston Society of Architects.[39] Like his colleagues in Boston's emerging Arts and Crafts movement, he advocated for restrained designs and decorative handwork of artisans. The Schwab House gables are enhanced by carving on the bargeboards, and windows on the first story have leaded glass.

During the last two decades of the nineteenth century, apartment buildings were constructed in Boston that catered to professionals and businessmen, and by century's end, this building type began to appear in the streetcar suburbs. Cram, Goodhue, and Ferguson took the

Of the various types of commissions that architects with Arts and Crafts interests might pursue, a contract for a church building was especially desirable. These projects appealed to the architects' academic interests in English medieval churches—interests that were reinforced by extensive study trips during which they documented what they saw. Warren paid special attention to the English parish church in his teaching at Harvard, and Cram and Walker wrote books about the topic.[45] Brown published a volume filled with photographs of "modern" English churches that American architects could examine and put to use.[46]

Two years after the Society of Arts and Crafts was founded, Warren designed a place of worship for his fellow Swedenborgians. The New Church Theological School chapel (1899–1901), located in Cambridge, Massachusetts, served students and a local congregation (fig. 1.11).[47] With a pitched roof and a bell cote, it was modeled after the Gothic parish churches that Warren had known from his upbringing. Split fieldstone walls of the chapel blend a subtle assortment of colors, the selection of which required the aesthetic judgment of the mason. At close range, the visitor notices carved stone ornament, including corbel sculptures of human heads, the work of Hugh Cairns (1861–1942). A founder of the Society of Arts and Crafts, Cairns also sculpted stone angels for a reredos inside. Irving and Casson supplied wood paneling and pews, Mercer delivered tile, and Donald MacDonald (1841–1916) provided grisaille glass, designed in collaboration with Warren. The chapel was well-publicized and exemplified Arts and Crafts architecture as advanced by the society.

Cram excelled at church design and, working in partnerships and then on his own, attracted commissions throughout New England and across the country.[48] Devoted to the Society of Arts and Crafts, he chaired its Ecclesiastical Work Committee, and he encouraged the organization's artisans to make liturgical objects. As in England, these pieces were often designed by architects. In 1907 Cram launched a magazine, *Christian Art,* that described such collaborations and gave credit to both architects and the makers. He regularly published articles about Gothic architecture, and in 1925 he encouraged the founding of the Medieval Academy of America, later serving as president.

When a budget for a new church wouldn't go far enough, Cram and his partners demonstrated a talent for figuring out how to maximize the effect of quality materials and craftsmanship. At St. James Episcopal Church (1907–8) in Woodstock, Vermont, by Cram, Goodhue, and Ferguson, the firm returned to the concept of positioning a massive square tower at the front of the building (fig. 1.12). The result is a simplified version of the scheme used at All Saints, Ashmont. Variation in the colors of split fieldstone, quarried nearby in Quechee, enhances the sheer walls. Moldings and tracery seem to be stone, but in fact they are cast concrete from the Economy Manufacturing Company of New Haven, Connecticut.[49] Although Cram once subscribed to Ruskin's view about honesty, rejecting imitations of different materials, by now he and his colleagues were persuaded that concrete had virtues. It resisted water better than limestone, and it didn't hurt that it was cheaper. Economy sold a respectable product. For sculptural decoration, the company employed Lee Lawrie, the artist of the fountain sculpture at Richmond Court, and it's likely that he made the models of a pilgrim's bag and scallop shell, symbols of St. James, that were cast and installed on the tower just under its parapet.

Cost was not an issue when the young millionaire John Nicholas Brown, Jr., engaged Cram to design a Perpendicular Gothic chapel for St. George's School (1924–28) in Middletown, Rhode Island (fig. 1.13).[50] Brown was a graduate of the school and a student at Harvard when he started to think about the project. In a class on medieval sculpture, taught by the renowned Arthur Kingsley Porter, Brown met Joseph Coletti (1898–1973), a son of Italian immigrants. In his teens, Coletti had worked as a stone carver under John Evans.[51] When construction began on St. George's in 1924, Cram and Brown were committed to having it embellished lavishly by sympathetic craftsmen. Coletti sculpted limestone figures, while other stone ornament was carved by Andrew Dreselly (1893–1985), working under Kirchmayer. Dreselly also carved decorative components in wood, which were shipped to Bedford, Indiana, where limestone for the church was being quarried. There the wooden models were copied in stone by Harry Thomas Easton, a native of Cambridge who had apprenticed under Evans. Ornamental iron came from Philadelphia's Samuel Yellin (1884–1940), a member of the Boston society. Stained glass, installed after the church was dedicated, was made by Wilbur H. Burnham and Joseph G. Reynolds. Both had learned their craft from Harry Goodhue, and both belonged to the Society of Arts and Crafts. The chapel

FIGURE 1.11. Warren, Smith, and Biscoe, New Church Theological School chapel (Swedenborg Chapel), Cambridge, Massachusetts, 1899–1901.

FIGURE 1.12. Cram, Goodhue, and Ferguson, St. James Episcopal Church, Woodstock, Vermont, 1907–8.

today is a spectacular example of the ideals of the Boston-based Arts and Crafts movement. Through the society and in their practices, the architects nurtured two generations of craft workers. It should be acknowledged, however, that the concept of collaboration did not go very far. In reality, as Dreselly later pointed out, a distinct hierarchy existed.[52] Most of the artisans labored in workshops that other artisans owned and ran, and the shop owners in turn reported to staff architects who worked in the offices of architect-business owners. Talented as designers, these top architects were also successful entrepreneurs, individuals with a knack for promoting both their firms and themselves.

In the opening decade of the twentieth century, several Boston architects landed commissions to plan large campus complexes. For these projects, they were drawn to the beauty of Perpendicular Gothic. The emergence of "Collegiate Gothic" in the United States began in Philadelphia, as acknowledged by R. Clipston Sturgis and Cram.[53] Stylistically, Collegiate Gothic drew upon several phases of English architecture, including Tudor, Jacobean, and English Renaissance, in order to evoke associations with the distinguished campuses of Oxford and Cambridge. What the Boston architects contributed was the idea of a soaring Perpendicular tower that would become the focal point of a campus.

The concept was introduced in April 1909 when Boston College announced the winning entry of a competition for a new campus.[54] The plan was the work of

Charles D. Maginnis (1867–1955), a native of Ireland, who had established a partnership with Timothy Walsh. Maginnis was active on committees of the Society of Arts and Crafts and joined the governing council that year. Prior to the competition, the leadership of the Catholic school had decided to relocate from the city to suburban Newton. Unimpeded by existing buildings, the architects concocted a scheme inspired by the characteristics of a cathedral, with a site plan organized around cross axes that suggested a nave and transept arms. Visitors to the campus were to enter main gates and proceed along a road covered by a canopy of trees that would create a natural vault. Where a cathedral's crossing would be located, a central academic building rose up, carrying a two-hundred-foot-tall Perpendicular bell tower. Construction of this building, Gasson Hall, began in the fall of 1909, and it opened in 1913 (fig. 1.14). Evans produced molds for cast concrete ornament, and a Jesuit brother painted murals.[55]

Many such towers followed on American campuses, with the Boston architects among the first to embrace the idea.[56] In the summer of 1909, Cram planned Princeton University's Graduate College, organized around Cleveland Tower, rising 173 feet in height. In August 1909 Sturgis sketched his idea for a 180-foot-tall Perpendicular tower at the center of a new campus to be built by Perkins Institution for the Blind in Watertown, Massachusetts, completed in 1912. All of the buildings and their towers were English in form and decoration. The fact that this stylistic choice was acceptable for Boston College, an

FIGURE 1.13. Ralph Adams Cram, St. George's School chapel, Middletown, Rhode Island, 1924–28.

FIGURE 1.14. Maginnis and Walsh, Gasson Hall, Boston College, Newton, Massachusetts, 1909–13.

institution that served Irish Catholic students, is worth noting when we consider that across the Atlantic, the Irish were struggling mightily against the yoke of the English. When University College Cork erected the Honan Chapel, opening months after the 1916 Easter Rising in Dublin, it reflected the Arts and Crafts idea of affirming one's own heritage.[57] Its design and interior decoration were revivals of Hiberno-Romanesque churches and Celtic art. But the story was different for Boston College. Here, English Perpendicular was not only acceptable, but considered appropriate, for a campus in New England.

COLONIAL REVIVAL AS ARTS AND CRAFTS

Through the 1890s, while Arts and Crafts concepts were catching on, Boston architects were studying the region's early buildings and applying what they learned to Anglo-Colonial Revival projects. In addition to designing Colonial Revival houses and churches, they referred to the eighteenth and early nineteenth centuries for civic buildings, in particular town halls and libraries.[58] Colonial Revival structures could be modest, built with local materials and little decoration, or they could be substantial, built with costly materials and handcrafted embellishment. Yet in all cases, the architects and their clients respected the mission of the Society of Arts and Crafts, which subscribed to an aesthetic marked by "restraint."

Hired to design the William Fogg Library (1906–7) in Eliot, Maine, Walker delivered a building that declares its civic importance by its siting on a rise in the land and its classical portico supported by four Ionic columns (fig. 1.15). A broad hip roof with three small pedimented dormers shelters the building. Erected with fieldstone, the library responds to its rural setting and satisfies the Arts and Crafts objective of reflecting its locale. In an unusual community effort, the citizens were asked to donate stone walls on their property to be used in the library's

FIGURE 1.15. C. Howard Walker, William Fogg Library, Eliot, Maine, 1906–7.

FIGURE 1.16. Lois Lilley Howe, Skyfield, Harrisville, New Hampshire, 1916.

FIGURE 1.17. Lois Lilley Howe, Cornish House, Cambridge, Massachusetts, 1916.

construction.[59] For the foundation and trimmings, local granite was chosen. Inside are two wooden columns, while the rest of the woodwork consists of flat stock and moldings. Walker was the critic of the jury of the Society of Arts and Crafts, a body that met with the artisan members and chose what the shop would sell. The library in Maine illustrates Walker's views about successful design based on employing natural materials, harmonious proportions, and a little well-chosen ornament.

Lois Lilley Howe (1864–1964) studied architecture at MIT and founded her own practice. By and large, clients hired her for residential work, which was typical for early female practitioners. She served on committees of the Society of Arts and Crafts and on its governing council. For Mrs. Edward C. Jones of New Bedford, Massachusetts, Howe designed a majestic country house, named Skyfield, in Harrisville, New Hampshire, built in 1916 (fig. 1.16).[60] Howe shared her colleagues' interest in measuring and drawing New England's historic houses, and Skyfield has the taut exterior, symmetry, and small forms, including the dormers and primary entrance, of eighteenth-century sources. At the same time, it reveals her familiarity with England's Neo-Georgian architects such as Ernest Newton, Arts and Crafts leaders who folded Georgian architecture into the movement.

In New England, a new twist on the Colonial Revival came about as the architects directed their attention to surviving seventeenth-century dwellings. In 1916 Howe designed a house for Louis C. Cornish that is likely the earliest example of the revival of First Period colonial

FIGURE 1.18. Warren and Smith, Slocumb Hall, exposed trusses, Proctor Academy, Andover, New Hampshire, 1909.

architecture in Cambridge, Massachusetts, where it is located (fig. 1.17).[61] With multiple gables and gabled dormers, the house is sheathed in clapboards stained a dark brown and has an overhanging second story and pendants at the corners. Yet it is unmistakably a twentieth-century house, with banked double-hung windows bringing in daylight for the pleasure of the occupants.

By the end of the nineteenth century, the architects in New England's Arts and Crafts movement were attracted to organizations and projects that involved the preservation of historic buildings. Longfellow, Howe, and Cram were among the first members of the Society for the Preservation of New England Antiquities, founded in 1910; the Boston Society of Architects became an institutional member.[62] When a mid-seventeenth-century house in Cambridge was threatened, Howe was one of five people who helped raise funds for the preservation society to purchase it.[63] In her practice, Howe was hired to restore and update historic houses for clients.

Historic buildings from the eighteenth and early nineteenth centuries, mostly frame and fairly small, were adapted for private clubs and academic institutions. In Connecticut, the Graduate Club employed Sturgis to oversee the restoration and an addition to the 1799 Jonathan Mix House (1901–2), overlooking the New Haven Green. Warren, in partnership with F. Patterson Smith, restored an early nineteenth-century farmhouse and transformed a barn into a social hall for the Winchester Country Club (1916) in suburban Boston. In 1909 Proctor Academy, a boarding school in rural Andover, New Hampshire, hired Warren and Smith to convert a livery stable into a gymnasium.[64] With its rectangular plan and pitched roof, the stable offered a large open space that was easily modified for its new purpose. The clapboarded exterior was retained, while at either end of the building, large rectangular windows with small panes were inserted, increasing the natural light inside. From the outside, Slocumb Hall retains the essence of a simple New England service building. The interior, however, is entirely unexpected and stunning. Hammerbeam trusses were constructed to support the roof, evoking the elaborate truss systems of medieval English halls and churches (fig. 1.18). An unassuming building, Slocumb Hall brings together the architects' interests in the Colonial Revival, English medieval architecture, and historic preservation.

For the architects who promoted the Arts and Crafts movement in New England, revivals of English and colonial architecture were favored. When working on residential commissions, however, they were sometimes more adventurous. Following trends in England, the architects designed large, simplified volumes, selected stucco as an exterior finish, and limited the use of ornament and moldings. In 1904 Warren designed and built a house for his family in Cambridge (fig. 1.19).[65] On the main elevation, a steeply pitched roof with a cross gable marks the entrance. Classical pilasters and half-columns frame the front door, above which are an entablature and three windows under a pediment. Built with brick at the foundation, the body of the house is clad in stucco. While it conjures up associations with regional architecture, it is entirely original and modern. Maginnis designed his family home in Brookline in 1920 (fig. 1.20).[66] It also features a steeply pitched roof, has a large gable over the entrance, and is covered in stucco. Pilasters flanking the door are capped by consoles with carved leaves, while an iron railing from the shop of Frank Koralewsky (1872–1941) rests on the entablature.[67] Although the exteriors of both houses are minimally ornamented, the interiors reflect the commitment of the architects to collaborating with craft workers. Warren's house includes Mercer tiles, carved mantelpieces, and bull's-eye and leaded glass, while the Maginnis House features stained glass in leaded windows, wrought-iron hardware, and an enchanting Gothic column carved in wood, its capital inscribed with the names of the architect's children.

The Arts and Crafts movement had a long run in New England, beginning in the early 1890s and extending into the 1920s. Quiet and conservative, buildings associated with the movement responded to English Arts and Crafts theories while also reflecting Yankee values. In rejecting ostentation, the architects who advanced the movement shared an Emersonian outlook. In promoting artists and artisans through a large, formally organized Society of Arts and Crafts, the architects took ideas from Ruskin and Morris and nurtured them, so they could eventually root and flourish in buildings throughout the region.

FIGURE 1.19. H. Langford Warren, Warren House, Cambridge, Massachusetts, 1904.

FIGURE 1.20. Charles D. Maginnis, Maginnis House, Brookline, Massachusetts, 1920.

2 Empire Statements

In anything written about New York state, on just about any topic, New York City plays the leading role. Yet when it comes to studies of the Arts and Crafts movement throughout the state, several smaller urban centers and rural communities have taken the spotlight, and the giant metropolis has remained in the shadows. Indeed, New York City never became a major center for Arts and Crafts activities; however, Arts and Crafts ideas did circulate in Gotham. Like the Bostonians, residents of New York City easily reached England by steamship and were conversant with the emerging movement, while residents living farther north and west rode the train to the port city before making the journey across the ocean.

Generally speaking, Arts and Crafts leaders in New York state were not as close to colleagues in England as their New England counterparts were, and New York's architecture was more varied. The state's middle and upper classes were more ethnically diverse, descending from Dutch and German as well as English stock, and its Arts and Crafts proponents were receptive to more stylistic approaches. These included not only English medieval revival styles, but also simple rustic structures. Reflecting the state's different approaches to Arts and Crafts architecture, New York produced some of the nation's most influential authors and editors, who were diverse in their approach, from sophisticated to homespun.

ARTS AND CRAFTS THINKING IN NEW YORK CITY

By the early 1890s, with the popularity of the Queen Anne and Romanesque revivals petering out, New York City's architects and clients gravitated to contemporary French architecture—favoring classical designs that were richly ornamented and that reflected the teaching at the École des Beaux-Arts in Paris.[1] Commercial buildings, town houses, and apartment buildings acquired an aristocratic aura through references to French sources. French-inflected architecture, especially in Manhattan, expressed the vast wealth that American businessmen and industrialists were accumulating during the Gilded Age. In 1892 a group of architects who shared an enthusiasm for French training founded the Society of Beaux-Arts Architects, based in New York City and modeled on the teaching at the École.

At the same time, several Arts and Crafts groups were organized in the city. A precursor was the Society of Decorative Art, founded in 1877 by Candace Wheeler to provide women with work and instruction in the applied arts.[2] Support for the handicrafts was furthered by the Guild of Arts and Crafts of New York, established in 1900, which maintained a home at the Guild House on East Twenty-Third Street, where they held regular exhibitions.[3] In 1906 the National Society of Craftsmen was organized.[4] These groups were detached from the architectural community.

Yet an interest in the Arts and Crafts movement was spreading among the local architects. By the late 1890s, the Architectural League of New York City embraced the Arts and Crafts cause, albeit in a distinctive way that fit its history and membership. Organized in 1881, the league sponsored its first exhibition in 1885.[5] During the early years, entries consisted of architects' drawings of their projects and sketches and watercolors of historic subjects. In 1887 Boston's Charles Eliot Norton lent the league artwork by J. M. W. Turner and John Ruskin, signaling that the professor's influence had made inroads into New York.[6] Ten years later, when the Society of Arts and Crafts was founded in Boston, entries chosen for the league's annual exhibition in New York City responded to a heightened interest among the architects in the applied arts.[7] Stained glass, mural designs, and sculpture accompanied displays relating to architecture. Viewers also could see a sketch for a candlestick and a design for a lace curtain. Nevertheless, most of the exhibits showcased the work of architects. They hailed mainly from New York City, while others came from Rochester, Buffalo, Boston, and Philadelphia. Many of the architects were prominent, and they favored styles from the period's opposing camps, from classicists such as McKim, Mead & White and Carrère and Hastings to medievalists such as Cram, Wentworth, and Goodhue. Selected entries also came from architects in France and England, reflecting the two strains of influence in New York City. In the 1897 catalogue, the roster of members included a few fine artists such as sculptors Augustus Saint-Gaudens and John Quincy Adams Ward; however, artisan members were missing altogether. Thus the Architectural League adopted the Arts and Crafts goal of supporting artists and craft workers through their exhibitions while carrying on as an organization run by and for architects, with a handful of token artists as members. Treating designers from all fields as equals wasn't attempted.

One can also chart the advancement of the Arts and Crafts movement in the city by examining the pages of the *Architectural Record,* which debuted in 1891. The magazine was a business venture of an unlikely entrepreneur, Clinton W. Sweet, who made a fortune as a "pioneer" in manufacturing overalls.[8] Recognizing another pioneering opportunity, Sweet envisioned a periodical that would appeal to a general as well as professional readership, and he hired wisely. The editor he picked was a twenty-eight-year-old journalist, Harry W. Desmond, who brought on board Herbert Croly and well-regarded critics Russell Sturgis and Montgomery Schuyler.[9] Both Sturgis and Schuyler were Ruskinians, and through them Ruskinian ideals moved into the pages of the *Record* at a time when the classical wave hit New York. In September 1897, a few months after the founding of the Society of Arts and Crafts in Boston, Schuyler published an anonymous letter in the *Record* that satirized the classicists. A facetious Schuyler explains, "If we were still doing Gothic or Romanesque, an architect would have no time to himself at all." By contrast, he continues, the classical formulas are "the greatest labor-saving devices of which the history of architecture gives any account."[10] Other perspectives, however, were welcome in the *Record,* and Desmond devoted space to classicism and even Art Nouveau.

An interesting detail emerged when the index for volume twelve came out at the end of 1902. The title page read: "The Architectural Record: A Monthly Magazine of Architecture and the Allied Arts and Crafts."[11] The *Record* was not and would never be an organ that advanced a Morris-inspired platform. As if to confirm this point, in a book co-authored by Desmond and Croly in 1903, they write that "the school of William Morris had very little influence on this side of the water."[12] Despite this assertion, as time went on, more and more articles and illustrations in the *Record* included the work of artists and artisans. In 1907 Pasadena architect Elmer Grey published an essay called "The Architect and the 'Arts and Crafts,'" discussing how architects would benefit from closer collaboration not only with craft workers but also those in the building trades.[13] An Arts and Crafts perspective held by the *Record*'s editors and contributors, many of them New York City architects, can be seen in the index headings for the magazine's illustrations. Naturally, headings appear for building categories such as "Commercial and Monumental Architecture" and "Domestic Architecture." But another substantial category of illustrations is dedicated to the "Allied Arts" such as mural painting, sculpture, and stained glass, while yet another category is devoted to "Details," highlighting finely executed doors and carved wood ornament.[14]

MANHATTAN, THE OUTER BOROUGHS, AND BEYOND

In surveying New York City's turn-of-the-century architecture, one can identify buildings that are indebted to stylistic developments associated with the Arts and Crafts movement in England and elsewhere in the United States.[15] In other, more subtle ways, the city's built environment shows the influence of Arts and Crafts concepts that were interpreted with original results. Designed by New York City architects, both well-known and relatively obscure, these examples appear in Manhattan, the outer boroughs, and country estates beyond the city limits.

One of the most familiar illustrations of the influence of the Arts and Crafts movement in the metropolis is located underground—in subway stations decorated by the architectural firm of Heins and La Farge.[16] Engineers were responsible for planning and constructing the Interborough Rapid Transit system, the city's first subway line, which opened in 1904. Each stop was embellished by colorful, durable ceramics. George Lewis Heins (1860–1907) and C. Grant La Farge (1862–1938) had met in Boston when they were architecture students at MIT.[17] Grant's father was John La Farge, the artist employed by Henry Hobson Richardson to design the murals and several windows for Trinity Church. After MIT, Grant stayed in Boston to work for Richardson, absorbing the master's Arts and Crafts proclivities. In 1886 Heins and La Farge, now living in New York City, formed their partnership, attracting national attention in 1891 when they won the competition for the Cathedral of St. John the Divine. After they were hired to work on the subway stations, the architects developed design concepts for tile friezes, panels that named the stops, and ornamental plaques that were made by the Grueby Faience Company of Boston and the Rookwood Pottery Company of Cincinnati. Grueby provided ceramics for seventeen stations, including plaques for Astor Place depicting a beaver gnawing on a tree, alluding to the Astor fortune that came from fur-trading, while Rookwood supplied ceramics for six stations, including Fulton Street, where the plaques illustrated Robert Fulton's steamboat (fig. 2.1).[18]

An affirmation of local history, a concept at the heart of the English Arts and Crafts movement, guided the design of subway entrance structures also by Heins and La Farge. Brick and terra-cotta control houses (1904–5), one at Battery Park and another at West Seventy-Second Street, are revivals of Flemish architecture, honoring the city's origins as a Dutch colony (fig. 2.2). An interest in Flemish and Dutch designs emerged in the city during the 1880s, evident in buildings topped by the curved and stepped parapet gables of the Low Countries.[19] In the 1890s, several fire engine houses were erected in Flemish and Dutch Revival styles. Examples in Brooklyn include a station in Bensonhurst (1895–96) and another in Bushwick (1896–97), both by the Parfitt Brothers.[20] As English immigrants, they would have understood the Arts and Crafts desire to design buildings with a reference to local history—buildings that spoke of Dutch Colonial New York, even if the fanciful modern structures weren't like anything the colonists would have seen.

The city's most magnificent expression of the Arts and Crafts movement is St. Thomas Episcopal Church (1905–13), designed by Cram, Goodhue, and Ferguson (fig. 2.3). Prominently sited on Fifth Avenue, it represents the last major project of Ralph Adams Cram and Bertram Goodhue before their relationship ruptured at the end of 1913, at which point Goodhue established an independent practice in New York.[21] As a Boston firm, the men served clients around the country, but when they won the 1903 competition to expand the campus at West Point, overlooking the Hudson River, they needed to open a New York City office. As a young man, Goodhue had trained in

FIGURE 2.1. Grueby Faience Company, tile in the Astor Place station of the New York City subway system, circa 1904.

FIGURE 2.2. Heins and La Farge, West Seventy-Second Street control house of the New York City subway system, 1904–5.

the city under James Renwick, and now he willingly moved to Manhattan.

In 1906 the firm won the St. Thomas competition to replace a church that had burned. As Cram recounted, the first plans were "quite English," with fan vaulting and Perpendicular tracery.[22] Upon receiving the award, he revised the scheme, producing "something more specifically French, of the latest, almost Flamboyant, type."[23] Cram's commitment to reviving Perpendicular Gothic, based on English Arts and Crafts theory and the English Gothic Revival, faded away. Goodhue, however, was not at all in agreement, and the partners went back and forth, sparring with designs. In January 1911, when the plans were finally set and the corner stone about to be laid, Schuyler wrote about the firm in an issue of *Architectural Record* devoted to their work. Regarding St. Thomas, he queried, "Is it early or late? Is it even French or English, this front . . . as of Amiens or the transept of Chartres, this Tour St. Jacques with English details?"[24] Schuyler lambasted scholarly purists and praised the partners for approaching the Gothic Revival with freedom.

While prominent features of St. Thomas, such as the rose window with flame-like tracery over the main portal, are clearly French, the church embodies the English Arts and Crafts ideal of collaboration between architects and artisans—incorporating work from exceptional shops in operation at the turn of the twentieth century. Schuyler credited both the architects and artisans for their "mutual knowledge" that enabled them to deliver such superior results.[25] Goodhue was behind most of the decoration. Like Cram, he joined the Society of Arts and Crafts in Boston in 1897, and he maintained his membership through two decades, long after moving to New York.[26] Lee Lawrie handled the sculpture for the St. Thomas façade and the enormous reredos, while Ardolino Brothers did the carving (fig. 2.4). Henry Chapman Mercer supplied tile for the chancel. Woodwork, including choir stalls, the pulpit, and lectern, came from Irving and Casson–A. H. Davenport, a merger of companies based in Cambridge, Massachusetts, that Boston's Arts and Crafts architects favored.[27] When stained glass windows were installed, beginning in 1927, most of them came from

FIGURE 2.3. Cram, Goodhue, and Ferguson, St. Thomas Episcopal Church, New York City, 1905–13.

FIGURE 2.4. Lee Lawrie, reredos, carved by Ardolino Brothers, St. Thomas Episcopal Church.

James Powell and Sons, Whitefriars, London, a company associated with the Arts and Crafts movement there.[28]

As could be seen in the cities of England and other American urban centers, wealthy residents of New York City at the turn of the century were erecting expansive country houses to escape the congested streets where they made their money. Many of these dwellings were formal and ostentatious, inspired by French and Italian architecture in the classical tradition, while others were informal and conveyed a sense of warmth, inspired by English architecture and the Romantic tradition.[29] Harrie T. Lindeberg (1880–1959) was a New York City architect who was widely admired as a designer of country houses.[30] Having worked early in his career for McKim, Mead & White, he could produce a beautiful Italian-style villa or a stately Georgian home. Even so, he became best known for designs that captured the flavor of England's leading Arts and Crafts proponents such as Ernest Gimson and Edwin Lutyens.

For James A. Stillman, president of National City Bank, Lindeberg oversaw the development of a remarkable ensemble of buildings for an estate in Pocantico Hills, north of New York City in Westchester County. Mondanne, as it was named, was built between 1906 and 1910, when Lindeberg was in partnership with Lewis Colt Albro (fig. 2.5). The house has been demolished, but it was extensively publicized and illustrated in periodicals, including the *Architectural Record*.[31] Rustic in effect, the residence was constructed of local fieldstone and flanked by low half-timbered wings. Its most memorable feature was its enormous pyramidal roof with shingles installed over rounded edges to create the illusion of thatch. Ruskin would have been appalled by the deception. Moreover, the scale of Mondanne was hardly humble or cottage-like—defying the concept of the charming rural house behind the English Arts and Crafts revivals. The *Record* called it a "Thatched Palace."[32] The main house extended three hundred feet in length, and around it were outbuildings including a superintendent's house, a gardener's house, and chicken houses. The result was like an English village. Mondanne was outlandish, but it was not unique. In 1911 *Country Life in America* presented it as one of several sizable examples of "the English cottage style."[33] These houses, noted the author, reflected "the value of simplicity," a unifying interest of Arts and Crafts architects. The style was perplexing, however, when the so-called cottages were, in fact, so large, and their "simplicity" was clearly a pretense.

FIGURE 2.5. Albro and Lindeberg, Mondanne, Pocantico Hills, New York, 1906–10.

The Tudor Revival was another option for Anglophile New Yorkers who were following architectural trends and planning a country estate.[34] Through the 1920s, the half-timbered Tudor, typically combined with stone, brick, or wood shingles, remained popular, while at the same time architects and their clients embraced a revival of the Jacobean house, erected in England at the tail end of the Gothic period. Like the Tudor houses with half-timbering, these Jacobean revivals were picturesque, with multiple gables, tall chimneys, and handcrafted ornament, but they were more refined. Goodhue designed an example of the type for John E. Aldred, named Ormston (1913–18), in Lattingtown, New York (fig. 2.6).[35] Located on Long Island Sound, the estate of 119 acres of grounds and gardens was landscaped by the Olmsted Brothers. Aldred was a self-made man, a native of Lowell, Massachusetts, who left school as a teenager to work in the textile mills, eventually accumulating eighty million dollars as an entrepreneur in public utilities. The Gold Coast country house positioned him and his wife in the company of New York City's weekend and summer society.

Asymmetrical in plan and elevations, the mansion has cross gables and steeply pitched roofs. Contributing to an air of informality are its thick slates and random-coursed fieldstone walls of varying colors. All the windows are leaded glass. While the medieval aspects of the mansion are dominant, it also has classical elements, recalling the transitional character of Jacobean houses. A double staircase on the entrance façade is especially impressive. Guests ascend from the ground-level courtyard to a terrace and continue through a round-arched doorway, reaching the mansion's main level. Other elevations include arcades, one of which is supported by hefty columns. Once inside the house, visitors enter a great hall with a stone fireplace, an organ, and paneling with extensive carving. The dining room, covered by a segmental-arched ceiling, has plasterwork molded with strapwork and English roses, while windows have insets of antique stained glass. Goodhue brought together a team of designers and artisans, as he did at Manhattan's St. Thomas Church. One collaborator may have been Francis H. Bacon—for just prior to receiving the commission for Ormston, Goodhue designed the Kitchi Gammi Club (1910–13) in Duluth, Minnesota, a Jacobean Revival building with many similarities to the Aldred mansion, which Bacon is known to have decorated.[36] An architect-turned-decorator, Bacon worked in Cambridge for A. H. Davenport before opening his own firm.

FIGURE 2.6. Bertram Grosvenor Goodhue, Ormston, Lattingtown, New York, 1913–18.

Like London, New York City was struggling with an exploding population and inadequate housing, leading philanthropists and architects to seek solutions that could be imitated elsewhere. English reformers and architects associated with the Arts and Crafts movement, concerned about the negative aspects of urban life and convinced of the restorative power of nature, promulgated theories and erected model communities. One of these models, Hampstead Garden Suburb, built near London and planned by Barry Parker and Raymond Unwin, provided an inspiration for the planned community of Forest Hills Gardens (1911) in the borough of Queens, designed by Frederick Law Olmsted, Jr. (1870–1957) and Grosvenor Atterbury (1869–1956).[37] The English development, conceived to bring together a mix of classes, was founded in 1906 by Henrietta Barnett a little more than two decades after she and her husband, Samuel, established Toynbee Hall, the settlement house in London's East End. Residents of Hampstead Garden Suburb enjoyed attractive homes designed by architects on streets that curved and opened to small parks. The project in Queens was initiated in 1909 by the Russell Sage Foundation, created two years earlier by the widowed Olivia Sage. From the beginning, the premise for building Forest Hills Gardens was to shelter the middle class. It would "set an example" and be managed "with due regard for profit."[38] In addition to houses and apartments, the development would include an inn where people could live as boarders as well as retail spaces for a few shops (fig. 2.7). A central green, small parks, and winding roads reflect Olmsted's study trip to England and the Continent, which he made just before the foundation hired him.

Atterbury was an obvious candidate to be invited as the project architect.[39] Drawn to housing reform, he had designed the Phipps Model Tenement (1907) in Manhattan and would design other such buildings. In 1907 he also had worked on a project funded by Olivia Sage—the restoration of the Governor's Room of New

FIGURE 2.7. Grosvenor Atterbury, Forest Hills Inn, Forest Hills Gardens, New York, 1911.

York City Hall. His lifelong engagement with housing and historic preservation aligned him with Arts and Crafts architects in both England and the United States. For Forest Hills Gardens, Atterbury was responsible for the first buildings, which introduced a palette of materials that would give the community its coherence. In 1911 he showed studies for the development in the Architectural League's annual exhibition, including a bird's-eye view.[40] Red tile roofs, dormers, and porches created picturesque streetscapes. One author observed in 1915, "The eaves overhang, after the fashion of many of the peasant cottages in rustic England." And to the credit of the development, there was "nothing arrogant or affected" about it.[41] As was the case with the thatched palace of Mondanne, rustic English architecture was intended to convey humility. Despite the quaint allusions, Atterbury took a modern approach to Forest Hills Gardens. The first houses were constructed quickly with modular concrete units. Furthermore, unlike a medieval English village, the community did not spread out around a parish church and market square. Rather, it was planned to serve twentieth-century commuters, who left in the morning from Station Square to take the fifteen-minute ride into Manhattan. Many of them merchants and clerks, they returned in the evening to socialize with like-minded residents. As was frequently the case with planned developments, people with artistic leanings also were drawn to it. At Forest Hills Gardens, Frederic W. Goudy, the renowned typeface designer, bought one of the houses and ran a press from his home (fig. 2.8).[42]

FIGURE 2.8. Grosvenor Atterbury, Goudy House, Forest Hills Gardens, 1913.

UPSTATE AND INFLUENTIAL

Several influential leaders in the American Arts and Crafts movement emerged in upstate New York, beginning in the 1890s. Elbert Hubbard (1856–1915) was the visionary behind the Roycroft community, located in East Aurora, twenty miles southeast of Buffalo.[43] Benefiting from his flair for marketing schemes, Hubbard spent the first half of his adult life as an executive at the Larkin Company in Buffalo. Cashing out in 1892, he aspired to a career as a writer. Two years later, he voyaged to England and Ireland, stopping along the way at Morris's Kelmscott Press in Hammersmith. In 1895 he launched *The Philistine: A Periodical of Protest,* a platform for his cultural commentaries, and the Roycroft Press, based in East Aurora.

Ever enterprising, Hubbard decided to build a print shop to handle the growing circulation of the periodical and the work of the press. Erected between 1897 and 1898, the print shop did not resemble an industrial building but rather an English country church.[44] Featuring a pitched roof and dormers, Gothic lancet windows, and a small cupola, the structure was shingled and simple. Inside, the trusses were visible in the manner of a church, while a large brick fireplace lent a domestic quality to the workspace. Hubbard's success was such that in 1899 he undertook construction of a "Chapel," in actuality a meeting hall, and a new print shop, finished in 1901 (fig. 2.9). Medieval English in character, both buildings are fieldstone and roofed in red tile, with castellated towers and Gothic windows, and the print shop has half-timbering. Both buildings have exposed trusswork inside.

Inspired by Ruskin and Morris, Hubbard had a benevolent attitude toward the men and women he employed. In truth, he was running a commercial operation, but he provided opportunities and an environment that were attractive to many. Eventually the community numbered about five hundred people. Hubbard also had a nose for artistic talent, and he recruited designers and artists to join him. They included designer-craftsmen William "Dard" Hunter and Karl Kipp as well as artists William W. Denslow, Alexis Jean Fournier, and Jerome Connor (1874–1943). On a gable of the north side of the "Chapel" is a terra-cotta face of the North Wind, a bas relief that Connor modeled (fig. 2.10).[45] The original print shop was

FIGURE 2.9. Elbert Hubbard, "Chapel," Roycroft community, East Aurora, New York, 1899–1901.

FIGURE 2.10. Jerome Connor, North Wind on Roycroft "Chapel."

FIGURE 2.11. Edward Austin Kent and William Winthrop Kent, First Unitarian Church, Buffalo, New York, 1904–6.

eventually incorporated into the Roycroft Inn, decorated by murals that Fournier painted. Hunter designed the inn's stained glass and sets of light fixtures.

In 1905 a wide porch with square columns was built across the front of the inn, called the Peristyle, possibly based on the pergola of the house built for Darwin D. Martin in Buffalo (see fig. 2.12). Frank Lloyd Wright (1867–1959) designed Martin's Prairie style home in 1903, and it was completed two years later. Hubbard and Martin had worked together at the Larkin Company, and they stayed in contact after Hubbard left the business. The Roycroft campus grew to fourteen buildings where artisans produced furniture, ceramics, and metalwork—most notably copper. Architects were never brought into Hubbard's Roycroft community, and the buildings he erected were rustic and basic. Yet the result was a pleasing ensemble. In 1915 Hubbard and his wife died on the *Lusitania*. Even without their charismatic leader, the community survived, but it couldn't make it through the Great Depression. Today, artists and artisans have returned to the campus in a village that honors the spirit of the Arts and Crafts movement.

At the opening of the twentieth century, Buffalo was thriving as a center for Great Lakes shipping and rail transportation, positioning it as the second-largest city in New York state and the eighth-largest city in the country.

Wealthy citizens commissioned sizable Tudor houses designed by local architects who followed current trends in Eastern seaboard cities and England.[46] Also popular were ecclesiastic buildings that called forth associations with England.

An elegant example of the English influence is the First Unitarian Church (1904–6), conceived as Early English Gothic in style (fig. 2.11).[47] It was designed by Edward Austin Kent (1854–1912) and William Winthrop Kent (1860–1955), brothers who were raised in Buffalo and educated in the East, Edward at Yale and William at Harvard.[48] Edward continued his studies at the École des Beaux-Arts and in London at the South Kensington School of Art, while William trained in Richardson's office in Brookline. Edward entered into a brief partnership with Joseph Lyman Silsbee and then set up practice on his own in Buffalo, while William settled in New York City. They worked together on the church.

When the building was illustrated in the *Inland Architect and News Record,* it was described as "like a quiet English parish church of 'ye olden tyme.'"[49] It has a large square central tower, buttressed at the corners, with a recessed Gothic portal, a lancet window above it, and battlements at the top. The door is oak and has wrought-iron strap hinges, probably designed by William, who published a book on architectural wrought iron in 1888. Departing from an Arts and Crafts preference for local materials, the architects chose Indiana limestone. Like a medieval church, the interior walls and flooring are stone. Overhead is a hammerbeam roof, which extends from the nave into the sanctuary. Stained glass windows were part of the original project, made by the workshop of Harry Goodhue of Boston. Aside from two figures, one of Isaiah and one of the Good Shepherd, the attraction of the windows is foliate decoration that reflects the influence of glass by Morris and his associates.

In Buffalo one confronts the diversity of styles that marks the American Arts and Crafts movement. Darwin D. Martin's Prairie style house (1903–5) was built when the Unitarian church was under construction (fig. 2.12).[50] Wright designed the house to be massed horizontally and covered by broad, low roofs with deep eaves, evoking the spreading landscape of the Midwest. The Martin House alludes neither to the western New York locale nor to an English heritage. Wright took a liberal view in interpreting this particular Arts and Crafts principle of building in a manner that affirmed a regional heritage, and as his practice grew beyond the Midwest, he promoted the new style as American. On the other hand, he was committed to the Arts and Crafts desire to integrate a dwelling with nature, designing the Martin House with banked windows to maximize the connection with the outdoors, a large veranda, the pergola admired by Hubbard, and planters. Writing in the *Architectural Record* in 1908, Wright advocated for the Arts and Crafts interest in simplicity.[51] Moreover, he retained an Arts and Crafts attitude in establishing relationships with favored artisans and artists.[52] Among his collaborators at the Martin House were Frank L. Linden (1859–1934) and the Linden Glass Company of Chicago, the source of the art glass (fig. 2.13); Chicago artist Blanche Ostertag and artisan Orlando Giannini, responsible for the fireplace mosaic; and Winslow Brothers of Chicago, metalworkers who supplied bronze firewood boxes. The Martin House thus speaks of the Arts and Crafts movement that developed in Chicago.

Rochester deserves to be recognized as a city where one of the earliest Arts and Crafts societies was organized in the United States. As in London and Boston, architects were active proponents. In March 1897 architects Harvey Ellis (1852–1904) and Claude F. Bragdon (1866–1946) joined three other people in founding the Rochester Arts and Crafts Society.[53] Ellis, an artist and illustrator as well as an architect, was elected president, and Bragdon, a prolific author, volunteered as treasurer. The Rochester Society would never sponsor large and influential exhibitions like those that contributed to Boston's reputation, but the founders believed that mounting exhibitions was part of their mission. By May 1897 the Rochester group presented a show of Japanese prints and modern French posters.[54]

Ellis, observed Bragdon after his friend's death, hadn't left "a single notable building" behind. Nevertheless, he was revered by his peers for his "architectural pen-drawings."[55] Ellis respected Morris's writings, and his "taste was Gothic rather than classic."[56] Early in life, between 1879 and 1885, Ellis partnered with his architect brother Charles in a Rochester-based practice, then left to work for architects in the Midwest, ultimately returning to Rochester during the 1890s. In 1903 he moved to Syracuse, where he was hired by Gustav Stickley as a writer and illustrator for *The Craftsman.*[57]

Bragdon trained with several architects, including Charles Ellis in Rochester and Bruce Price in New York City, before eventually settling in Rochester.[58] Captivated at a young age by the writings of Ralph Waldo Emerson,

FIGURE 2.12. Frank Lloyd Wright, Darwin D. Martin House, Buffalo, New York, 1903–5.

FIGURE 2.13. Frank L. Linden and Linden Glass Company, art glass doors in the library, Martin House.

he was intrigued by the philosopher's view that beauty could be achieved through "geometry, instead of expense."[59] As an architect, ideal proportions became one of Bragdon's interests. At the same time, he was drawn to Morris and an aesthetic that favored simplicity. Bragdon designed his own house, named Cro' Nest, in 1902 (fig. 2.14). He gave it a gable-on-hip roof with overhanging eaves, shingles that were stained gray "like the tree branches," and shutters that were painted "leaf green," he wrote in an article about it. Lacking any applied ornament, its aesthetic appeal was due to its "justness of proportion." Inside the house, one found stained cypress, leaded glass windows, and "plain oak furniture." The result was "a little austere and bare," but it was harmonious and restful, he wrote, adding Morris's admonition to value usefulness along with beauty.[60] Arts and Crafts elements included a stained glass window with a crow perched on a grapevine, a fireplace surround with a large Grueby tile representing a sailing ship, and andirons that Bragdon designed.[61]

Within a few years, Bragdon's thinking about beauty and ornament evolved. In *Projective Ornament,* published in 1915, Bragdon argued that mathematical patterns found in nature should provide the basis for a new ornamental language.[62] Unrelated to historical styles, this new ornament would be universal. In his buildings, Bragdon's interest in patterns can be seen in brickwork and in tiles with geometric decoration. Like many Arts and Crafts theorists, Bragdon was motivated by a progressive outlook; however, by embracing a mathematical approach to design, he became an advocate for regular, repetitive ornament, which Ruskin and Morris would have rejected as rigid and unnatural.

Gustav Stickley (1858–1942), best known as a manufacturer of Arts and Crafts furniture, also advanced Arts and Crafts ideals in American architecture.[63] Reared with only a grammar school education, he found a calling making furniture, ultimately establishing his own business near Syracuse in 1898. Ambitious and energetic, he was willing to partner with individuals who were better educated and more talented as designers than he.

In 1900 Stickley hired a young architect, Henry W. Wilkinson (1869–1931), to assist him with a new line of furniture. Wilkinson was born in Syracuse and earned a degree in architecture from Cornell University in 1890.[64] He spent his first year of practice in Boston, where he leased an office next to Shepley, Rutan, and Coolidge, Richardson's successor firm.[65] He also joined the Boston Architectural Club, absorbing the growing interest of his Yankee colleagues in the Arts and Crafts movement.[66] After a stint in New York City, Wilkinson moved back to Syracuse. While working with Stickley, he is credited with developing the simple furniture that would become famous. All the while, the links among progressive designers in upstate New York were becoming stronger. Bragdon befriended Wilkinson, met and married Wilkinson's sister Charlotte, and settled with her in Rochester at Cro' Nest.

FIGURE 2.14. Claude Bragdon, Cro' Nest, Rochester, New York, 1902.

Stickley and his company flourished, and in 1900 he bought a newly built house in Syracuse, a Queen Anne designed by local architect Wellington Tabor.[67] On Christmas Eve of 1901, a fire broke out, which led to the reconstruction of the dwelling in the new year. It was completed with many of the features that Stickley would encourage. One enters the house through a wide chestnut front door, surrounded by flat casings. On the first floor, the spaces of the rooms flow together, from the entry foyer and living room, to a wide hall, and then to the dining room (fig. 2.15). Characteristic of Stickley's preferences are chestnut paneling, built-in seating and cabinets, exposed ceiling beams, and an inglenook. Very little ornament is to be found; nevertheless, artisans made a few contributions, evident in a metal fireplace hood and Grueby tiles. The house was "singularly free from pretension," observed one writer, specifying a virtue associated with Arts and Crafts architecture.[68]

As Stickley's business took off, he changed the firm name so that it was no longer identified with him. In 1901 he rebranded it as "The United Crafts" to suggest that it was a shared venture of the workers. In fact, he remained the company owner. Also that year, he hired Irene Sargent to write for him.[69] She came from the region, but her family roots were in New England and she had studied in Boston. During that time, she attended art history lectures by Charles Eliot Norton at Harvard. In the years ahead, she would distinguish herself as a professor at Syracuse University teaching Romance languages and art and architectural history. When the first issue of *The Craftsman* was issued in October 1901, Sargent wrote all the articles. Devoted entirely to the "life, art, and influence" of Morris, they were substantive, directed to an educated middle-class audience. Through the spring of 1905, Sargent remained the monthly magazine's editor, managing contributors including Harvey Ellis. Topics ranged from home furnishings and gardening to jewelry. Designs for houses began appearing in 1902, and articles on residential architecture as well as house plans ran through 1916, when the magazine shut down.[70] The many ways in which Arts and Crafts ideas took form in American architecture were documented by *The Craftsman.* Bungalows were a favorite type. Readers learned about Forest Hills Gardens in 1911, and they read about "The Home of the Future" in articles by Goodhue and Lindeberg in 1916.[71] The magazine's tent was a big one.

Another Syracuse resident prominent in the nation's Arts and Crafts movement was the ceramic artist Adelaide Alsop Robineau. In 1903 she built a pottery studio on a hillside overlooking Onondaga Lake, and a year later she and her husband erected a house next door (fig. 2.16).[72] Called Four Winds, it was designed by architect Katharine Cotheal Budd (1860–1951).[73] Both women started out as artists and formed their friendship when they studied

FIGURE 2.15. Gustav Stickley, Stickley House, hall looking toward the dining room, Syracuse, New York, 1901.

FIGURE 2.16. Katharine Cotheal Budd, Four Winds, Syracuse, New York, 1904.

painting with William Merritt Chase. Budd would pursue art throughout her life, but she redirected her professional ambitions to a career in architecture, training in New York City and Paris before opening her practice in New York. In 1924 she became the first female member of the New York City chapter of the American Institute of Architects.

Four Winds evokes a cozy cottage in England, with a steeply gabled roof that overhangs the entrance. Its shingles on the upper story-and-a-half and clapboards on the first story were allowed to weather, while vines were planted to climb around the windows, creating a close relationship between the house and nature. Along the driveway, Robineau placed cement flower pots that she had made. The interior rooms of the house included many popular Arts and Crafts elements, such as fumed chestnut paneling, built-in cabinets, and a settle bench on each side of the fireplace. A high narrow shelf wrapped around the living room walls to display Robineau's pottery, and a large built-in desk provided the space she needed to edit the magazine *Keramic Studio.* After the house was finished, she made tiles, some representing wisteria, to enhance the living room fireplace. The furniture was "mission in type," created by a friend.[74] In its decoration, Robineau told the author of an article in *American Homes and Gardens,* the cottage carried out "William Morris's precept" about usefulness and beauty.[75] Simplicity was desired, and nothing was "for show"—except, of course, Robineau's own ceramic creations.

FIGURE 2.17. Ralph Radcliffe Whitehead and Bolton Brown, White Pines, Byrdcliffe, Woodstock, New York, 1903.

RUSKIN IN WOODSTOCK

Byrdcliffe, a summer arts colony in the Catskills, wasn't especially influential, but it warrants attention as a variation on the theme of the utopian Arts and Crafts community.[76] Located near the hamlet of Woodstock, it was founded in 1902 by Ralph Radcliffe Whitehead (1854–1929), a wealthy Englishman who married an American. Whitehead had studied with Ruskin at Oxford, and he embraced Ruskin's belief in artistic expression as essential to a rewarding life.[77] When Whitehead decided to underwrite an arts community, he also responded to Ruskin's love of remote mountain scenery, purchasing seven mountainside farms for his colony. To assist him in the development, he turned to Bolton Brown, an artist and educator. Brown had earned degrees at Syracuse University and established the art department at Stanford. Together, the two men planned the site and erected five buildings by the beginning of 1903.[78]

Construction advanced rapidly that year, resulting in about thirty structures that served the colony, including a spacious art studio, a library, shops for pottery, metalwork and woodwork, a boarding house, and a large home for Whitehead and his family, named White Pines (fig. 2.17).[79] In keeping with much Arts and Crafts architecture, the buildings were simple in design, employing local pine and stone, and linked to nature with porches and balconies. They also had low sloping roofs with overhanging eaves and horizontal siding, reminiscent of the chalets of Austria and Switzerland. In that the reference was to foreign rather than native architecture, Whitehead and Brown departed from mainstream Arts and Crafts thinking. This choice would have originated with Whitehead, who was described as Byrdcliffe's "absolute monarch."[80] Even though Byrdcliffe was not a business enterprise, it was hardly a utopia in the way in which it was governed. After a few summers, many of the original colonists became disillusioned and decided not to return.

In New York state, the Arts and Crafts movement caught fire in multiple centers. This phenomenon was different from what happened in other regions around the nation. Generally, the leading figures who promoted an Arts and Crafts philosophy came from major American cities and had a greater impact than the people who lived in small cities and towns. But in New York state, Hubbard, Bragdon, Stickley, and Whitehead all found the ideas of Ruskin and Morris compelling and became known. On the other hand, New York City's architects and clients were not especially attached to England, and many of the wealthy were enthralled by France and showy architecture. Simplicity wasn't what they wanted, and the architects responded accordingly. Yet even though New York City never saw a fervent commitment to an Arts and Crafts philosophy, architects there absorbed it. Ultimately, the Empire State's most significant contribution to architecture and the Arts and Crafts movement was through publications, notably the *Architectural Record* and *The Craftsman,* which reached subscribers around the country.

3 Visionaries in the Mid-Atlantic

By the end of the nineteenth century, large swaths of the Mid-Atlantic region were changing, altered by expanding commuter rail networks and the intensifying subdivision of land near the train lines leading to New York City and Philadelphia. Developers turned to architects and landscape architects to plan well-designed buildings and communities that would cater to upper-middle-class residents. Many developments were idyllic retreats, with the winding streets and picturesque houses that Arts and Crafts principles encouraged. Outstanding examples appeared in New Jersey and towns around Philadelphia. Along the Mid-Atlantic, visionaries who embraced Arts and Crafts ideals also founded places with utopian goals. In Philadelphia, these architects and the city's elite generally identified themselves with England. Like their colleagues in Boston, the Philadelphia architects were conversant with trends in English architecture and were in contact with designers at the forefront of the English Arts and Crafts movement. At an early date, Philadelphia architects embraced the Tudor Revival. As in Boston and New York City, Philadelphia architects were hired to design impressive country estates, the largest of which were compounds inspired by Arts and Crafts thinking. But where Philadelphia architects earned special recognition was for establishing a vision for Collegiate Gothic campuses, a stylistic approach that colleges and universities would imitate across the United States.

AT HOME IN NEW JERSEY

Of the many burgeoning suburbs in New Jersey at the end of the nineteenth century, Millburn was one of the most attractive. Founded in 1857, the town appealed to affluent newcomers seeking comfortable homes near commuter rail service to Newark and New York City. Potential residents also would have heard about the initiative in the early 1890s to protect the South Mountain, located partially in Millburn, as a nature reserve. At one of the township's edges is the neighborhood of Wyoming, where a teenaged Joy Wheeler Dow (1860–1937) moved with his widowed mother and sister in 1878.[1] Although never formally trained, he became a respected architect and writer. For the next thirty years, he remained in Wyoming.

Dow solidified his reputation through the publication of *American Renaissance: A Review of Domestic Architecture*, issued in 1904. He was no fan of John Ruskin, whom he disparaged as an "old fogy," and he never mentioned William Morris.[2] Nevertheless, Arts and Crafts themes run through the book's chapters. Above all, Dow conveys his admiration for the early, modest architecture of his own heritage—that is to say, American houses of the colonial and federal periods, which he calls the "American Renaissance." In these "olden times," he explains, the architect and the builder were often the same person, which to his mind was advantageous.[3] In taking this view, he responded to the high esteem held by English Arts and Crafts theorists for the medieval master builder. Dow didn't say so, but we can guess that he was intrigued by the idea that individuals who lacked formal training, such as himself, could be superior designers. Also reflecting an Arts and Crafts outlook, Dow railed against commercialism in American architecture. While on the topic, he wanted his readers to know that we'd be better off without skyscrapers.[4] Throughout his book, he identifies early American architecture as a reflection of Anglo-Saxon culture, and he concludes by saying that in his own designs, he strives to express Anglo-Saxon "home feeling."[5]

Often Dow's starting point for a residential project was an English or early American house, which he adapted to suit the locale and modern needs. Rabbit House (1904), erected in the Wyoming neighborhood for his family, was his interpretation of Sparrow's House in Ipswich, England, a late medieval building with a seventeenth-century front elevation (fig. 3.1).[6] Much as Dow admired its pargeting, an ornamental plasterwork, he knew the treatment wouldn't survive the winters in New Jersey. As a substitute, he ornamented Rabbit House with a carving of a rabbit and rabbit images inset in leaded glass. What he took from Sparrow's House and applied to Rabbit House were second-story oriels and casement windows, the sashes reduced in size for better function. By emphasizing "adaptation" as a design strategy in his writing and in his work, Dow promoted a method that was shared by English and American Arts and Crafts architects.

FIGURE 3.1. Joy Wheeler Dow, Rabbit House, Millburn, New Jersey, 1904.

Two miles to the west of Rabbit House is a courtyard house named The Close (1912–13), designed by M. H. Baillie Scott (1865–1945), one of the leading figures of the English Arts and Crafts movement (fig. 3.2).[7] Commissioned by Henry Binsse, it's located in leafy Short Hills, established in 1874 by Stewart Hartshorn, an inventor and manufacturer.[8] Hartshorn steadily assembled parcels of property, and in preparing for development, retained the rural qualities and natural grades of the land. His goal, he explained, was "to create a harmonious community filled with people who appreciated nature." His concept was well-executed but not original, clearly taking as its model Llewellyn Park in nearby West Orange, begun in 1853 and designed by Alexander Jackson Davis. This and other residential parks, undertaken during the Victorian period, reflect an attachment to nature that carried into the planned communities of Arts and Crafts proponents.

As its name suggests, The Close is organized around a green, its principal rooms located on one side in order to capture the sun, while attached outbuildings including a laundry, garage, kennel, and "tool house" extend along two other sides. At the open end of the central space is a low garden wall, beyond which was a sizable vegetable garden. Baillie Scott liked the scheme of a courtyard with a close-cropped lawn, having successfully incorporated this feature into other houses. He also employed it for a large project at Hampstead Garden Suburb, Waterlow Court (1904–9), a group home of fifty flats for working women.[9] When The Close was built, chestnut trees on the property were taken down and used, as in traditional building practice. They were felled, shaped, and pegged to frame the house, which was Tudor in style. Stucco covered brick

FIGURE 3.2. M. H. Baillie Scott, The Close, Short Hills, New Jersey, 1912–13.

infill, and handmade tile from England covered the roof. The Close was thus both indigenous and English.

About fifteen miles northwest of Millburn, Gustav Stickley began buying farmland in 1908 to create a utopian farm, workshop, and school as well as a new home for his family.[10] By this time, he was living in New York City, having decided to move his business operations there, while his wife and children remained in Syracuse. The land that he bought in Parsippany-Troy Hills was commuting distance to New York yet still rural, dotted with large estates. He named his property Craftsman Farms. What he envisioned for it responded in many ways to Arts and Crafts values. First and foremost, Craftsman Farms would promote the simple life, refuting Victorian extravagance. It would preserve the agricultural use of the land, while its buildings would be designed to harmonize with nature. It also would be an educational center, where boys could learn to farm and receive training in the manual arts. The vision never came to fruition.

Stickley first built structures to support the farm and serve the community he hoped to attract, including worker cottages, two barns, and a location for dairy processing. Between 1910 and 1911, he erected a building that he conceived as a clubhouse; he expected to add an estate house for his family at a later date. But even before construction began, he modified the design so the building could function as the family residence.[11] Upon its completion, his wife and children left Syracuse to join him in New Jersey. At the time, the Craftsman furniture business and *Craftsman* magazine appeared to be thriving, motivating Stickley to invest in a Manhattan showroom and offices and to open a home-building service.[12] Retail sales

FIGURE 3.3. Gustav Stickley, Craftsman Farms, Parsippany-Troy Hills, New Jersey, 1910–11.

were starting to falter, however, and by 1915 he was forced into bankruptcy, lost Craftsman Farms, and returned to Syracuse.

Yet for a few short years, Stickley succeeded in publicizing his utopian vision and his idea of the Arts and Crafts house through his magazine and his company. "The ruling principle of the Craftsman house is simplicity," Stickley informed his readers in 1913.[13] Like the furniture that he sold, the lines of his ideal dwelling should be simple and avoid "elaborate ornamentation."[14] As a result, the house would not only be beautiful but also would exert a positive influence on the family it sheltered, especially the children. The building should be designed to harmonize with its environment. It also should employ wood to advantage, with beamed ceilings, built-ins, and wainscoting. Stickley, readers were reminded, was "perhaps the leading authority on the proper use of our native woods and their treatment for decorative purposes."[15]

Consistent with these ideas, the house at Craftsman Farms was constructed with wood from chestnut trees on the property (fig. 3.3). In this respect, it is like The Close by Baillie Scott. But Stickley erected a log house, not an English half-timbered house. It was rustic outside and inside, evoking the cabins of American settlers. In massing, the house is a low one-and-a-half-story box, with a one-story kitchen attached to the rear. Fieldstone chimneys and diamond-paned windows are the main enhancements. Running across the width of the house is a large living room, dominated by fireplaces at either end. Copper fireplace hoods and copper light fixtures are handcrafted embellishments—useful and beautiful. Upstairs, light-blue Grueby tile surrounds a bedroom fireplace. Stickley's company provided furnishings for the house, including a custom-designed piano and a dining room sideboard. The effect was simple, in harmony with nature, and American in spirit. But as Stickley learned, realizing a utopian vision proved not to be a simple matter. In truth, it could only be supported by an elaborate business enterprise—and briefly at that.

PHILADELPHIA, PENN, AND THE T SQUARE CLUB

Along with Boston and New York City, Philadelphia at the turn of the twentieth century had become one of the country's most important centers for the architectural profession. Its practitioners were highly trained, at home and abroad, and many were formally educated. Visual artists had established a foundation for the architects to build upon. In 1805 the Pennsylvania Academy of the Fine Arts was launched as a school and museum, the first such institution in the United States. The Philadelphia Sketch Club started in 1860, followed by the Philadelphia Museum of Art, originating with the Centennial Exhibition of 1876. In 1877 the Philadelphia Society of Artists and the Art Club of Philadelphia were organized. Also during this decade, in 1874, the University of Pennsylvania asked the university architect, Thomas W. Richards, to open an architecture program to meet a growing demand for well-designed buildings. Penn was the fifth institution in the United States to offer such a curriculum, following MIT, the University of Illinois, Cornell, and Syracuse.[16]

Several energetic architects saw the benefit of gathering regularly to discuss their projects and ideas. In 1883 they organized the T Square Club, the second such group in the country, founded two years after the Architectural League in New York. Subsequently clubs were organized in Chicago in 1885 and Boston in 1889. Unlike their colleagues in Boston or London, the Philadelphia architects did not take the lead in forming an Arts and Crafts society. Instead, it was art students from the Drexel Institute who gathered in 1904 to start the Daedalus Arts and Crafts Guild. By 1911 it evolved into a juried group of craft workers, and they changed the organization's name to the Arts and Crafts Guild of Philadelphia.[17]

Nevertheless, Philadelphia architects were very much oriented toward trends in English architecture, and the T Square Club encouraged an Arts and Crafts ethos. Among the founders were Walter Cope, Frank Miles Day, Wilson Eyre, William L. Price, and John Stewardson, all sympathetic to the Arts and Crafts movement.[18] In 1893 the T Square Club sponsored its first exhibition, motivated by the examples set by the Architectural League in 1885 and the Boston Architectural Club in 1890. Within a few years, the club's exhibitions promoted Arts and Crafts concerns. Cope was a key figure. For the show that ran from the end of December 1896 through January 1897, he chaired the jury.[19] Then in the spring of 1897, he served on the committee for the Boston Architectural Club's exhibition that coincided with Boston's first Arts and Crafts exhibition.[20] A distinction of the Philadelphia show was its inclusion of entries from the Department of Interior Decoration at Penn's School of Architecture. Reflecting the Arts and Crafts emphasis on well-crafted ornament and furnishings, examples of stained glass, furniture, tile, and room designs were displayed.[21] Leading members of the English Arts and Crafts movement contributed to the T Square Club exhibitions. For example, in 1899–1900, entries came from C. R. Ashbee and Walter Crane.[22] The architects' commitment became explicit when they broadened the scope of the 1906–7 show to cover "Architecture and the Allied Arts."[23] It included tile, pottery, metalwork, stained glass, and mosaics, bringing craft workers and architects together.

"EXPRESSIVE OF DOMESTICITY"

Like Boston's Robert Peabody, Wilson Eyre (1858–1944) admired the Tudor style and applied it to his country houses before the style was widely adopted in the United States.[24] An early example of Eyre's interest is Wisteria, the Charles A. Newhall House, built between 1884 and 1885 in the Chestnut Hill neighborhood of Philadelphia (fig. 3.4).[25] Above its stone foundation, the dwelling was constructed of several materials: red brick, shingles, and Tudor half-timbering with stucco. On the garden elevation, the second story jetties over the first, the gabled attic jetties over the second story, and a small turret projects on one side. The massing is asymmetrical, and the effect is an informed interpretation of the domestic work of Richard Norman Shaw. Eyre's Tudor design for Wisteria had staying power. In 1900 the garden elevation was illustrated in *Architecture* magazine.[26] The same issue included a photograph of Old Moreton Hall, a sixteenth-century half timbered house in Cheshire, providing readers the opportunity to study an English example.[27] Writing in *Country Life in America* in 1913, Eyre explained why he favored the "Elizabethan" style. It was "expressive of domesticity," allowed for flexible floor plans, and was practical in that its stucco could be applied over stone, hollow tile, or brick.[28]

The entrance façade of Wisteria is dominated by a large, broad Flemish gable on the right. In 1884 Eyre designed a similar brick gable on an urban townhouse in Camden, New Jersey, for Dr. Henry Genet Taylor.[29] The form was uncommon in the United States at this time, but again it reflected Eyre's kinship with English architects including Shaw, Ernest George, and Baillie Scott, who frequently used this Jacobean component.[30]

By the 1890s, Eyre distanced himself from his "first eccentricities."[31] He still drew upon England's manor houses with gables and dormers, but his rooflines and elevations became simpler, and he used fewer materials. The informal plan of the English country house continued to appeal to him. Writing in 1917 to Frank Chouteau Brown, editor of the Boston-based *Architectural Review,* Eyre observed that the "people in England live more nearly the kind of life we lead."[32] Eyre took an Arts and Crafts approach to craftsmanship that was similar to Brown's in his Boston practice. Eyre wanted the textures of the worker's hand to be evident, whether in the joints of masonry, the adzed dressing of timber, or the rough surfaces of plaster. Widely admired, Eyre was hired to design substantial country houses, yet he always aimed to avoid pretentiousness.

For his own family homes, William L. Price (1861–1916) turned to the Tudor Revival.[33] He and his brother Francis trained with Frank Furness, and in 1882 the Prices opened an office. The following year, they participated in founding the T Square Club. Over the course of the decade, the young architects pulled away from the expressive approach of Furness and embraced the new trends in England and the northeastern United States. When Will bought out his brother in 1893, he had married and started a family. During this period, he and a developer began working on a planned residential community in northwest Philadelphia that they would market to a professional class. Called Overbrook Farms, it was adjacent to an existing commuter rail line.[34] The timing was right for Price. He was tasked with designing a model house that would set the tone for the Main Line development. When

FIGURE 3.4. Wilson Eyre, Wisteria, Philadelphia, 1884–85.

FIGURE 3.5. William L. Price, Kelty, Lower Merion, Pennsylvania, 1900–1901.

the house was finished in 1894, the Price family moved in.[35] The Tudor dwelling is two-and-a-half stories, stone on the ground level and half-timbered and stucco above, with a cross gable over an entrance enlivened by elaborate carving on the bargeboards.

Two years later, Price traveled to England and the Continent.[36] In England he visited Ashbee and members of the Guild of Handicraft. He was drawn to the example of the architect working alongside the artisans, and he was attracted to the writings of Morris. When his father died in 1899, Price pursued these interests. Having come into an inheritance, he planned a spacious home, much larger than the Overbrook residence.[37] He acquired a lot in Lower Merion, four miles to the northwest, and again chose the Tudor style, blending a stone first story with half-timbering above. Called Kelty (1900–1901), the house includes ornamental work by two of Philadelphia's leading craftsmen: glass by Nicola D'Ascenzo and iron sconces by Samuel Yellin (fig. 3.5).[38] Most of the rooms are Gothic in décor, including beamed ceilings and doorways with pointed arches. On the third floor is a small theater, supported by hammerbeam trusses.

Rambling Tudor country houses were especially popular with Philadelphia's well-to-do, and they

FIGURE 3.7. Wilson Eyre, Neill and Mauran House, Philadelphia, 1891.

clients. In 1905 Frank Miles Day (1861–1918) was hired to restore an early nineteenth-century house and barn on a neglected Mount Airy farm in northwest Philadelphia for artists Violet Oakley, Elizabeth Shippen Green, and Jessie Willcox Smith, along with a fourth friend and family members.[48] The house had succumbed to a fire, and after an attempt to save parts of it, the remains were torn down. Day then designed a new center-entrance Colonial Revival dwelling, completed in 1906. The barn was in poor shape, but Day managed to preserve its stone walls. A new roof was erected and the interior reconstructed to accommodate three studios for the women, who named their home Cogslea (fig. 3.8).

Day, a native of Philadelphia, was born to an English father and was oriented toward England.[49] After graduating from Penn, he studied in London at the South Kensington School of Art and at the Royal Academy of Art, and then worked for the architect Basil Champneys. It's not surprising that when he wrote a critique of modern American houses, he commented approvingly on our "latter day Colonial" architecture inspired by Georgian houses, which "our forefathers brought from England."[50] He must have admired English preservation activities and the effort of his colleagues in Boston when they campaigned to restore the Massachusetts State House, completed in 1898. In 1899 Day chaired a committee of the

Philadelphia chapter of the American Institute of Architects to research and devise a plan to preserve Congress Hall, built from 1787 to 1789, which served as the United States Capitol during the 1790s.[51] Restoration was finished in 1913. When designing one of the studio windows at Cogslea, in which muntins define a tall, round-arched shape, Day must have been thinking of the tall, round-arched windows at Congress Hall.[52]

In 1906 Oakley was completing a mural cycle for the Pennsylvania capitol building at Harrisburg.[53] She subsequently was commissioned to paint murals for two more chambers of the capitol, and she hired Day to expand her studio.[54] He opened one of the barn walls on the upper level and enlarged the space, undertaking the work in 1914. Three large, squat stuccoed columns helped carry a fifty-foot-square room that was twenty-four feet high. Much as Day and Oakley were pleased to retain the old barn, they were willing to make extensive changes to it. This relaxed attitude toward preservation was in line with the philosophy in New England, where architects R. Clipston Sturgis and H. Langford Warren were freely adapting colonial and federal buildings for clubhouses and a school gymnasium during these same years.

UTOPIAN COMMUNITIES

Several people with rare imaginations drew upon Arts and Crafts concepts to bring designers and craft workers together in places that were at some distance from Philadelphia, but connected to it. Price was one of these visionaries. In sympathy with Morris and Ashbee, he embraced their social concerns as a founder of the utopian communities of Arden, Delaware, and Rose Valley, Pennsylvania. Both were conceived as villages that put all residents on an equal footing, providing them with shared greens, woodlands, and public halls.

In 1900 Price's friend Frank Stephens, a sculptor, bought 162 acres of Delaware farmland six miles north of Wilmington. There, a year later, Stephens, Price, and others established a village, naming it Arden after the magical forest in Shakespeare's *As You Like It*.[55] Residents would lease, not buy, the land, following the "single tax" theory of economist Henry George, and the property would be managed by trustees. Price produced a plan for the village that respected the rustic setting. At its center was a Village Green, while a stream valley and wooded areas were designated to remain in their natural state. Artists and craft workers arrived, living during the first years in tents and

FIGURE 3.8. Frank Miles Day, Cogslea, Philadelphia, 1905–6.

FIGURE 3.9. William L. Price, Green Gate, Arden, Delaware, 1909.

rudimentary cottages. In 1902 Red House was built, providing a place where guilds of the community assembled. Named for the brick dwelling erected by Morris for his family forty years earlier, Arden's small frame Red House was unremarkable. Its construction was followed by an outdoor theater-in-the-round in 1906 that was similarly rudimentary. Three years later Joseph Fels, millionaire soap manufacturer and philanthropist, provided funds to underwrite sturdier buildings. Stephens, Arden's founder, erected a house on the green in 1909 using hollow tiles covered with stucco and half-timbering. On a beam of the façade was carved the motto "Tomorrow Is a New Day" from Ralph Waldo Emerson. Price designed several houses, including Green Gate (1909), which was stuccoed and ornamented with tile (fig. 3.9). As more residents arrived, the community needed a larger meeting place than Red House. Taking the route of other Arts and Crafts designers, in 1910 Price rebuilt an 1850s barn, named the Gild Hall. To serve the growing number of artisans, Price designed the Craft Shop, dating from 1913 (fig. 3.10).

Just when Price was outlining a vision for Arden with Stephens and overseeing the completion of Kelty, the large house for his family in Lower Merion, he bought an abandoned mill village southwest of Philadelphia near Media. It was incorporated in July 1901 as the Rose Valley Association, a community dedicated to craft production.[56] Like Morris, Price rejected the factory system and wanted to promote the well-being of the laborer. Furniture production would be a central activity of the community, supervised by carver John Maene. Price began by renovating an existing row of worker houses, covering their rubble stone walls with stucco, and moved his family into one of the residences right away. He also put other existing structures in the village to use, including several houses and the remains of two water-powered mills. A Victorian house, remodeled, became his long-term family home. In 1901 one of the mill buildings was turned into a woodshop, and a year later the second was rebuilt as the Guild Hall (fig. 3.11). Price also designed new houses. Constructed with native stone and stucco made with local sand, the buildings of Rose Valley harmonized visually

FIGURE 3.10. William L. Price, Craft Shop, Arden, Delaware, 1913.

with each other, creating an impression that was similar to the unified appearance of villages throughout England. Tying them together further, Rose Valley's buildings were roofed with red tile and decorated with ornamental tile from Henry Chapman Mercer's pottery in Doylestown.

In 1903 Price began issuing a magazine, *The Artsman.* Published and printed in Philadelphia, it was a vehicle for him to promote his ideas. An early essay was entitled "The Relation of Arts and Crafts to Architecture."[57] Price explained, "We talk of a renascence of architecture. But first we must have a renascence of artisans."[58] He believed, as did Morris, that by starting with the workman and treating him well, "beauty in architecture and in all arts" would come about as "the natural expression of a beautiful life."[59] Unfortunately, the cost of Rose Valley furniture was prohibitive, wages couldn't be met, and in 1906 the workshops were closed. As was often the case, Arts and Crafts idealism collided with reality, and reality came out on top.

Social reform was not a driving objective for Henry Chapman Mercer, founder of the Moravian Pottery and Tile Works in Doylestown, north of Philadelphia.[60] Most compelling for him was the region's pre-industrial past. As an undergraduate at Harvard, he encountered Arts and Crafts ideas when he studied fine arts with Charles Eliot Norton. He also met classmates who would become active in Boston's Society of Arts and Crafts.[61] After settling in Doylestown, he began collecting antique tools, which led to an interest in craftsmanship, and then a desire to make tiles by hand.

In the late 1890s, encouraged by both William De Morgan, one of England's leading ceramists, and Eyre, Mercer succeeded in forming tiles with local clay fired in a kiln on an indulgent aunt's property. He named his company Moravian Pottery and Tile Works for the Pennsylvania Germans who settled in eastern Pennsylvania, whose craftsmanship he admired. Architects in Philadelphia and Boston began ordering Mercer's tile, and it was exhibited and sold by the Society of Arts and Crafts in Boston.[62] In 1901 Mercer became a Craftsman member of the Boston society, and he was elevated to Master status a year later.

FIGURE 3.11. William L. Price, Guild Hall, Rose Valley, Pennsylvania, 1902.

His success was such that he bought property and built a large tile works on it, relocating the business there in 1912 (fig. 3.12).[63] Designed with three segments that create a courtyard and arcades along the inner walls, it evokes a cloister. At its closed end is a three-story wing, resembling a chapel. Like the tile made on the premises, the complex itself was hand-crafted. Outside and in, one sees walls, floors, and vaults of exposed concrete, all of which was hand-mixed. Vaults were made by workers who mounded earth, covered it with sand, and inserted mesh and reinforcing rods before pouring concrete.[64] In 1916 Mercer added a tower crowned by a low hipped ogee roof enhanced by red barrel tiles. With rounded gable parapets at its ends, the building is reminiscent of California missions—not a regional reference, and in this aspect out of step with a widely accepted Arts and Crafts tenet. Also out of step with Arts and Crafts philosophy was the fact that Mercer was the sole designer of his tile (fig. 3.13). In order to produce large quantities, he trained and employed farm laborers living nearby.[65] The hierarchical social order was entirely different from the community that Price sought to create. At the tile works, Mercer's domain was the chapel-like wing that functioned as his studio and showroom, while his business manager enjoyed a vaulted, handsomely tiled office. Yet it should be acknowledged that through the rest of his life, Mercer ran a viable operation that stayed afloat when others failed.

"JOINT PARTNERS WITH THE ARCHITECTS"

Arts and Crafts ideas were behind the construction of Bryn Athyn Cathedral, built between 1913 and 1919, as well as ancillary structures completed in 1928 (fig. 3.14).[66] The cathedral, located in the borough of Bryn Athyn, north of Philadelphia and south of Doylestown, is the ecclesiastical center for the General Church of the New Jerusalem, whose adherents follow the teachings of Emanuel Swedenborg. In 1897 Swedenborgians from Philadelphia moved to Bryn Athyn, where John Pitcairn, Jr., a wealthy industrialist and president of the Pittsburgh Plate Glass Company, established a religious and educational community on property he had bought. Eleven years later, he donated funds to build a cathedral.

FIGURE 3.12. Henry Chapman Mercer, Moravian Pottery and Tile Works, Doylestown, Pennsylvania, 1912.

FIGURE 3.13. Henry Chapman Mercer, tile made by the Moravian Pottery and Tile Works, set in the building's exterior wall.

FIGURE 3.14. Ralph Adams Cram and Pitcairn workshops, Bryn Athyn Cathedral, Bryn Athyn, Pennsylvania, 1913–19.

As planning moved forward, the project piqued the interest of Pitcairn's son Raymond (1885–1966).[67] He approved of the decision to employ a Gothic style, but he was not pleased with what he saw in the preliminary drawings. The church, young Pitcairn thought, should be English Gothic, and for this reason in 1912 he wrote to Ralph Adams Cram, the leading medieval designer of the era, asking whether the architect might want to take on the project.[68] He most certainly did. The relationship presented a unique opportunity, and Cram proposed to put into practice his theories about the medieval guild system whereby the artisans would be "joint partners with the architects."[69] Construction began in 1913, and within a few years, workshops were erected around the cathedral grounds for stone and wood carvers, cabinetmakers and joiners, metalsmiths, and makers of stained glass. Pitcairn was enthusiastic about the artists and artisans working together, and he grew increasingly committed to building the cathedral in a collaborative manner. Plaster models were prepared, studied on site, and modified. Cram, occupied in Boston and serving clients elsewhere, was removed from the decision-making and was slowly sidelined. By the spring of 1917, the church terminated the relationship with him. Writing about the experience a year later, Cram concluded, "In architecture at least there must be a final and an unquestioned authority, and that authority is the architect himself."[70] Nevertheless, as time passed, Cram judged the project at Bryn Athyn positively, even if it didn't end well for him. Bryn Athyn Cathedral, he wrote, was "one of the most picturesque and romantic architectural compositions in the country."[71]

Stylistically, the church is relatively severe, reminiscent of early Gothic designs of the twelfth and thirteenth centuries. Across its west front is a wide porch, which visually balances the lofty tower that rises over the crossing. Stone walls are constructed of granite from a quarry that was opened half a mile away. Also local in its source is the timber for the roof, which came from white oak trees that were found in eastern Pennsylvania. The Arts and Crafts love of variety, promulgated by Ruskin and Cram, was encouraged by Pitcairn. Artisans evoked natural flora and fauna, whether carving stone rosettes or fabricating metal screens and hardware, while avoiding repetition. As construction of the cathedral was underway, slight curves were introduced for aesthetic effect in elements such as stringcourses and cornices—an unusual and time-consuming process. Cram understood that this approach was too expensive to be repeated elsewhere, but he considered it a success. All in all, Bryn Athyn was the "epitome" of medieval English church-building.[72]

Given the Anglophile culture of Philadelphia, it's not surprising that its architects would turn to England's early academic buildings as an inspiration for campus projects.[73] Walter Cope (1860–1902) and John Stewardson (1858–1896) developed a romantic vision of Collegiate Gothic architecture that was emulated across the nation through the early decades of the twentieth century.[74] The partners took their first steps in this direction at Bryn Mawr College, west of Philadelphia on the Main Line, with their design for Radnor Hall (1886–87). Other commissions for Bryn Mawr followed, which brought the men to the attention of Princeton University in New Jersey and led to their designing Blair Hall (1896–98) and Little Hall (1899–1901).

When a new administration was installed at the University of Pennsylvania, erecting undergraduate dormitories was prioritized. In 1894 Cope and Stewardson, both on the architecture faculty, were charged with the project (fig. 3.15). For the urban setting of West Philadelphia, the partners preferred buildings that would run along the street edges to form quadrangles with interior lawns, following the examples at Oxford and Cambridge.[75] As at Bryn Mawr and Princeton, the dormitories were to be built of gray stone. During the summer of 1894, Stewardson's vision for Penn changed dramatically. Traveling in England, the architect was swept away by St. John's College, Cambridge. Excited by what he saw, he proposed building Penn's quadrangles in red brick and limestone, materials that also would be in keeping with the fabric of Philadelphia. The style of the Quadrangle Dormitories would still be Collegiate Gothic, but in a variation that was Jacobean with Renaissance motifs. Prominent roofs and gables, tall chimneys, and oriel windows would be medieval in origin, while a Palladian archway would recall the move toward classicism in sixteenth-century England. In keeping with their Arts and Crafts orientation, the firm's architects collaborated closely with the men who executed the ornament, which includes bosses set in belt courses on the new buildings (fig. 3.16). Office architect John J. Borie drew comical little people and animals, artist Henry F. Plasschaert modeled them in clay, and Edward Maene (1852–1931) and his workshop carved them from the limestone blocks.[76] Among the carvers trained by Maene was his nephew John, who went on to head the furniture shop at Rose Valley.

Although there were quibbles, Cope and Stewardson's Collegiate Gothic buildings were critically acclaimed. Montgomery Schuyler declared that the architects' work at Penn was "a pronounced success," even though he was bewildered by the way it charmed him.[77] He groused, "We may admit that there is something unscrupulous in this picturesqueness and this amusingness."[78] Of the architects' work at Bryn Mawr, Princeton, and Penn, Cram wrote, "This is poetry, sheer, unmitigated romance."[79] Day reinforced the Collegiate Gothic style of Princeton's campus when he designed the Holder Hall quadrangle (1908–10). As experts in this niche of collegiate work, Philadelphia firms competed with Boston firms. Day was hired to work at Wellesley College near Boston, while Cram was hired at Princeton. What they shared was a view that in the United States, it made sense to erect campus buildings that were, in Cram's words, "scholastic of the type that is ours by inheritance; of Oxford and Cambridge, not of Padua or Wittenberg or Paris."[80]

FIGURE 3.15. Cope and Stewardson, Quadrangle Dormitories, University of Pennsylvania, Philadelphia, begun 1894.

FIGURE 3.16. Workshop of Edward Maene, carved boss, Quadrangle Dormitories.

SOUTHWEST IN THE KEYSTONE STATE

In the southwestern corner of the Keystone State, 250 miles from Philadelphia, Pittsburgh offered opportunities for ambitious architects. As one of the nation's major industrial centers, dominated by steel production, the city was experiencing a rapidly expanding economy that fostered the construction of large institutional buildings, commercial buildings, and residences. The Boston firm of Longfellow, Alden, and Harlow opened an office there and was hired to design a library and music hall complex, and Cram and Bertram Goodhue received plum commissions for churches.[81]

During the same years, Frederick G. Scheibler, Jr. (1872–1958), born and raised in the city, devoted his career to less prestigious projects—by and large, apartment buildings and houses.[82] Nevertheless, his designs were exceptional in their originality. While the better-educated and better-traveled architects from the coastal cities of the Northeast embraced English and French trends, Scheibler adopted ideas from avant-garde Germanic architects and blended them with English Arts and Crafts elements. His Old Heidelberg apartment building (1905), located in the city's East End, illustrates how he synthesized turn-of-the-century sources (fig. 3.17).[83] Through published illustrations, Scheibler absorbed the innovations of Joseph Maria Olbrich, a member of the Vienna Secession. The massing, materials, and decoration of Olbrich's houses in Darmstadt, Germany, find their way into the Old Heidelberg. Reflecting those examples, the apartment building has a high tiled roof, abstracted forms, exposed I-beams, and details such as whimsical hearts in plaster relief on column capitals. Cutout squares on the center porch and on plate rails in the apartments reflect Scheibler's debt to Glasgow's Charles Rennie Mackintosh. Scheibler also studied the work of Baillie Scott, whose influence is apparent in the apartment's red tile, white stucco, visible timberwork, and round entry arches. It can be seen in the art glass of apartment doors

FIGURE 3.17. Frederick G. Scheibler, Jr., Old Heidelberg apartments, Pittsburgh, 1905.

FIGURE 3.18. Charles Z. Klauder, Cathedral of Learning, University of Pittsburgh, 1924–37.

and windows and in the copper fireplace hoods in the living rooms.

In nearby Oakland, American Collegiate Gothic architecture reached its zenith with the construction of the Cathedral of Learning for the University of Pittsburgh (fig. 3.18).[84] Designed by Charles Z. Klauder (1872–1938) of Philadelphia between 1924 and 1925 and dedicated in 1937, this Gothic Revival tower brings an Arts and Crafts ethos to a steel-framed skyscraper. Klauder had worked with several Philadelphia architects, including Cope and Stewardson, before settling in with Day, becoming his partner in 1911. Academic buildings and campus master plans became Klauder's specialty, and he published an authoritative book on college architecture.[85]

The concept of a tower anchoring the Pitt campus came from its chancellor, John Bowman, who arrived in 1921 and identified Klauder as the best choice for the commission. Land was provided through the largesse of the Mellons. Classrooms, libraries, and offices would be accommodated within a structure of forty-two stories rising to a height of 535 feet. The sheer walls, setbacks, and aluminum spandrels between the windows reflect Art Deco trends of the 1920s. Yet the limestone-clad building also owes much to the Arts and Crafts movement. Passing under pointed arches, first-time visitors widen their eyes when they see a vast Perpendicular Gothic Commons Room, devoted to quiet study. Its vaults soar to a height of fifty-two feet, rising from shafts that support ribs as in medieval construction. Hand-wrought iron, including light fixtures, railings, and gates, were crafted by Philadelphia's Yellin (fig. 3.19). Embellishments in stone were conceived by Joseph Gattoni, whose designs represented native plants of the region, carved by Edward Ardolino. Charles J. Connick was contacted to make stained glass medallions—a project that fell through.[86] But when Heinz Memorial Chapel was built on the campus between 1936 and 1938, designed by Klauder, Connick glass filled its walls. Around this time, Connick also created a window for the Cathedral of Learning. When the building was under construction, different ethnic groups in Pittsburgh accepted an invitation to decorate the classrooms. The earliest "Nationality Rooms" opened in the late 1930s, showcasing old world decorative arts traditions of working-class immigrants. Thus the city's residents—plutocrats and laborers—united English and ethnic traditions along with medieval construction and modern steel framing, resulting in an enduring Pittsburgh landmark.

FIGURE 3.19. Workshop of Samuel Yellin, iron gates, Cathedral of Learning.

While living in the Mid-Atlantic region, at rustic Craftsman Farms, Stickley broadcast an Arts and Crafts message to the nation. He delivered an Arts and Crafts philosophy and promoted Craftsman houses to readers of his magazine. He latched on to the ideal of simplicity, embodied by inexpensive houses that were well-suited to America's expanding suburbs. Philadelphia provided an environment where architects were predisposed to advance Arts and Crafts values, in keeping with the English movement. Although the architects didn't join forces with artisans to form an Arts and Crafts society, they demonstrated their support for the movement through their T Square Club exhibitions and in their practices. As Anglophiles, they were advocates of building designs that revived English styles, especially the Gothic and Tudor revivals. Cope and Stewardson became known for Collegiate Gothic campuses, as at Penn, and Klauder became renowned for academic commissions, including the Cathedral of Learning at the University of Pittsburgh. As proponents of the Arts and Crafts movement, these architects oversaw sophisticated projects. Eyre and Day contributed to the Anglo-Colonial Revival, based on their admiration of Philadelphia's colonial and federal buildings. Day, in charge of restoring Congress Hall, shared the value that Ruskin and Morris placed on historic preservation. Price pursued the socialist angle of the movement by planning utopian communities at Arden and Rose Valley, while an idealism of a different stripe guided Pitcairn in the construction of the Gothic Revival cathedral at Bryn Athyn, where all involved strove to work on the same level. The Mid-Atlantic was home to some of the country's most visionary people—individuals who absorbed the principles of the Arts and Crafts movement and applied them in novel and influential ways.

ST. JAMES
CITY HALL

4 The New South

The American South beckoned. As the nineteenth century drew to a close, winter-weary Americans—middle-class and wealthy residents of industrial cities where Arts and Crafts ideas were gaining traction—packed their bags and departed to more hospitable climates. Sunny and green, with palmetto trees and live oaks breaking through blue skies, the southern states were markedly different from the all-too-often chilly and gray North and Midwest. Some people just wanted a brief respite, while others traveled in pursuit of new homes. To meet the demand, small southern cities, like the large cities in the North, were expanding with new residential developments. Finer neighborhoods included houses that architects designed in the Arts and Crafts styles of the Northeast and Chicago. Ambitious southern women also participated in the movement: one of them designed houses and published plan books in Atlanta, and a larger number of women decorated pottery in a facility erected for them in the Garden District of New Orleans. Although far from the country's major centers of Arts and Crafts advocacy, the trends affected the South, which we can observe in what people there built.

RELAXATION AND RECREATION IN NORTH CAROLINA

Temperate, not tropical, North Carolina emerged as an attractive location for retreats from the bitter cold. A notable example is the village of Pinehurst, located about seventy miles south of Raleigh.[1] It began as a philanthropic project by a Boston manufacturer of soda fountain equipment, James Walker Tufts, who hired Boston architects and landscape architects to realize his dream. Although Pinehurst wasn't established as an Arts and Crafts community, the men involved in its creation applied Arts and Crafts concepts circulating in New England to the Carolina village.

Between 1895 and 1896, Tufts bought nearly six thousand acres of depleted sand hills where pine trees had been harvested.[2] There, he erected a health resort for Yankees. At first, he welcomed guests with mild tuberculosis, but within a year they were banned. Pinehurst was not a sanitarium. The people Tufts wished to help were working and middle class, worn down by winter but unable to afford the southern resorts that the wealthy patronized. In Boston, Tufts supported programs for the needy that dovetailed with Arts and Crafts values. He funded a mutual benefit association for his employees, and he was a director of the North End Union, which served Italian immigrants. Taking a different approach, Tufts embarked upon the creation of Pinehurst to lift the lives of people who were not charity cases, but whom he regarded with compassion.

The plan of Pinehurst was developed in 1895 by Warren H. Manning (1860–1938), assisted by John Charles Olmsted (1852–1920), a partner in Olmsted, Olmsted, and Eliot.[3] In February of the following year, the project was turned over to Manning when he launched an independent practice. His challenge was to plant a landscape that would be evergreen through the winter and blossom early in the spring, before visitors went north for the summer. Pine trees, oaks, magnolias, and mountain laurels achieved the objective. To preserve the natural topography, streets wound through the terrain, the roadsides softened by broad planting beds for trees and shrubs. Pinehurst's streets were, as the *New England Magazine* reported in 1896, "beautiful as well as useful," employing the words of William Morris.[4] From the beginning, the village offered lodging options of varying costs and types, including an inn, cottages, and apartments. At the center of the community was the Village Green, intended to evoke the small towns of New England. With Pinehurst's emphasis on relaxation and recreation, residents could avail themselves of tennis, croquet, and horseback riding. In 1897–98 a golf course was built, and in 1900 Donald Ross arrived, designing more sophisticated courses and cementing Pinehurst's reputation.

Wanting to elevate the appearance of village buildings, in 1897 Tufts hired the architect Bertrand E. Taylor (1856–1909).[5] Many of Taylor's Boston colleagues were active in the Society of Arts and Crafts, and he would become a member.[6] Typical of architects designing model villages, he sought to unify the new buildings stylistically; however, the Arts and Crafts inclination to draw upon vernacular traditions was cast aside. Most of the longtime residents of the region were impoverished and lived in log cabins and tumbledown shacks. Taylor therefore turned his attention to local materials, the climate, and topography. He designed apartments, cottages, and a village store with hip roofs, deep overhanging eaves, porches, and lap siding of local pine. When Tufts decided to erect the full-service Carolina Hotel (1899–1900), it was Colonial Revival in style, painted yellow and white, with Tuscan columns and a cupola on the roof, again evoking New England (fig. 4.1).[7]

Tufts shared an appreciation for local history with Arts and Crafts leaders in Boston. In 1895 he arranged for an early nineteenth-century Carolina log cabin to be dismantled and reinstalled under Taylor's eye at the edge of the Village Green.[8] Operated as a museum, it displayed historic local tools, reflecting an interest in bygone craft skills that Henry Chapman Mercer in Pennsylvania also held. In 1923 the operation of the cabin was assigned to the Sandhills Woman's Exchange, where the organization sold crafts made by poor local women.

Unlike utopian colonies and planned communities in the North, Pinehurst was racially mixed, populated by

FIGURE 4.1. Bertrand E. Taylor, Carolina Hotel, Pinehurst, North Carolina, 1899–1900.

FIGURE 4.2. Fred L. Seely, Grove Park Inn, Asheville, North Carolina, 1913.

Blacks and whites.[9] The Black residents, however, were all workers and very much subservient, living in separate cottages from white workers. Some of them, such as cooks and cleaners, were invisible, whereas golf caddies were in close proximity to the white residents. After Tufts died in 1902 and his son took charge, Pinehurst started selling lots for houses, carrying restrictive covenants that excluded Blacks and Jews.

At the western end of North Carolina, in Asheville, the Grove Park Inn also attracted people who were seeking relaxation and recreation (fig. 4.2).[10] Strictly a business endeavor, it was conceived and financed by Edwin W. Grove of St. Louis, who amassed a fortune purveying Grove's Tasteless Chill Tonic, a quinine-laced concoction to combat malaria. When he was recovering from bronchitis, Grove visited Asheville, and he established a second home there. A trip to Yellowstone National Park in 1910 gave him another idea for an investment. At Yellowstone he had admired the Old Faithful Inn, which opened in 1904, and it inspired him to erect a large, well-appointed retreat on Sunset Mountain, where he owned land overlooking Asheville (see fig. 7.2). Architect Henry Ives Cobb (1859–1931) provided the first design concepts for the Asheville inn, including suggestions to build with granite rocks from the mountain and to use red tile roofing; however, Grove preferred a sketch by his son-in-law, Fred L. Seely (1871–1942). Grove dropped Cobb and hired Seely to oversee the project. An architect-engineer, G. W. McKibbin (1860–1927), also assisted, but Seely is generally considered the building's primary designer.[11]

In July 1913 the inn was ready for guests. Rustic in appearance, it seems to be at one with nature, a widely held ideal for Arts and Crafts architecture. The main block, constructed with granite rocks, rises to a height of four stories, and two more floors are sheltered under a tiled roof with dormers. Especially memorable are the roof's undulating eaves and rounded edges, imitating the thatched roofs found on English cottages. The treatment is similar to that of the well-publicized "thatched palace," Mondanne, completed in 1910 by Harrie T. Lindeberg in New York's Westchester County (see fig. 2.5). Inside the inn is a great hall with a massive fireplace at each end, also fashioned with native boulders. Although the huge rocks suggest primitive construction, the inn was erected with reinforced concrete and is entirely modern. To decorate the inn, Seely approached Elbert Hubbard and the Roycrofters. He knew their capabilities, having visited the Roycroft Inn in East Aurora, New York, and he commissioned them to supply him with furniture and light fixtures.

The Grove Park Inn served an affluent clientele. For recreation, it offered guests an indoor swimming pool and a bowling alley, along with access to golf at a nearby club. Anyone who was tired could expect a tranquil environment. Children were discouraged from visiting, and no dogs of any size were allowed. The Grove Park Inn also let it be known that it was not a sanitarium, and consumptives should not register.

Ultimately Grove and Seely had a falling-out, and Seely needed to find new work. In 1917 he bought a craft enterprise that had been launched by George and Edith Vanderbilt, owners of the Biltmore Estate (1889–95), to train local youth. Over time the operation evolved to employ artisans who specialized in woodworking and the production of homespun wool cloth. When Seely took charge, he renamed the company Biltmore Industries.[12] On property next to the Grove Park Inn, he built six cottage-like structures, stuccoed and covered by red shingled roofs with rounded edges, which connected the buildings visually to the inn. As at Roycroft, mottos painted on the walls and carved on doors and beams addressed the workers. At Biltmore Industries, the words of inspiration came from John Ruskin and the fertile mind of Fred Seely.

IN FLORIDA'S GLINTING SUNSHINE

Florida was another alluring state for Americans in the Northeast and Midwest, and many who made the trip became permanent residents. Small cities, flourishing in the glinting sunshine, were appealing destinations for enterprising individuals. One of them was the architect Henry John Klutho (1873–1964), who arrived in Jacksonville at the beginning of the twentieth century.[13] Klutho was a midwesterner, raised in an Illinois town near St. Louis, where he studied art and could admire Adler and Sullivan's Wainwright Building of 1891. When he was in his twenties, he moved to New York City, traveled in Europe, and returned to New York to set up practice. Then, in 1901 his life took a turn. Reading the news, he learned that a devastating fire had leveled Jacksonville. Wasting no time, he relocated there and was immediately rewarded with major commissions. A few years later, Klutho met Frank Lloyd Wright, who was overseeing construction of the Darwin D. Martin House (1903–5) and starting work on the Larkin Administration Building (1903–6), both in Buffalo (see fig. 2.12). At some point between 1904 and 1907, Klutho and his wife visited Wright at his home and studio in Oak Park, Illinois.[14] Back in Jacksonville, Klutho gravitated toward the progressive design ideas of the age, and Jacob Cohen was a receptive client.

Cohen was a member of a German Jewish family that had settled in New York City after the Civil War and founded a successful dry goods company.[15] In 1867, seeing potential in Jacksonville, the family opened an outpost there, at first in a basic log cabin. The Florida business thrived, and the company improved and expanded the operation through the century. When its Florida building was lost in the 1901 fire, Cohen decided to erect a modern department store. He met with Klutho, who persuaded his client to invest in a project that was far more ambitious—the St. James Building (fig. 4.3). Built between 1911 and 1912, it would cover an entire city block and house the department store, retail shops, and offices.[16]

In certain respects, the St. James Building was at odds with Arts and Crafts values. It was a commercial building, and it lacked any visual relationship to its locale. That said, the exterior elevation's emphasis on structure and the designs of the terra-cotta ornament reflect the movement as its principles were absorbed and transformed by Louis Sullivan. Pronounced verticals of pilasters across its long façade echo Sullivan's work, as does the semicircular arch in the tall central pavilion above the main entrance. Also Sullivanesque are its terra-cotta capitals and escutcheons, designed by Klutho, with components that are spiky and abstract. Modeled and fabricated by the Conkling-Armstrong Terra Cotta Company of Philadelphia, the decorative pieces were illustrated in a 1914 issue of the *Western Architect*.[17] Unlike Sullivan's ornamental designs, which originated in nature, those by Klutho are purely geometric, including parabolas, spirals, and orbs. In their curves and vitality, however, they are organic in effect.

FIGURE 4.3. John Klutho, St. James Building (City Hall), Jacksonville, Florida, 1911–12.

FIGURE 4.4. Milton B. Medary, Jr., Singing Tower, Mountain Lake Sanctuary (Bok Tower Gardens), Lake Wales, Florida, 1927–29.

Wright's influence, and specifically the influence of the Larkin Building, can be recognized in the St. James Building interior. Klutho designed a seventy-five-foot-high atrium covered by a skylight, encouraged, no doubt, by the Larkin's atrium. Also indebted to Wright's work are Klutho's cast bronze elevator cages with patterns of straight lines and squares. Although Klutho was mainly inspired by innovations in Chicago, he may have been thinking of Vienna in the spandrels and frieze of the façade, where he embedded checkerboard patterns of green and white terra-cotta. When he built his own house in Jacksonville (1908–9), he emulated Wright directly.[18] The dwelling has a shallow hip roof, six-foot-deep overhanging eaves, and art glass in the stairwell, all responding to Wright's Prairie School houses and their Arts and Crafts characteristics.

In the lake region of central Florida, Philadelphia's Edward W. Bok brought together a leading architect and artisans from the Quaker City to build a marble-faced tower in a botanical garden. Erected between 1927 and 1929, the Singing Tower, as he called it, was designed by Milton B. Medary, Jr. (1874–1929), and holds a carillon (fig. 4.4).[19] Bok was a self-made man who came from the Netherlands to the United States as a boy. Despite receiving little formal education, he advanced to become editor of the Philadelphia-based *Ladies' Home Journal.* In its pages, he encouraged progressive causes relating to education, health, and conservation; he also featured attractive, moderately priced houses. Shortly after retirement, in 1922 he bought a site in Lake Wales to build what he called a sanctuary "for humans as well as for birds"—a retreat designed by landscape architect Frederick Law Olmsted, Jr., working in partnership with his half-brother John Charles Olmsted.[20]

Plans for Mountain Lake Sanctuary were set and planting was proceeding when Bok decided that the garden would be enhanced by a bell tower, and he asked Medary to meet him in Florida. During his years at *Ladies' Home Journal,* Bok encouraged Arts and Crafts ideas, and the tower would reflect them. Stylistically it was Gothic Revival. The Singing Tower rises to a height of 205 feet from a square base to a buttressed octagon and a flat top with pinnacles and sculpture carved by Lee Lawrie and his shop. Framed in steel, the tower is structurally modern. Nevertheless, it adheres to the Arts and Crafts preference for regional materials in its exterior cladding, with pink and gray marble from Georgia and coquina, a limestone of shellfish and sand, from Florida. Ornament on the tower also connects it to the region. Sculpture and faience allude to Florida plant and animal life.

At the same time, the tower may be construed as an example of the Arts and Crafts movement and its visionaries in Philadelphia. Medary, the Philadelphia architect, orchestrated the effort, Samuel Yellin fabricated the ironwork and brass door, and J. H. Dulles Allen's Enfield Pottery and Tile Works made the panels for the top of the tower and the flooring inside.[21] The tower also reflects Bok's personal identity rather than the identities of people in Florida. For his client who came from the Low Countries, Medary designed a Gothic Revival structure that was inspired by a fifteenth-century tower in Mechelen, Flanders. Yet that non-native allusion didn't detract from its beauty. In creating a retreat from the world, a landscaped sanctuary where carillon music wafted through the air, Bok provided visitors a chance to escape for a few hours to an Arts and Crafts paradise. White visitors, we should understand. During its first decades, this paradise was not a gift for all people, at least most of the year. Through the 1930s and 1940s, only on "Negro Day" were Black visitors welcomed into the sanctuary.[22]

HOMES FOR THE SOUTHEAST

The growth of southern cities in the early twentieth century presented opportunities for an individual who wished to pursue a career as a residential designer. Open fields were being transformed into middle-class subdivisions, and houses were going up that reflected many of the facets of American Arts and Crafts architecture. Bungalows were widespread. Georgia architect Leila Ross Wilburn (1885–1967) devised plans that she sold to builders throughout the South.[23] Born in Macon, she studied at what was then Agnes Scott Institute in Decatur, apprenticed with an Atlanta architectural firm, and opened an office in the city in 1908. Rather than pursuing commissions for custom houses, she began working with local contractors.

Catering to this market proved to be successful, leading her to publish her first plan book, *Southern Homes and Bungalows,* in 1914. Addressing its readers, she explained, "This book is published with the idea of supplying Southern people with homes suitable for climatic conditions of the Southeast."[24] Her interest in designing in response to regional conditions, an Arts and Crafts

FIGURE 4.5. Leila Ross Wilburn, Carr House, Atlanta, 1919.

priority, translated into plans with sizable verandas, relatively spacious rooms that allowed for better air circulation, and sleeping porches. With a focus on "moderate-cost" houses, she embraced another priority of the movement. Her plans included "useful built-in furniture and artistic effects," an echo of Morris's call for both the useful and beautiful.[25] Achieving this aim for moderately priced houses wasn't easy. Just a few of her designs incorporated Arts and Crafts decorative components such as tile or art glass, but she routinely specified beamed ceilings and built-in bookcases. Stylistically, many of her bungalows were indebted to the English cottage, with steep rooflines and large dormers finished with half-timbering and stucco. Overall, the simplicity of these houses conveyed the humility that was valued by Arts and Crafts proponents.

Wilburn included plans for grander houses in *Brick and Colonial Homes,* published in 1921, but she favored restraint for them, too.[26] One of the published houses, erected for Harry J. Carr, president of a building company, in the Olmsted-designed development of Druid Hills in Atlanta, is brick with a red clay tile roof and porches across the front and to one side (fig. 4.5).[27] Completed in 1919, it has visible rafter tails, low segmental arches at the front porch and porte cochere, and a two-story bay that breaks through the roof. The lack of any ornament is consistent with Wilburn's strategy for her smaller houses. In light of the market she sought to attract through catalogues, Wilburn could not offer plans that required specialized craftsmanship such as custom stone or wood carving, nor could she succeed with novel architectural concepts.

Noah Webster Overstreet (1888–1973) took a bold approach when he designed a Prairie house for himself in Jackson, Mississippi (fig. 4.6). Born near Hattiesburg, he received a degree in architectural engineering at the University of Illinois, then settled in Jackson in 1912.[28] He would become the first registered architect in Mississippi and the first president of the state's chapter of the American Institute of Architects, chartered in 1929. In 1913 he bought a parcel of land in a new residential development a mile north of Jackson's downtown.[29] It would be named Belhaven and is considered the city's first suburb. The house was built by 1914 and demonstrates Overstreet's familiarity with trends in Chicago.[30] A high first story is brick while a shorter second story is finished in textured stucco, with tile covering a low hipped roof. A distinctive touch, reflecting the influence of Wright and the Prairie School, is the raking of the horizontal joints in the brick, craftsmanship that reflects the collaboration between the young architect and an anonymous mason. In its massing, the house is conservative—symmetrically massed and boxy, without the cantilevers and interpenetrating volumes of Wright's most recent projects.

A NEIGHBORHOOD PARK

As southern cities prospered and sought to attract affluent buyers to newly planned neighborhoods, civic leaders and developers followed the national pattern of reserving land for parks. The Arts and Crafts appreciation for nature contributed to this direction in a general way, while occasionally the movement's influence could be seen more clearly. In Birmingham, Alabama, Rhodes Park presents such an example.[31] To serve an influx of residents, a new residential area was planned on the side of Red Mountain, designed with a landscaped boulevard, Highland Avenue, and three parcels to be maintained for the community. One of them, Rhodes Park, represents the collaboration of a landscape architect and an architect who were both connected to Boston. George H. Miller (1883–1943), the landscape architect, had been in charge of Warren Manning's office before opening his own practice on Beacon Street.[32] In 1909 Miller was hired to plan Fairfield, a model industrial town, just west of Birmingham, for the United States Steel Company. Notably, he called it a "garden city."[33] Bungalows for the workers were designed by William L. Welton (1874–1934), who was raised near Boston and studied architecture there before relocating to Birmingham in 1907.[34]

When Miller was hired to plan Rhodes Park in 1910, he needed to figure out what to do about the hollow—a natural depression around which Highland Avenue looped. Covering three-and-a-quarter acres, it wasn't especially large. Miller's plan retained the drop from the road while providing a few level gathering spots. Welton's job was to design the architectural features. As a young

FIGURE 4.6. Noah Webster Overstreet, Overstreet House, Jackson, Mississippi, 1913–14.

5 Big Shoulders in Chicago

In the years between 1880 and 1890, Chicago muscled past Philadelphia to become the country's second-largest metropolis, only behind New York City. As the transfer point for railroads and shipping that moved agricultural and manufactured products across the continent, the City of Big Shoulders was stretching and straining, generating wealth and poverty at new extremes. Its leading citizens were ambitious, founding the Art Institute of Chicago in 1879 and the University of Chicago in 1890, and they showed off their success when the city hosted the World's Columbian Exposition in 1893.

Able and willing to traverse great distances, several influential Chicagoans visited some of England's most important people and places associated with the Arts and Crafts movement.[1] One of the movement's fundamental concerns, the social ills that coincided with industrial growth, was shared by the city's progressive men and women. Observing so many struggling laborers, especially impoverished immigrants, activists responded by exploring how they could address the misery. Jane Addams and Ellen Gates Starr journeyed to London and investigated Toynbee Hall, a settlement house, and returned home to establish Hull-House in 1889. Others from Chicago met William Morris, viewed his Merton Abbey workshop, and spread his ideas. They included Joseph Twyman, an English-born furniture designer; Oscar Lovell Triggs, a literary critic and University of Chicago professor; and Charles Zueblin, a sociology professor at the university.[2] Walter Crane, the English artist and illustrator, arrived in Chicago in 1891 and lectured, and English architect C. R. Ashbee stopped in the city in 1900 on a tour of the United States.

The city that grew upward through the 1880s and 1890s at the edge of Lake Michigan would have appalled John Ruskin and Morris. They would have objected to its scale and the businesses that powered the expansion. In Chicago, office buildings were reaching new heights in the service of commerce and trade. Architects benefited and were in demand. Like their colleagues in the East, they sought out each other's company, and in 1885 they launched the Chicago Architectural Club. As the 1890s unfolded, a small circle of architects gravitated toward Arts and Crafts ideas, including brothers Irving and Allen Pond, Robert C. Spencer, Jr., and Frank Lloyd Wright. In October 1897 they participated in founding the Chicago Arts and Crafts Society at Hull-House.[3] The close relationship between architects and the Chicago Arts and Crafts Society was similar to the relationship that developed in Boston, where the Society of Arts and Crafts had been chartered in June. A year later, when the Chicago Architectural Club organized its annual exhibition, it invited the new Arts and Crafts group to participate with a show.[4] What came to characterize the Chicago Arts and Crafts Society was the organization's qualified acceptance of the machine, which was judged acceptable to the extent that it would relieve the workman from drudgery. Yet the Chicago society's constitution also declared that its members would insist that the machine would not "dominate the workman and reduce his production to mechanical distortion."[5]

Support for Arts and Crafts theories quickly gained momentum. In 1899 Ashbee's example of providing training for workmen inspired the founding of the Industrial Art League of Chicago.[6] Wright and Louis Sullivan both became members. Triggs was devoted to the league and championed the establishment of workshops and a salesroom on Michigan Avenue. While he embraced the Arts and Crafts platform that conjoined art and labor, he departed from the original English view by asserting that the machine could be a force for good. This belief would be reiterated by Wright. At the same time, an interest in Morris intensified.[7] In 1902 Twyman organized a showroom of Morris & Co. products at Chicago's Tobey Furniture Company, including two stained glass windows designed by Edward Burne-Jones, which were sold and installed in the Second Presbyterian Church. A year later, Twyman helped found a Morris Society, the first anywhere, to promote craftsmanship. Charter members included Triggs and Zueblin as well as Gustav Stickley. Ralph Radcliffe Whitehead, who established the Byrdcliffe arts colony in New York, was a vice president.

Architect members of the Chicago Arts and Crafts Society and the Chicago Architectural Club sought to reconcile Arts and Crafts principles with the innovations and modern building products that opened new possibilities for construction.[8] What they embraced were Arts and Crafts ideas about the virtue of simplicity, a respect for materials, and an appreciation for nature, especially as the basis for ornament. Like architects elsewhere in the United States and Britain, they hoped to better the life of the worker through their practices. Most notably, they pursued the Arts and Crafts interest in designing buildings that reflect one's own region—leading to the Prairie School. During the same years, Arts and Crafts buildings in the English tradition were commissioned. There was room for both stylistic approaches in the big-shouldered metropolis.

INSPIRED BY ENGLAND

One of the most creative American responses to the Arts and Crafts movement in England was the house that John J. and Frances Glessner built in Chicago on the corner of Prairie Avenue and Eighteenth Street, designed in 1885 by Boston's Henry Hobson Richardson and completed in 1887 (fig. 5.1). With round arches over the front and side entrances and broad expanses of stone walls, the exterior elevations are consistent with the architect's many adaptations of Romanesque architecture from France and Spain. Yet while these sources must be acknowledged, the fact of the matter is that the catalyst for the design of the Chicago house was English—a photograph owned by the Glessners of a vernacular stone building at Abingdon Abbey, south of Oxford.[9] Richardson saw the photo when visiting the couple in Chicago and suggested making this modest structure, a gabled stable entry attached to an old fulling mill, the "keynote" for their new home. That image was reworked to become the dwelling's austere side elevation that runs along Eighteenth Street. From there, Richardson designed the main elevation. It, too, is austere, with rusticated walls and boxy massing, very different from the extensively ornamented palaces favored by the wealthy neighbors. The unpretentiousness of Glessner House, inspired by a vernacular source from a rural English location, illustrates the architect's and owners' take on the Arts and Crafts movement. Moreover, while minimally ornamented, the building's exterior is enhanced by a sculpted tympanum and column capitals carved by John Evans and his Boston-based workshop. Evans, who would join in founding the Society of Arts and Crafts in Boston a decade later, frequently worked with Richardson.

Despite the somewhat forbidding impression made by its street elevations, the Glessner House is well lit and comfortable inside.[10] It's planned to wrap around an interior courtyard, with the main rooms facing south to overlook the yard. Upon entering the house, the aura of restraint continues with low beamed ceilings and simple oak paneling. To decorate the rooms, the Glessners chose Morris textiles and wallpapers as well as tile by England's William De Morgan. New furniture, including a custom-designed piano for Frances Glessner, came from the firm

FIGURE 5.1. Henry Hobson Richardson, Glessner House, sculpted tympanum and column capitals carved by John Evans and his workshop, Chicago, 1885–87.

of A. H. Davenport, whose chief designer was Francis Bacon, an architect by training and former Richardson employee. After moving into the house, Frances Glessner pursued the Arts and Crafts love of handicraft, retreating to her basement to make decorative pieces and jewelry out of silver.[11]

The social concerns of the Arts and Crafts movement were addressed head-on at Hull-House, situated in the midst of factories and tenements southwest of downtown Chicago. In 1889 Jane Addams and Ellen Gates Starr leased rooms in a dingy, leaky Italianate dwelling and took up residence to assist the neighborhood's beleaguered immigrants.[12] The women were inspired by Toynbee Hall, founded in London's East End five years earlier by Samuel and Henrietta Barnett and the first example of a social settlement house. New construction for Hull-House began in 1891 and continued over time, until twelve buildings wound around the entire city block (fig. 5.2). All of them were designed by brothers Irving K. Pond (1857–1939) and Allen B. Pond (1858–1929).

Writing in 1910, Addams expressed her gratitude to the Ponds for performing marvels "with a combination of complicated demands and little money."[13] Yet the buildings were worthy of respect. They "stated to Chicago that education and recreation ought to be extended to the immigrants."[14] Hull-House provided a public library branch, exhibition and studio space, an auditorium for lectures and performances, and rooms equipped for crafts such as woodworking and metalworking. When the first sales shop opened, Addams recalled, it was directed by residents who also were members of the Chicago Arts and Crafts Society.[15] Starr traveled to London to study bookbinding with T. J. Cobden-Sanderson and came home to establish a bindery and teach what she had learned.[16] Addams clarified, however, that Hull-House did not give young people trade-training but rather encouraged their latent aptitudes and exposed them to employment possibilities.

As architects for the settlement, the Ponds could not foresee what functions the buildings would serve nor what land would become available. Indeed, the structures changed in use, and sometimes they were extensively rebuilt.[17] Yet the brothers managed to create a coherent ensemble, designing red brick buildings that blended English and Anglo-Colonial traditions—some vaguely Jacobean with parapet gables and diaper patterns, and others reminiscent of Wren and American Colonial architecture with cupolas and pediments. The allusions were consistent with the stylistic choices of English Arts and Crafts architects and colleagues in the American Northeast. The architect Fiske Kimball admired Hull-House for its "absence of institutional character" and "true picturesqueness."[18] On the other hand, he criticized its quadrangle plan, arguing that with this scheme, Hull-House faced inward when "it should seek to assimilate itself to conditions of the neighborhood."[19] Nevertheless, with a stretch of lawn and a protected terrace, the courtyard became a green and tranquil refuge for a desperately poor community.

The summer house that Chicago architect Howard Van Doren Shaw (1869–1926) designed for his family might well have been built in the English countryside.[20] Ragdale, located north of the city in Lake Forest, was begun in 1897 and finished the following year (fig. 5.3). Shaw had studied at Yale and MIT, then furthered his knowledge by journeying through Continental Europe, concluding his tour in England in 1893.[21] He was especially attentive to houses designed by Edwin Lutyens and C. F. A. Voysey. When he began planning Ragdale, he pursued a direction that his overseas counterparts were exploring at the same time. The house that he designed includes a main elevation with two front-facing gables, a catslide roof, and a deeply recessed porch, the whole contained within a taut envelope covered in stucco.

On entering Ragdale, the visitor admires a hall with a barrel-vaulted ceiling, high oak paneling, and a screen of leaded glass that sparkles with light coming from the windows in the dining room. Both the dining and living

FIGURE 5.2. Pond and Pond, Hull-House, Chicago, begun 1891.

FIGURE 5.3. Howard Van Doren Shaw, Ragdale, Lake Forest, Illinois, 1897–98.

rooms have beamed ceilings and built-in benches, with an inglenook in the living room around the fireplace. Like many Arts and Crafts architects, Shaw designed furnishings for his home, including a trestle table in the dining room and andirons for the fireplace.

Shaw was devoted to several organizations that supported the arts in his native city. He was committed to the Art Institute of Chicago, serving as a trustee alongside John Glessner. As a member of the Chicago Architectural Club, Shaw assisted with the joint exhibitions that the architects held with the Chicago Arts and Crafts Society at the museum. Another endeavor to which Shaw contributed time was the Municipal Museum of Chicago, founded in 1904 to promote reform ideas through exhibitions and lectures. He and Jane Addams both sat on its board.[22] Writing about Shaw, Irving Pond observed that his friend felt a "strong sense of his obligation to society."[23] It might seem paradoxical that in his practice, Shaw served the wealthy, designing country houses and commercial buildings. But such was the case.

A MASTER OF ORNAMENT

As a young architect working in Chicago, Louis Sullivan (1856–1924) cast his gaze toward Richardson's new buildings.[24] He was already a master of ornament, his talent having been nurtured during a short period of employment with Philadelphia's Frank Furness and encouraged by his reading of Ruskin. Sullivan would have been impressed by the quality of carving at the Glessner House. The fact that the clients brought John Evans and fellow carvers from Boston to execute the exterior sculpture would not have been lost on him. For Sullivan to achieve the quality of craftsmanship that he wanted, he needed outstanding collaborators. First in partnership with Dankmar Adler and then on his own, he depended on them for projects including the Auditorium Building (1886–90); the Chicago Stock Exchange Building (1893–94); and the Schlesinger and Mayer department store (1898–1903; fig. 5.4). Among his preferred artisans and workshops were Kristian Schneider, a sculptor and modeler; Winslow Brothers Company, metalwork fabricators;

Healy and Millet, decorators specializing in stenciling and art glass; and William Henry Burke, a master of marble mosaic flooring.[25]

Even as he designed urban, steel-framed buildings, and even though he accepted the benefits of the machine, Sullivan did not "neglect to use hand work," reported *The Brickbuilder* in 1903. It continued, "He is an artist himself and has a following of skilled artists whom he uses in their proper vocation."[26] Taking his cue from Ruskin, Sullivan studied thistles and seedpods native to the American countryside, sketched them, and abstracted them, producing the "conventionalized" ornament for which he is admired.[27]

Through his involvement with the Industrial Art League, serving on its five-member executive committee, Sullivan participated in training a large number of craft workers. Both Crane and Morris articulated the philosophical views that the organization advanced.[28] In a membership brochure, Crane is quoted as urging art "in the humblest objects and materials." On the back of the booklet appears a plea from Morris, slightly reworded: "One day we shall win back art again to our daily labor; win back art, that is to say, the pleasure of life, to the people."[29] This focus on a return to creativity in the work of ordinary people was consistent with Sullivan's objectives as an architect and author.

FIGURE 5.4. Louis Sullivan, Schlesinger and Mayer department store (Carson Pirie Scott and Company), Chicago, 1898–1903.

In 1906 Sullivan addressed middle-class Americans when he published a three-part essay in *The Craftsman*.[30] Readers were informed by its editor, Gustav Stickley, that Sullivan's study was a "clear exposition of all *The Craftsman* stands for."[31] One might have assumed that an architect of steel-framed commercial buildings would be poles apart from a promoter of bungalows and rustic houses, yet as theorists, the two men were in sympathy. To begin with, Sullivan invoked the demand for "simplicity," one of the most widely shared clarion calls of Arts and Crafts leaders and a watchword for Stickley.[32] In elaborating, Sullivan expressed his admiration for buildings that are "modest, truthful and sincere," buildings that are natural and democratic.[33] After castigating the benighted American people, Sullivan offered a remedy: "individual honesty."[34] For the nation to achieve its potential as a democracy, he urged his readers to look to nature for "creative energy." With integrity of thought, he argued, the American people would lead their architects to deliver a superior architecture "for the common good."[35]

When Rochester architect Claude Bragdon wrote his foreword to Sullivan's *The Autobiography of an Idea,* he closed by calling its author "a friend and fellow craftsman."[36] Identifying themselves as craftsmen rather than architects represented a deliberate choice of wording—a choice made by Bragdon that put some distance between them and their wayward fellow professionals. The two men were reform-minded, designers who broke from the academy to find solutions that would more appropriately reflect modern America.

THE PRAIRIE HOUSE TAKES FORM

The rejection of historic architectural styles and the search for a new direction, suitable to the Midwest, was led by Frank Lloyd Wright (1867–1959) after he bade farewell to Adler and Sullivan in 1893 to start his own practice. For Wright, the question was how to digest Sullivan's ideas and apply them to his residential projects.[37] Having participated in founding the Chicago Arts and Crafts Society, he also was interested in the concept of collaboration. After he erected and opened a studio in 1898 adjacent to his suburban Oak Park home, he adopted this principle by bringing architects and artists together. His commitment to an Arts and Crafts philosophy was reinforced when he met Ashbee in 1900, establishing a friendship with the English Arts and Crafts leader. By this time, Wright was thinking about how to engage with the movement in ways that would make sense in the machine age.[38] As the 1890s drew to a close, he continued to refine his vision for an ideal midwestern house.

By February 1901 Wright had arrived at a prototype. Featured as "A Home in a Prairie Town," his design appeared in the *Ladies' Home Journal,* the Arts and Crafts–oriented magazine edited in Philadelphia by Edward Bok, who would fund a garden in Florida in the late 1920s (see fig. 4.4).[39] Wright's Prairie house was forward-looking, but it didn't seem out of place in an issue that included readers' hand-painted china and ads for women's shirtwaists and corsets. The house was to be moderate in cost and suited to the suburban lots that were attracting the magazine's subscribers. Like many Arts and Crafts houses of the period, the Prairie house was fairly simple. Finished in stucco, it had casement windows with diamond-shaped panes. Inside the house, rooms included beamed ceilings and high paneling capped by moldings to display artistic plates. The house also responded to the setting of the region, as promoted by Arts and Crafts thinkers, in the way it hugged the open land with its low profile, deep eaves, and breadth of massing. In his design, Wright introduced what would be distinctive features of his Prairie houses: extreme horizontality, a double-height living room with a gallery, and furnishings that were coordinated with the building.

In March 1901 Wright lectured to the Chicago Arts and Crafts Society at Hull-House on "The Art and Craft of the Machine," participating in a series of talks that included Addams and Sullivan. Like Triggs, Wright believed in the benefits of machines. The machine, Wright argued, was "the tool which frees human labor, lengthens and broadens the life of the simplest man, thereby the basis of Democracy upon which we insist." Not in his vision were the realities of mechanization and the harsh conditions endured by workers in the nation's industrial centers. He did acknowledge Morris, however. Morris, Wright stated, "pleaded well for simplicity as the basis of all true art."[40] When considering the potential of the machine, he explained, it was well-suited to this aesthetic.

Wright's dream client signed on with him in 1902 to build an extravagant, fully realized version of the Prairie house. A year after the death of her father, Susan Lawrence Dana commissioned Wright to remodel her family home in the Illinois capital of Springfield.[41] When the work ended in 1904, the original Italianate house had all but disappeared, with only its foundations and one room remaining (fig. 5.5). Located on a residential street and next to train tracks, the new Prairie house wasn't in view of any prairie, but Wright was wedded to a design that alluded to the region. Horizontal massing made this connection. The residence was planned to run along the street, its length exaggerated by a porch and conservatory that connect to a studio and library. The decoration of the house, including art glass and a painted mural, evokes the beauty of the plains in autumn.[42]

While well-removed from the medieval past that was at the heart of Arts and Crafts architecture, the Dana House retains vestiges of the movement's beginnings. The round arch at the front entrance as well as the ribbed barrel-vaulted ceilings of the dining room and studio echo Romanesque forms, filtered through Richardson and Sullivan.[43] Gothic in spirit are stained glass windows with abstracted shapes based on sumac leaves and butterflies, installed in bands that appear to float under shallow-pitched roofs. Artists and craft workers were essential to realizing Wright's vision, including the sculptor Richard Bock (1865–1949) and designer George M. Niedecken (fig. 5.6). In 1898 Niedecken contributed an entry to the Chicago Arts and Crafts Society that was displayed in a Chicago Architectural Club exhibition. At the Dana House, Niedecken painted a mural, and he provided designs for the glass and furniture.[44] Stunning though it all is, the Dana House did not emerge from an entirely contented workshop.[45] Much as the architects and artists employed in Oak Park admired their master, he could treat them shabbily. When Bock, installed in the studio mezzanine, was working on a clay model that didn't please Wright, the architect pulled it apart, bringing the sculptor to tears. For Niedecken, residing in Milwaukee, the challenge was surviving on the low pay. Ultimately he felt compelled to open his own company. Young architects came and went. In reality, the Dana House was not the creation of the joyous artists and artisans of Arts and Crafts mythology but of people who "frictionalized and fraternized," as Bock later said.[46]

Considered from another perspective, the Dana House illustrates how Wright's Prairie style contributed to twentieth-century architecture. In its materials and construction, the house is modern. What appear to be caps and belt courses of stone accenting the brick exterior are in fact tinted concrete. Large interior rooms, including the entry hall, dining room, and studio, are supported by structural steel. Also significant is the way exterior and

FIGURE 5.5. Frank Lloyd Wright, Dana House, Springfield, Illinois, 1902–4.

FIGURE 5.6. Richard Bock, *Flower in the Crannied Wall,* Dana House, 1904.

interior spaces are manipulated, flowing into each other. In his treatment of space, Wright may have been influenced by M. H. Baillie Scott, but he approached space with more daring.[47] Within a few short years, Wright's innovative merging of exterior and interior spaces culminated in the Frederick C. Robie House (1908–10), in Chicago, distinguished by deep cantilevered roof eaves.

PRAIRIE SCHOOL VARIATIONS

Wright would prove to be the most brilliant of the architects associated with the Prairie School, but the early success of the group was due in large part to Robert C. Spencer, Jr. (1864–1953). As a writer and a leader, he publicized the designers' ideas and their buildings. In his practice, he blended elements of English Arts and Crafts architecture with concepts from Sullivan.[48] A native of Milwaukee, Spencer earned an engineering degree from the University of Wisconsin, where he crossed paths with the younger Wright. Spencer then headed to Boston to study architecture at MIT, followed by employment with architects including Shepley, Rutan, and Coolidge, Richardson's successors. His talent was recognized when he was awarded the Rotch Traveling Scholarship, which enabled him to explore Europe for two years.

Throughout his career, Spencer never broke from the past.[49] He maintained an interest in his English peers, especially Voysey and Baillie Scott.[50] Like them, he produced buildings that were grounded in the Tudor Revival and abstracted. In 1894 he designed a Tudor house, an early date for the style in Chicago. Built for J. Stanley Grepe in Evanston, the house was finished in stucco and had casement windows—Tudor features that he would retain for Prairie School houses.[51]

Also in 1894, Spencer opened his office in Chicago and reconnected with Wright. A few years later, they moved to an office building called Steinway Hall, where they joined other reform-minded architects who were sympathetic to Sullivan.[52] At the beginning of the new century, the group maneuvered to take control of the Chicago Architectural Club, and in 1901 Spencer was elected president. He also served as one of three members of the jury for the club's 1902 exhibition, contributing to its domination by the Steinway Hall architects.

During this period, Spencer approached his East Coast contacts to publish articles in professional and popular magazines. In 1900 he wrote the first major article on Wright, which ran in the Boston-based *Architectural Review,* and a year later he helped Wright place his first essays in the *Ladies' Home Journal.* Writing in the *Architectural Review,* Spencer praised Wright's houses for expressing "certain ideals of home and of quiet, simple homelife," employing language that reflected Arts and Crafts values. He continued, "Our beautiful buildings must not be the forced fruits of an artificial civilization, but must be the natural bloom of a hardy native growth with its roots deep in the soil."[53] Spencer thus restated Sullivan's call for a new American architecture while he advocated for an organic architecture, growing naturally from its locale—a goal that Wright would advance.

By and large, Spencer's residences were marked by repose, massed horizontally with shallow hipped roofs and overhanging eaves. In 1907 he was hired by Edward and Caroline McCready to design a brick house for a corner lot in Oak Park (fig. 5.7).[54] In plan it is configured as an L, similar to Richardson's Glessner House (see fig. 5.1), to maximize the southern light that reaches the interior garden. The front elevation is balanced, although not symmetrical, with the low hipped roof that Spencer favored. Roman brick of gold shades was laid with joints that were deeply raked to emphasize the building's horizontality. What animates the façade is a projecting center mass in which the front door is offset to the left and staircase windows are on the right. Casement windows, promoted by Spencer in his writing and in a business venture, include decorative art glass, while the entry is enhanced by a limestone door surround and a substantial lintel, both carved with geometric patterns that reflect Sullivan's influence.

Of the many capable architects associated with the Prairie School, Walter Burley Griffin (1876–1937) was one of the most adventurous.[55] After receiving a degree in architecture from the University of Illinois in 1899, Griffin began working for the Steinway Hall architects. Two years later, he was hired by Wright to join the Oak Park studio, and by 1902 he was managing the office. Ultimately the men had a falling-out, and in 1906 Griffin left to open his own practice. He headed back to Steinway Hall where Spencer, the Ponds, and other sympathetic souls were ensconced.

Griffin developed a version of Prairie School architecture that was weighty, typically designed with hefty piers and solid walls. His first independent residential project, for William H. Emery, Jr., dates from 1903 and was erected while Griffin was still working for Wright (fig. 5.8).[56] Located in the Chicago suburb of Elmhurst, it forecasts his future direction. The house retains vestiges of the Tudor Revival but is distinctly original—an imposing rectangular block of brick that supports a second story of stucco with wood trim. Sharing his colleagues' interest in concrete, Griffin set the house on a concrete base and incorporated concrete string courses and concrete caps to enliven and finish the brick. Like Wright and others of the Prairie School, he employed casement windows that were grouped in bands. But he turned away from the ground-hugging approach of Wright and others in the Prairie School, designing the Emery House with a gabled roof and large piers at the corners. Moreover, whereas Wright conceived of spaces that flow together horizontally, Griffin connected spaces vertically. The idea originated with the client and Griffin embraced it, producing a plan in which the dining room, living room, and den are on different levels, tied together by stairs. He would pursue a vertical integration of spaces in subsequent work.

On the exterior, the Emery House is austere. Inside, however, rooms are warmed by an extensive use of natural

FIGURE 5.7. Robert C. Spencer, Jr., McCready House, Oak Park, Illinois, 1907.

FIGURE 5.8. Walter Burley Griffin, Emery House, Elmhurst, Illinois, 1903.

oak, the boards left flat to show the grain, as Wright had advocated. Spencer thought highly enough of the dwelling's decoration to select photographs of the living room and dining room for an article on woodwork.[57] The colors of the rooms, noted Spencer, included olive, old gold, and cream. Art glass is used extensively on windows, doors, and cabinets. Griffin also designed sconces of art glass and brass that were so successful that more of them were crafted for the Dana House.

Like Wright, Griffin wanted to develop a new American architecture. When an article about Griffin's houses ran in the *Architectural Record,* the author wrote that Wright's style is "so very personal that its imitation is dangerous." But the writer complimented Griffin for his work and said that the style was worth perpetuating "because it is the result of a sincere and intelligent attempt to make the modern American house an honest, simple and effective architectural unit."[58] Those objectives were familiar as Arts and Crafts objectives and would have resonated among readers as they perused the magazine pages.

ARCHITECT MARION MAHONY

The Arts and Crafts ideal of architects, artists, and artisans who labor together was realized by architect Marion Mahony (1871–1961) early in her career. A native of Chicago, she studied architecture at MIT and in 1894 became the second woman to complete the program.[59] A year after returning home, she started working for Wright, and when he opened his studio in 1898, she joined him there. For the Dana House, she and Bock shared responsibility for a wall fountain called *The Moon Children*.[60] The sculptor provided Mahony with an initial sketch, and she assisted him in refining his concept. The result is a tondo in terra-cotta of nudes and toddlers, the circular relief anchored visually to the wall by representations of thin clouds. Mahony also designed planters to flank the fountain and a hexagonal basin.

When Wright left for Europe in September 1909, abandoning his family for the wife of a client, he needed someone to take over his unfinished commissions.[61] Presented with the offer, Mahony turned him down. But after the business went to Hermann von Holst, she agreed

FIGURE 5.9. Marion Mahony, Adolph Mueller House, Decatur, Illinois, 1910–11.

to work for him in a contractual arrangement. She was tasked with building an enclave of three houses in Decatur, east of Springfield, called Millikin Place.[62] One of the dwellings was based on Wright's initial scheme, while the other two were entirely hers.

Of the three, the Adolph Mueller House (1910–11) was the last to be erected and illustrates her work (fig. 5.9).[63] Its primary living spaces are arranged on a long horizontal axis with a pair of vertical buttress-like forms at one side of the front façade. Like many Prairie School houses, the Mueller House is stuccoed and has casement windows with colored glass in geometric patterns. In the living room, a pitched, tentlike ceiling is inset with large panels of art glass. During this period, Mahony and Griffin became romantically involved, marrying in 1911, and Griffin served as landscape architect for the development. The third designer working on the houses was Niedecken, whom Von Holst hired to oversee their decoration.[64] Mahony and Niedecken had collaborated on projects when they were employed by Wright, and by this time, Mahony had enough clout that she must have been satisfied with Niedecken's role. For the Adolph Mueller House,

Niedecken designed Prairie-style draperies, rugs, and furniture as well as ceramics and embroidered textiles.[65]

THE NORTH SHORE'S KENILWORTH

The village of Kenilworth, on Chicago's North Shore, presented opportunities for Chicago architect George W. Maher (1864–1926) to influence its public spaces and to design more than three dozen houses guided by Arts and Crafts values.[66] Quite different from Roycroft or Rose Valley, which fostered craft production, the development at the edge of Lake Michigan was a commuter suburb, akin to Forest Hills Gardens in New York City, but more exclusive. Like all of these communities, Kenilworth was a place where nature and beauty were emphasized, to provide a more uplifting way of life.

Maher trained with Chicago architects before opening his practice in 1888.[67] Although he never worked at Steinway Hall, he shared an admiration for Sullivan with the architects who fraternized there, and he embraced the master's call to develop an architecture in response to local conditions. A living architecture, Maher wrote in 1900, "must be part of the mind of the community." Picking up on Morris, he continued, "Originality is desired in the composition, but all trending toward the union of utility and the beautiful." Maher was an advocate for restraint and cautioned architects to avoid "vanity and untruthfulness."[68] As a member of the Chicago Architectural Club, he encouraged reform in design. When he spoke before the group in 1906, he criticized the "reactionary spirit" of architects in the East and asserted that their buildings in revival styles were "lamentable."[69]

In 1891 Maher designed a couple of houses for the newly established village of Kenilworth, and two years later he built his family home there. As a resident, he advocated for beautifying the landscape.[70] One place that needed attention was the entrance to the commuter rail station, and he followed up by designing it with a fountain in a central square. He and fellow residents also encouraged planting trees along arterial streets, reflecting the Arts and Crafts desire to bring nature to everyday living.

Fifteen years after Kenilworth's founding, a venue for community gatherings, frequently built in model communities, was erected on land that the developer donated.[71] Maher designed what became known as the Kenilworth Assembly Hall (1906–7). One story in height, it has a low hipped roof with the deep overhanging eaves that the Prairie School architects favored. On one side of the building was the hall, outfitted with a stage, and on the other a meeting room and library. A recessed entrance enabled the preservation of an existing elm, and planters were installed under the windows, both gestures reflecting a desire to keep nature in close proximity. Mainly stucco with exposed vertical timbers, the building is ornamented with a repeating motif of stemlike forms that sprout into diamond shapes. Maher believed in developing a motif that he could repeat in a building to reflect his client and unify a project. At the Assembly Hall, he thought, the stem-and-diamond device would represent the character of Kenilworth. When the motif was deployed for stenciling and stained glass, the diamonds were colored green and blue and included abstractions of leaves to reflect the natural setting of the village (fig. 5.10). If Kenilworth was exclusive, it also was inclusive, and the hall, funded privately, welcomed all residents and their organizations.

CONTRASTS IN ARTS AND CRAFTS CHURCHES

Like architects in England and the American Northeast, Chicago architects who subscribed to the Arts and Crafts movement viewed church commissions as extremely desirable. Church-building gave architects and artisans opportunities to collaborate in fields ranging from sculpture to stained glass. Also appealing was the social purpose of these buildings, which involved caring for church members and people in the greater community. Inspired by Arts and Crafts principles, Chicago architects created churches that were exceptional in design while contrasting with each other dramatically in terms of their styles.

When the Oak Park Unity Church burned in June 1905, Wright eagerly sought the job to plan the new edifice.[72] He was at an advantage in that he and his wife belonged to the Unitarian congregation, and it was progressive in outlook. Challenged by a tight budget, Wright proposed constructing a sanctuary and parish house that would be entirely concrete. The idea was unusual for a church building, but what was especially bold was his intention to avoid facing the concrete with brick or stone or even to use them as trim.[73] Moreover, Wright's design did not make any overt references to historic sources. Completed in 1908, Unity Temple, as the new building was called, was essentially a cube of exposed concrete (fig. 5.11).

On a visit to Chicago that year, Ashbee saw it and liked it. He praised Wright's project as "sound and wholesome and truthful," echoing Ruskin's call for truth.[74] Pointing out its "truthfulness in structure," Ashbee appreciated how the design reflected the realities of poured and molded concrete. He also responded favorably to the way in which Unity Temple illustrated "the principle for which the arts and crafts movement stands: namely 'discrimination' in what is and is not the province of the machine." He continued, "In this building, anything that savored of hand detail imitated by machinery had been as rigidly excluded as it would have been from an English 'arts and crafts' building."[75] Ashbee was intrigued by the conviction, advanced in Chicago, that mechanical tools could be used appropriately in architecture and decoration. Machine-cut bands of stained wood softened Unity Temple's sanctuary and parish house interiors—a simple treatment that Prairie School architects also specified for their houses.

Wright's achievement was in fact one of many minds and hands, collaborating in his Oak Park studio and on the job site.[76] For example, in working out the decorative treatment of the columns that would be installed at the sanctuary clerestory and on two sides of the parish house,

FIGURE 5.10. George W. Maher, Kenilworth Assembly Hall, interior view of windows in the main hall, Kenilworth, Illinois, 1906–7.

FIGURE 5.11. Frank Lloyd Wright, Unity Temple, Oak Park, Illinois, 1905–8.

Wright started out by sketching a foliate motif for the upper ends of the shafts. The concept then was developed further by Wright, builder Paul Mueller, and the sculptor Richard Bock.[77] Ultimately they settled on a design with right angles, suited to the wooden molds that shaped the concrete. What began as leaves evolved into brick-like blocks placed in pairs along flat stalks.

For the sanctuary and parish hall, Wright designed art glass, working with the Temple Art Glass Company in Chicago.[78] The pieces of glass are rectilinear shapes that originated in nature and were "conventionalized," as Wright and Sullivan would have said. Right-angled shapes were essential for an innovative process in which the glass pieces were fused together with zinc strips in a chemical solution. At the same time, Wright embraced the medieval method of glassmaking in which pigments were added to the molten glass. When a window was finished, the artistry was achieved solely through colored and clear glass, without applied enameling—demonstrating his respect for the material. In this way, Wright accepted an approach to glass that was encouraged by Arts and Crafts designers, going back to Morris and Philip Webb.

Long after Unity Temple was built, the Gothic Revival was what clients typically wanted for ecclesiastic projects. Between 1912 and 1914, Chicago's Fourth Presbyterian Church was erected to plans by Boston's Ralph Adams Cram and its parish buildings to plans by Howard Van Doren Shaw. In 1914 Bertram Goodhue, who had parted with Cram and Boston for New York City, designed a small Arts and Crafts gem, St. Andrew's Chapel, for Chicago's St. James Cathedral. Around this time, Goodhue began angling for a much larger prize—the

2328

6 Crossing the Heartland

Chicago, of course, wasn't the only place that was booming in the Midwest at the end of the nineteenth century. Cities by the edges of the Great Lakes, in farm regions, and along the banks of the Mississippi and Missouri rivers were rapidly expanding as hubs of commerce and industry. Well aware of trends in Chicago and the East, Americans in the nation's heartland joined architects, artists, and artisans to form Arts and Crafts organizations. In Detroit, a Society of Arts and Crafts was launched in 1906, and a decade later its members erected a headquarters, signifying their success. In Minneapolis, the Chalk and Chisel Club, established in 1895, evolved after four years to become the Arts and Crafts Society of Minneapolis. The Handicraft Guild of Minneapolis, founded in 1904, solidified the movement in the Land of Ten Thousand Lakes. When Midwestern architects designed residential and institutional projects, they sometimes looked to the Prairie School for inspiration, employing its salient features such as broad roofs and bands of casement windows. Other midwestern clients hired architects with Arts and Crafts sympathies to create grand Tudor Revival houses. Along similar lines, several midwestern universities commissioned a leading Chicago firm to design impressive Gothic Revival buildings for their campuses.

A POTTERY FOR A DETROIT CERAMICS ARTIST

One of the most ambitious individuals contributing to Arts and Crafts endeavors in Detroit was Mary Chase Perry (1867–1961), a ceramics artist. In 1903 she partnered with a businessman, Horace J. Caulkins, to open the Pewabic Pottery.[1] Having developed a high-heat furnace for firing dental products, Caulkins provided Perry with valuable expertise. Her enterprise took off, and in 1906 the two turned to William B. Stratton (1865–1938), a Cornell-educated architect working in the city, to design a pottery building east of downtown in the Jefferson corridor (fig. 6.1). The Pewabic Pottery opened in 1907 and has been operating continuously at this location ever since. Perry chose to stay in the neighborhood in the decades after it was built, which is notable because, by the 1920s, the building had become "fairly elbowed from its original setting by arrogant apartment houses and darkened by the downpouring soot of factories."[2] The presence of the pottery represented a genuine commitment to the people living in its vicinity.

FIGURE 6.1. William B. Stratton, Pewabic Pottery, Detroit, 1906–7.

Unpretentious in style and scale, the building is overtly English, "modeled after an old Kentish inn."[3] Featuring brick, stucco, and timber on the first floor and half-timber and stucco above, it has a high hipped roof covered in clay tile. The allusion to English architecture visibly associates Perry's endeavor with the origins of the Arts and Crafts movement, while colored tiles inset on one of the building's two chimneys advertise the products of the pottery. At a time when Detroit was reckoning with a new economy based on the assembly line production of automobiles, Perry resisted standardization even for large orders, adhering to the Arts and Crafts principles of originality and handicraft.[4] When she and the pottery won the competition for a tile pavement for Detroit's Cathedral Church of St. Paul (1908–11), by Ralph Adams Cram, she attracted widespread attention. Further recognition came in the 1920s when the Pewabic Pottery supplied ornamental tile to decorate the crypt of the National Shrine of the Immaculate Conception (1920–59) by architects Maginnis and Walsh in Washington, D.C.

Exhibitions preceded the founding of an Arts and Crafts society in Detroit. In December 1904 the Detroit Museum of Art presented the first such display in the city, and Perry served on the organizing committee.[5] Two years later, while Stratton was designing the pottery building, he, Perry, and Caulkins participated in establishing the Detroit Society of Arts and Crafts.[6] A wealthy newspaper publisher, George G. Booth, was the first president, and Stratton volunteered as vice president and treasurer. In 1916 Booth donated land to build a home for the organization, which was designed by members H. J. Maxwell Grylls and Stratton.[7] Like the Pewabic Pottery, the building evoked English Arts and Crafts architecture. Its roof was gabled and tiled and its masonry walls were stuccoed. Around this time, Perry and Stratton, long attracted to the same endeavors, found themselves attracted to each other and married in 1918.

A TUDOR REVIVAL HOUSE CALLED CRANBROOK

Booth's promotion of the Arts and Crafts movement in Michigan would be far-reaching, but he took a while to conceptualize and act on a strategy. Between 1907 and 1908, he and his wife built a Tudor Revival house, assisted by Detroit architect Albert Kahn (1869–1942). Located on a 175-acre farm in Bloomfield Hills, twenty miles northwest of Detroit, it was a showcase for the couple's commitment to art and craftsmanship (fig. 6.2). They called the house Cranbrook after the town in Kent that had been the home of Booth's father's family.[8] In designing the house, Kahn was guided by sketches from Booth, and the result blends various English sources. With a red tile roof, dominated by a pair of front-facing gables, and brick on the first story with half-timbering on the second, it recalls M. H. Baillie Scott's Red House (1889–1901) on the Isle of Man. The influence of C. F. A. Voysey and Edwin Lutyens also is apparent. Cranbrook was planned with a spacious center hall, a dining room to one side, and a living room on the other side. The dining room includes built-in cabinets to display silver by leading metalsmiths. In the late teens, Booth again hired Kahn, this time to expand the house with a large library wing and another wing with an even larger room for entertaining, called the Oak Room. Each of the rooms features the craftsmanship of nationally prominent artisans. In the library, the focus of the space is a spectacular wood overmantel, positioned above a Tudor-arched fireplace (fig. 6.3). Carved by Johannes Kirchmayer of Boston, it represents Cranbrook's craft workers alongside the regional bishop and Kahn, who stand at the center of the panel. In the Oak Room, the fireplace is faced with tiles from Henry Chapman Mercer's Moravian Pottery and Tile Works in Doylestown, Pennsylvania.

Booth's relationship with the Arts and Crafts movement in Boston was personal, as he was connected to it through his wife, Ellen, and her parents, James E. and Harriet Scripps.[9] James Scripps, born in London, grew wealthy in Detroit as a newspaper publisher. When he and his wife decided to erect a family mortuary chapel, they turned to the young Boston architect H. Langford Warren to design it.[10] The choice was logical in that Scripps wanted the chapel to adhere to English Gothic conventions, and Warren had trained in England before settling in Boston. Moreover, Warren happened to have been Harriet's first cousin.[11] In October 1885 Warren visited the family in Detroit to work out plans for the chapel, which would include ribbed groin vaults.[12] It was built in Woodmere Cemetery between 1886 and 1887. Ornamental carving was handled under Warren's oversight in Boston, almost certainly by John Evans. After Warren helped found Boston's Society of Arts and Crafts in 1897, Booth became a member.[13] The relationship of the Scripps and Booth families with Boston was enduring. In 1899 photographs of the Scripps chapel sculpture were exhibited in Boston, and in the years that followed, Booth patronized artists and artisans who belonged to the Boston society, including Kirchmayer and Mercer.[14] When the 1904 Arts and Crafts exhibition was organized in Detroit, Booth served on the committee, and he would have regarded Boston's exhibitions as a standard.[15] When Booth became the first president of the Detroit Society of Arts and Crafts in 1906, Warren was president of Boston's Society of Arts and Crafts.

With the passing of time, the death of Scripps, and increasing wealth, the Booths saw potential for their Bloomfield Hills estate and pursued it. Cranbrook became an educational center, an arts community, and headquarters for a foundation. Devoted to nurturing the human spirit in an Eden-like setting, the Booths, as faithful Episcopalians, decided to build a chapel.[16] Their selection to design it was New York City's Bertram Grosvenor Goodhue, who shared their devotion to art and handicraft. When he died in 1924, the couple pressed ahead with his associate, Oscar H. Murray. Christ Church Cranbrook (1925–28) was decorated with stone sculpture by Lee Lawrie that was carved by Edward Ardolino, stained glass by Nicola D'Ascenzo, Pewabic tile mosaics by Mary Chase Perry Stratton (fig. 6.4), painting by Hildreth Meière, wood carving by Johannes Kirchmayer and Alois Lang, and tapestries designed by English artist J. H. Dearle and woven by Morris & Co. at Merton Abbey in England. The chapel is gorgeous if conservative. Around this time, Booth's ideas about art and design were diversifying, and in 1925 he invited the Finnish architect Eliel Saarinen to Cranbrook to make preparations to open an art school.[17] In 1932 Saarinen became the first president of Cranbrook Academy of Art, and from this post, he would foster a modern interpretation of Arts and Crafts tenets that would challenge the more severe aesthetic of the Bauhaus in architecture and design.

FIGURE 6.2. Albert Kahn, Cranbrook, Bloomfield Hills, Michigan, 1907–8.

FIGURE 6.3. Johannes Kirchmayer, *Personification of the Arts,* wood overmantel in the library, Cranbrook, 1918.

FIGURE 6.4. Mary Chase Perry Stratton and Pewabic Pottery, mosaic installation on the baptistry vault, Christ Church Cranbrook, building designed by Bertram Grosvenor Goodhue, constructed under Oscar H. Murray, 1925–28.

THE DETROIT AREA THROUGH THE 1920S

Architects and clients in the Detroit area held fast to an Arts and Crafts ethos through the 1920s and patronized artisans associated with the movement. Grosse Pointe Memorial Church, located in the wealthy suburb of Grosse Pointe Farms, northeast of downtown Detroit, illustrates this attachment and displays exceptional Arts and Crafts workmanship (fig. 6.5).[18] Construction began in 1926 and was completed the following year. The architect, William E. N. Hunter (1868–1947), a native of Hamilton, Ontario, had become a respected specialist in Detroit for ecclesiastic projects.[19] A Latin cross in plan, the Grosse Pointe church is English Gothic Revival in style. Built with limestone, it includes a wide front elevation containing a single Gothic arch, tall clerestory windows, and a square tower that rises seventy-eight feet. Above a pair of doors at the entrance are carvings of the church's name, heraldic shields, and a band of branches and vines. A deep, long nave leads to a chancel with furnishings in dark wood. Lang carved figures and ornament on the reredos, clergy and choir stalls, lectern, and pulpit, an ensemble for which the church has become known. Born and raised in Oberammergau, Lang pursued a career as a wood-carver, following in the path of his older half-sibling Johannes Kirchmayer. Although Kirchmayer flourished in Boston, Lang stayed there only briefly, moved to Manitowoc, Wisconsin, and eventually settled in Grand Rapids, Michigan. A second distinction of the Grosse Pointe church is its stained glass. Between 1925 and 1926, Henry Lee Willet of Willet Stained Glass Studios in Philadelphia sketched images for the church windows that were medieval revival and influenced by Arts and Crafts ideals, including an emphasis on the leading. As donors came forward, the company made the windows and installed them.

A change in the wind, design-wise, during the 1920s is manifest in the building for Detroit's Scarab Club (fig. 6.6). It was erected between 1927 and 1928 to serve the city's artists, architects, musicians, writers, and friends such as George Booth.[20] Club member Lancelot Sukert

FIGURE 6.5. William E. N. Hunter, Grosse Pointe Memorial Church, Grosse Pointe Farms, Michigan, 1926–27.

(1888–1966) received the commission, while the other architect members acted as associates.[21] The main elevation of the three-story building is asymmetrical, with the entrance on the left and second- and third-story windows stacked vertically on the right, separated by heavy piers. Bold and simple, the façade combines Art Deco and Arts and Crafts components. Art Deco elements include the rectangular framing of the entry in brick that recesses in steps around double doors as well as tile grilles in geometric patterns mortared into the wall. In keeping with the Arts and Crafts movement in Detroit, a ceramic medallion of a scarab, the club's insignia, commands attention, installed high above the front doors. A Detroit sculptor, Horace Colby, modeled it, and the Pewabic Pottery glazed and fired it in turquoise, green, and gold.[22] To meet a goal of club members, all of whom were men, the plans included a comfortable lounge. Akin to the living rooms of Tudor Revival dwellings, the lounge was finished with beams, dark paneling, and a fireplace.

In central Michigan, owners of the Aladdin Company realized that a market was growing among working- and middle-class buyers who wanted to live in a home with an Arts and Crafts feeling.[23] Launched in 1906, the company was located in Bay City, near Saginaw Bay, southwest of Lake Huron. Aladdin became the first company in the nation to sell precut, mail-order houses. With extensive timber forests nearby, the operation milled and sawed the wood and then added plasterboard, hardware, and paint to the shipments. Upon delivery, buyers needed "no tool but a hammer" to assemble their new homes.[24] At first Aladdin's "kit" houses were basic one-story boxes with gabled roofs pitched at a ninety-degree angle. But in the spring of 1909, the catalogue offered a house that was fancier than the others and more in keeping with the times.[25] A story-and-a-half in height, like many bungalows, it was side-gabled and the front slope of its roof had a wide dormer. Diamond-paned windows were another enhancement. In the living room, the space opened to the

FIGURE 6.6. Lancelot Sukert, Scarab Club, Detroit, 1927–28.

FIGURE 6.7. Pond and Pond, Michigan Union, University of Michigan, Ann Arbor, 1910–19.

full height of the house, revealing its structural beams, and at its rear, stairs ran to a gallery and two bedrooms. Five years later, the Aladdin Company was marketing "The Pomona," described in a catalogue as a "bungalow-type" of house with an "overhanging roof."[26] Rafter tails were visible, another nod to fashion. After less than a decade in business, Aladdin was selling build-it-yourself houses to a somewhat more affluent market. Generally speaking, we may guess that the Pomona's buyers weren't familiar with Arts and Crafts theories, such as the premise that a building's exposed structure conveys honesty and truth. But some of them may have read Gustav Stickley's magazine *The Craftsman,* and they clearly admired the bungalows that were going up in better neighborhoods. Aladdin's houses didn't provide built-ins or fireplaces—standard features of house plans that *The Craftsman* and Georgia's Leila Ross Wilburn both sold. Instead, for buyers of the kit houses, affordability and simplicity were their virtues.

COLLEGIATE GOTHIC BY POND AND POND

Collegiate Gothic architecture, tethered to Arts and Crafts principles, was advanced with originality by the firm of Pond and Pond in their student union buildings, beginning with the union erected at the University of Michigan in Ann Arbor. Brothers Irving Pond and Allen Pond were raised in Ann Arbor and educated at the university before establishing a partnership in Chicago.[27] Successful and well-regarded, in 1905 they were elected fellows of the American Institute of Architects, and from 1910 through 1911 Irving served two terms as the institute's president. The commission for the Michigan Union building naturally came to them in 1910 (fig. 6.7). Ground was broken six years later, and the dedication took place in 1919.

An underlying goal of the university's leaders was a progressive desire to encourage social cohesion by bringing students together—or at least male students, for the union would be built exclusively for men.[28] By providing opportunities for socializing, the union would counter the negative influences of fraternities. The Ponds, supporters and architects of Chicago's Hull-House, which encouraged social solidarity among immigrants from different parts of the world, would have been predisposed to recognize the social merits of a student union.[29]

Michigan did not build the first student union in the United States; that distinction belongs to the University of Pennsylvania's Houston Hall, which was designed by Frank Miles Day and completed in 1896.[30] Michigan, however, would require a far bigger building. When the Ponds were hired, the university had the third-highest enrollment of any American campus, numbering more than five thousand students.[31] The Michigan Union would include an assembly hall, a swimming pool, a bowling alley, and guestrooms. An imposing seven-story tower dominated a principal structure of four stories.[32]

Spending their days at Chicago's Steinway Hall, the Ponds were aligned with architects and fellow tenants Howard Van Doren Shaw and Robert Spencer, who often based their designs on English architecture while transforming it for American clients. The Michigan Union is loosely Jacobean, brick and limestone, with parapet gables in the slate roof, mullioned windows of leaded glass, and carved stone ornament. The ornament, however, does not imitate historical examples but rather reflects the midwestern locale and modern times—an Arts and Crafts propensity. For the Michigan Union, Irving Pond devised an abstracted motif inspired by squash blossoms that was carved in stone and used on colored tiles.[33] Above the union's main entrance and below the tower, two sculptures were installed, one of "The Athlete" and the other "The Student," conceived and paid for by the architects. To execute the carving, they employed Michael Thomas Murphy, an Irish-born sculptor and a longtime member of the Art Workers' Guild in London who had immigrated to Chicago.[34]

Upon completion of the Michigan Union, other university leaders approached the Ponds to design union buildings for their campuses. Commissions came from Purdue University (1921–29), Michigan State University (1923–25), the University of Kansas (1926–27), and the University of Michigan for the Michigan League Building (1927–29), erected to serve women. Stylistically the buildings were Collegiate Gothic, brick trimmed with stone, and animated by sculpture at their entrances.

Well after the Purdue Memorial Union was completed in 1929, trustees of the West Lafayette, Indiana, university demonstrated a respect for the Ponds' Arts and Crafts ethos.[35] The Purdue union is brick and horizontally massed, featuring a hefty square tower over an entrance that is faced in stone (fig. 6.8). Leaded glass, indicating the architects' commitment to craftsmanship, fills the tympanum over the front doors and mullioned windows above. At the upper portion of the tower, bands of stone are carried by corbels that resemble squash blossoms, as at the Michigan Union. Over the entrance arch, large blocks of Indiana limestone were installed, with the expectation that they would be carved with figures of students. When the Great Depression hit, the plan for the stone blocks was derailed, and they were left unfinished. Finally, in October 1937 the trustees felt they could proceed with a "recommended sculptor."[36] At the beginning of the new year, Frances Rich presented herself to the trustees, and they agreed that she would prepare models for the job.[37] To assuage any doubts about her work, she would be supervised by Irving Pond; local architect Walter Scholer; and sculptor Carl Milles, a renowned Swedish artist teaching at Cranbrook. Rich most likely received this commission when someone from the university asked Pond to recommend an artist and he consulted Saarinen or Milles, who promoted the female sculptor. She had been Milles's student. In any case, Rich went ahead with the commission—reliefs of students, men and women, treated in an archaic manner. She finished the project in the fall of 1939, just weeks after Irving Pond's death.[38]

At this time, another Arts and Crafts embellishment to the union building was in the works. The widow of a former trustee donated funds for a stained glass memorial window, installed in 1940 (fig. 6.9).[39] It was designed and made by Charles J. Connick, who had attained national prominence in the Arts and Crafts movement, having just stepped down as president of the Society of Arts and Crafts in Boston.[40] Represented in the Purdue window are individuals holding a train, a bridge, and a tractor—all associated with academic disciplines at the university. While reviving medieval craftsmanship, the window honors modern education.

FIGURE 6.8. Pond and Pond, Purdue Memorial Union, Purdue University, West Lafayette, Indiana, 1921–29, with sculptures of students by Frances Rich, 1937–39.

FIGURE 6.9. Charles J. Connick, James H. Smart memorial window, Purdue Memorial Union, stained glass, 1940.

ART AND ARCHITECTURE IN INDIANAPOLIS

At the close of the nineteenth century, conditions in several midsize midwestern cities led arts-oriented citizens to promote Arts and Crafts ideas. Indianapolis was among them.[41] There the groundwork was laid by women, who founded the Art Association of Indianapolis in 1883. Four years later, a chapter of the American Institute of Architects was organized by local practitioners. Significantly, in 1892 the Art Association of Indianapolis held an exhibition on William Morris, and in 1898 an Arts and Crafts exhibition was held at a city high school, followed by another exhibition a year later.[42] In addition to displays of handicraft, architectural renderings were presented. By 1905 the Arts and Crafts Society of Indianapolis was chartered and opened a shop organized like the one in Boston.[43] It lasted just a year before closing, which might suggest a failure. But what should be understood is that the arts community shifted its attention to supporting a new art museum, the John Herron Art Institute. On the building's first floor were galleries dedicated to the applied arts, representing a strong commitment in Indianapolis to the Arts and Crafts movement.[44]

Over the course of three decades, properties along North Meridian Street, running northward from the center of the city, attracted wealthy residents who built English Tudor and Prairie style homes. Elements of both styles contributed to the design of the Rebecca Adams House (1903), by Chicago architect Robert C. Spencer, Jr. (fig. 6.10).[45] With a gable-ended pitched roof and a large front-facing cross gable, it was brick on the first story and

FIGURE 6.10. Robert C. Spencer, Jr., Adams House, Indianapolis, 1903.

FIGURE 6.11. Fermor Spencer Cannon, Wolfe House, Indianapolis, 1924.

FIGURE 6.12. Rubush and Hunter, Wadley House (Indiana Governor's Residence), Indianapolis, 1928.

half-timbered with stucco infill above. Although the house can be readily associated with the Tudor Revival, its bands of casement windows, including groups of windows tucked under the eaves, align it with the Prairie School. The widowed Adams, active in the Art Association of Indianapolis, had the wherewithal to ask Spencer to engage leading Chicago artists to embellish her new residence.[46] For art glass windows he brought in Giannini and Hilgart, and for a plaster bas-relief over the library fireplace he turned to A. L. Van den Berghen.[47] Illustrations of the house and its decoration were published in nationally distributed professional and popular periodicals.[48]

As development continued along the North Meridian corridor, Indianapolis architects and their clients erected many sophisticated houses.[49] Frank B. Hunter (1883–1958) designed a house in the spirit of the Prairie School, built in 1922 for Wesley E. Shea. The broad dwelling of brick and limestone recalls the designs of Spencer in its weight and clarity. Also reflecting Spencer's influence are its casement windows filled with art glass. The Arthur C. Wolfe House, dating from 1924, illustrates the long-lasting appeal of Prairie School architecture (fig. 6.11). It was designed by Fermor Spencer Cannon (1888–1973), a graduate of the architecture program at the University of Illinois. Cubic and austere, the house has brick walls and a low roof with deep eaves penetrated by a massive chimney. The dwelling's simple geometric form derives from Arts and Crafts thinking as the movement evolved. Yet Prairie School designs were never common in Indianapolis. When commissioning an architect to build a new home, wealthy clients favored the Tudor Revival. For example, Scott Wadley hired partners Preston C. Rubush (1867–1947) and Edgar O. Hunter (1873–1949) to design a sprawling, irregularly planned brick house, constructed in 1928, that represents the ongoing popularity of Tudors (fig. 6.12).[50] On the right of the façade is a buttressed porte cochere with an archway where guests entered on foot and a larger archway where visitors arrived in automobiles. To the left is a polygonal bay with mullioned windows and crenellations. In developing this scheme, Rubush and Hunter adapted the medieval house to modern living.

A SNUG BUNGALOW

For midwesterners who attained the status of solidly middle class, the snug bungalow emerged as an appealing choice for a dwelling. In Madison, Wisconsin, the type was introduced by a recently widowed woman, Cora Cadwallader Tuttle (1864–1948).[51] After losing her husband in 1906, she and her children joined family in Prescott, Arizona. Tuttle and her sons didn't remain in the Southwest very long, but Prescott's bungalows made a durable impression on her. By 1908 the Wisconsin native moved to Madison so that her eldest child could enroll in the state university. She was ready to build a house and settle down.

The property that Tuttle bought is located in the Wingra Park neighborhood, west of the city center.[52] Streetcar service to the area had opened in 1897, and the development was becoming highly desirable. Tuttle selected a parcel adjacent to what was then a new park and near Lake Wingra. Recalling the Prescott bungalows, she designed a family home. Upon its completion in 1909, it became the first bungalow in Madison (fig. 6.13). Her son, an engineering student, assisted, and Gustav Stickley's Craftsman houses may have guided her. Yet she had no training in architecture. Tuttle's bungalow has a low gable that extends over the entire width of the house and shelters an ample front porch. The general effect is rustic, with the body of the house sided in rough-cut boards, shingles installed in the gable field, and split fieldstone used for porch piers and a chimney. Double-hung windows are grouped on the main story and under the gable, and rafter tails and purlins are visible, typical of the Craftsman bungalow.

Tuttle said she had no ambition to become an architect, but her house attracted admirers.[53] After it was finished, she designed a bungalow for her sister in the same neighborhood, and over the next two decades, she produced at least fifteen more dwellings in Madison, mostly bungalows. In recent years, Tuttle has been recognized as the first known female architectural designer in the state.

About forty miles west of Madison, Frank Lloyd Wright built a house for himself and the woman he loved, Mamah Borthwick. In 1909 they left their families to live together in Europe, precipitating a scandal. On returning to the United States, they decided to make their home in Wisconsin near Spring Green, where Wright's grandparents had lived. Wright named the new house Taliesin (fig. 6.14).[54] Construction took place in 1911, and the couple moved in by the end of the year.

When a local newspaper editor referred to Wright's new house as a "bungalow," the architect protested, but that's how his home became identified.[55] Like all bungalows, including Tuttle's modest version, it had broad,

FIGURE 6.13. Cora Cadwallader Tuttle, Tuttle House, Madison, Wisconsin, 1909.

FIGURE 6.14. Frank Lloyd Wright, Taliesin, view toward the house at left and studio at right, Spring Green, Wisconsin, 1911.

spreading roofs. It also was constructed of stone, wood, and plaster, and it had covered outdoor spaces and groups of windows. Taliesin didn't incorporate any handcrafted ornament in its fabric, but craftsmanship was apparent in the way the masons laid courses of rock-faced ashlar, some of the blocks projecting slightly as if nature had dropped them there randomly. Artwork graced the entry court, where visitors encountered a cast of a sculpture that Richard Bock modeled for the Dana House. In his approach to furnishing, Wright followed the Arts and Crafts emphasis on handicraft by using furniture and vases that were made for him according to his designs. Wright's house also included built-in seating next to the fireplace and built-in cabinetry, typical of better bungalows.[56]

But Taliesin was so much more. In keeping with an Arts and Crafts philosophy, Taliesin was truly at one with the land, built with local limestone and plaster mixed with local sand. Its sloping hip roofs reached toward the earth, like the rolling hills around it. Whether the occupants were inside or on terraces, they looked out toward a panoramic view of the valley and the Wisconsin River. While the dwelling was a discrete structure, it was connected by a loggia to a studio and farm buildings, an ensemble that wrapped around the brow of a hill, extending to gardens, orchards, and open land. Like Wright's Prairie houses, Taliesin reflected the sweeping Midwest and the breadth of the American nation. The "bungalow" did not last long. In 1914 a distressed servant killed Borthwick and six other people, set fire to the house, and destroyed it. Wright would build a larger house, which would suffer through another fire, and he would rebuild yet again.

WOMEN IN MINNEAPOLIS

It was women in Minneapolis who established Arts and Crafts organizations and sponsored exhibitions in the city, doing so at an early date.[57] In January 1895 women who were designers and woodcarvers began the Chalk and Chisel Club, and in the fall of 1898 they sponsored Minnesota's first Arts and Crafts exhibition. The display included works sent by prominent artisans from other states and England. A year later the club reorganized as the Arts and Crafts Society of Minneapolis, continuing as a group run by women. Before long, several women determined that there was a demand in the region for formal training in the applied arts, leading eleven of them to found the Handicraft Guild of Minneapolis in 1904. The guild's workshops soon became known for ceramic and metal wares. Because the organization was run by women and mainly served them, it's not surprising that their activities were only loosely linked to architecture, the territory of men. Even so, Handicraft Guild members made and sold products such as tile and metal light fixtures for architects' projects.

In order to offer classes, studios, and a salesroom, the guild leased space.[58] With continued success, in 1906 the directors announced plans to erect a building at a downtown site. The Handicraft Guild's new home was designed by Minneapolis architect William Channing Whitney (1851–1945) and was finished in November 1907 (fig. 6.15).[59] The three-story building contained a sales and display room, a luncheon room, studios, and an assembly hall. On the exterior, the style is Anglo-Colonial Revival, a choice that would have been made by Arts and Crafts

Minneapolis in 1907. Toward the end of 1909, Sullivan was forced to contract his office further, and Elmslie joined Purcell and Feick in Minneapolis.

Shortly after reorganizing, the partners were commissioned to design the E. L. Powers House, built in 1910 on a site near Lake of the Isles in a prime neighborhood southwest of the city (fig. 6.17).[69] As seen from the outside, the house is severe and seemingly unlike its Tudor neighbors. In accord with Prairie School architecture, it has deep eaves and groupings of windows. Yet its brick first story, stucco second story, and dark wooden trim are rooted in the Tudor Revival. Also reminiscent of medieval architecture is the polygonal bay on the main elevation, supported by brick buttresses. The house is unusual and site specific, planned so that visitors enter it midway along the side elevation. At the rear is the living room, located to overlook the garden and lake, while the dining room is at the front. Elmslie's skill at generating ornament, nurtured during his years with Sullivan, was used to advantage and illustrated in the January 1913 issue of *Western Architect,* devoted entirely to the firm's projects.[70] Terra-cotta reliefs, inspired by plants, embellish the formal entrance and the living room fireplace, while art glass in geometric patterns was designed and made for built-in bookcases and doors. Elmslie also took charge of furnishings for the dining room, crafted by woodworker Gustav F. Weber. Born in France and of German descent, Weber had settled in Minneapolis in 1903.

A few blocks away, also near the lake, Purcell and his wife, Edna, built their own home, completed at the end of 1913 (fig. 6.18).[71] With a nearly flat roof, the residence was striking to passersby. Indeed, Purcell later recalled that "the neighbors never got wholly used to it."[72] The boxy massing and sheer walls of the stuccoed exterior are what one first sees, but a visitor who approaches the house and enters is won over by its artistry. Running across the first story is a screen of tall leaded windows that bring eastern light into the living room. Stepping through a front-yard

FIGURE 6.17. Purcell, Feick, and Elmslie, Powers House, Minneapolis, 1910.

FIGURE 6.18. William Gray Purcell, Purcell House, Minneapolis, 1913.

garden and nearing the entrance, the visitor notices a carved beam, and at the door, leaded glass sidelights tease with the words "Peek a Boo." Purcell deferred to Elmslie to design the art glass for the house, which they had made by E. L. Sharretts of the Mosaic Art Shops in Minneapolis. Elmslie developed designs for stenciled friezes, applied to exterior and interior walls, and he contributed patterns for curtains that Edna embroidered. Custom-designed furniture came from the firm of George M. Niedecken of Milwaukee, a favorite of the Prairie School architects. Pendant light fixtures, conceived by Elmslie as half-spheres, were fabricated by Robert Jarvie of Chicago. Artists added yet another level of embellishment to the dwelling. For the wall over the living room fireplace, Charles Livingston Bull, a renowned illustrator, painted herons. For a ledge on a low wall separating the living and dining rooms, the Purcells commissioned Richard Bock to make a sculpture. Cast in patinated plaster, it represents a boy astride a goose, the subject taken from a popular children's book.

In 1915 Elmslie was contacted by a friend with whom he had worked in Sullivan's office.[73] William L. Steele (1875–1949), practicing in Sioux City, Iowa, had landed the job of designing a new county courthouse, and he needed to associate himself with a firm that had more experience and staff. In the end, the Woodbury County Courthouse was erected with Steele as the "executive head" and Elmslie in charge of planning and design (fig. 6.19). Purcell coordinated the artists. When it opened in 1918, the building was a masterpiece of Prairie School architecture and a marvel of the Arts and Crafts movement in the Midwest.

Entirely unlike the conventional courthouses of the era, the building is neither white nor classical. A square

FIGURE 6.19. Purcell and Elmslie with William L. Steele, Woodbury County Courthouse, Sioux City, Iowa, 1915–18.

block of buff-colored Roman brick with a tower at the center, it is impressive in its own way, enriched by art and ornament outside and in. Above the main doors is a terra-cotta bearded and muscular "Spirit of the Law," flanked by a procession of men and women of different ages and types, interpreted in an archaic manner. The sculpture has long been credited to Chicago artist Alfonso Iannelli, but more recently his wife, artist Margaret Iannelli, has been credited as a partner in his projects.[74] At the rear of the building, above the jail entrance, are terra-cotta bison heads by Kristian Schneider. Additional terra-cotta ornament, some glazed in vibrant colors, was designed by Elmslie, and he designed leaded glass for the building's casement windows and a dome over the lobby. On the walls of the lobby mezzanine are murals painted by John Warner Norton of Chicago, two of which represent farm and urban scenes that alluded to the daily lives of residents in the region.

In an essay in Gustav Stickley's *Craftsman,* published in 1912, Purcell and Elmslie argued, "Creative power in any field of activity is indigenous to the soil." They vigorously objected to the revival styles that their colleagues employed. In their view, America was "a virgin field for a great democratic architecture."[75] The courthouse in Sioux City, close to the Missouri River, exemplifies this conviction.

OMAHA, ST. LOUIS, AND KANSAS CITY

At the very heart of the nation's heartland, in Omaha, Nebraska, St. Louis, Missouri, and Kansas City, Missouri, virgin fields around dense centers presented all sorts of possibilities for architects and builders. The "great democratic architecture" as envisioned by Purcell and Elmslie was not, however, what most clients wanted. Neither was it advocated by two of the Midwest's leading architects, one in Omaha and another in St. Louis, who were trained in the East. Their work mirrors the conservative strain of the Arts and Crafts movement. Yet design ideas popularized by the Prairie School architects did make inroads.

During the first two decades of the twentieth century, Thomas Rogers Kimball (1862–1934) was the most highly esteemed architect in Omaha.[76] Although born in Ohio, his ties to New England were strong. His father's family was from Maine, and his mother was from New Hampshire. In 1871 his parents moved to Omaha when his father was rising through the ranks of the Union Pacific Railroad, eventually to be appointed a vice president. In 1880 young Kimball was sent to Boston to study art and architecture, entering MIT as a special student in 1885. He roomed with Dwight Perkins, a future participant in the Prairie School, and studied with C. Howard Walker, a founder and future president of Boston's Society of Arts and Crafts. Like many MIT architecture students, Kimball left the city to enroll at the École des Beaux-Arts in Paris. Back in Boston in 1888, he joined Henry Bates in publishing MIT's *Technology Architectural Review.* Walker must have thought highly of Kimball, for he invited Kimball to become a partner with him and Herbert R. Best. Upon Best's death, the firm became Walker and Kimball, and Kimball returned to Omaha to open a branch office.

The year was 1891, and Kimball's success was immediate. Shortly after his arrival, he received the commission to design the Omaha Public Library, and three years later he and Walker were designated architects-in-chief to oversee construction for the Trans-Mississippi Exposition, held in Omaha in 1898. During the same period, Kimball designed Omaha's Burlington Railway Station, commissioned in 1896. His approach, like Walker's, was not limited to English medieval or Anglo-Colonial revival styles, and these projects drew upon the classical tradition. What they took from the Arts and Crafts movement was its emphasis on restraint and quality of ornament. For the sculpture on the Burlington station's pediment, Kimball collaborated with Richard Bock.[77] Although Kimball never joined an Arts and Crafts organization, he would have been well-versed in the principles of the movement, especially as they were articulated by his Boston colleagues.[78] Respected by his peers, Kimball was elected president of the American Institute of Architects, serving two terms from 1918 to 1920. In 1928, seeking to reduce his workload, he invited William Steele to join his firm, and Steele moved from Sioux City to Omaha.[79] In no way did Kimball disapprove of Steele's projects influenced by the Prairie School.

When designing a house for his widowed mother and a sister in Omaha, Kimball produced a knowledgeable interpretation of the Jacobean country house (fig. 6.20).[80] Mary Rogers Kimball and her daughter moved into their new home in 1905. Constructed of buff-colored brick with limestone trim, it has a crow-stepped gable over the front entrance. Never common, the feature appeared in Boston in H. Langford Warren's 1888 design of the Charles J. Page House, built when Kimball was living in the city.[81] Visitors to Mary Kimball's house would have admired carved oak and mahogany as well as leaded-glass bookcases and a marble mantelpiece in the living room. From the main hall, guests ascended a staircase to reach the third floor and a theater, where Mary Kimball provided opportunities for local performers.

During this decade, John Lawrence Mauran (1866–1933) designed two elegant Tudor Revival houses on Portland Place in St. Louis. Portland Place and a parallel street, Westmoreland Place, were developed on former pastureland in 1888, with narrow parks running down the middle and gates at their entrances to limit public access.[82] Located to the west of the city's center, the residences were tightly controlled by covenants, but the architecture was varied in style. One of the Tudor houses that Mauran designed was for Charles and Sadie Stix, whose wealth was amassed through the Stix, Baer and Fuller Dry Goods Company (fig. 6.21).[83] Active in the St. Louis Jewish community, the Stixes also were accepted by the city's Protestant elite. Charles was admitted to the Missouri Athletic Club, and he and his wife were listed in the city's social register.[84] In building a Tudor Revival house, erected in 1909, Charles and Sadie Stix were embracing a fashionable image—a style that entered the country in the 1880s, encouraged by East Coast architects who were of English descent, for clients of English descent. Tudor was a comfortable choice for the civic-minded Stixes. Grounded in the Arts and Crafts movement, the style exuded an aura of warmth, contrasting with the off-putting neoclassical mansions in the neighborhood.

The house that Mauran created for the Stixes is a textbook example of the Tudor Revival. Brick with limestone trim, it is two-and-a-half stories high and dominated by a parapet gable that projects from a steeply pitched, slate-covered roof. Carving enhances the limestone of the Tudor-arched entrance, above which is a limestone oriel with battlements. The left side of the house has an overhanging half-timbered second floor, while the right side has a two-story polygonal bay with banked windows and a tall Tudor chimney. Half-timbered dormers on each side of the center gable balance the façade's picturesque asymmetry.

Mauran was one of the city's star architects. A native of Providence, he received his degree in architecture from MIT in 1889, worked with Shepley, Rutan, and Coolidge in Boston and Chicago, and opened a branch office in St. Louis before launching an independent practice with two partners.[85] In 1902 and 1903 he was elected president of the local chapter of the American Institute of Architects, and he served two terms as president of the national organization from 1916 to 1918, after which he was succeeded by Thomas Kimball.

Prairie School architecture in the heartland cities was not widespread, but even so, the style appeared well into the 1920s. In Rosedale, Kansas, southwest of downtown Kansas City, Missouri, a prominent lawyer erected a Prairie School house on a street of Craftsman-inspired bungalows (fig. 6.22). It was built between 1922 and 1923 for Louis R. Gates, a representative in the Kansas state legislature.[86] The architect of his new home was Clarence E. Shepard (1869–1949), who had worked as a draftsman

FIGURE 6.20. Thomas Rogers Kimball, [Mary Rogers] Kimball House, Omaha, 1905.

FIGURE 6.21. John Lawrence Mauran, Stix House, St. Louis, 1909.

FIGURE 6.22. Clarence E. Shepard, Gates House, Rosedale, Kansas, 1922–23.

7 Mountain States and Rustic Living

Remote and unspoiled, rising high above the midwestern plains, the Mountain States awed America's citizens. As the twentieth century opened, the craggy Rocky Mountains, covered with timberlands and capped with snow, were a wonder to be seen and explored.[1] Newly laid railroad tracks and newly built roads enabled more and more tourists to journey west—to hike, to fish, to hunt, to ride on horseback. In Wyoming, entrepreneurs erected lodges and dude ranches that appealed to a popular enthusiasm for the picturesque and all things rustic. Wealthy clients employed architects to design getaway retreats, conceived to reflect the magnificence of the West. In Colorado, institutional clients hired architects who reconsidered the revival styles that were fashionable in the East and identified new historic sources that they believed were more appropriate for the locale. Appropriately enough, the Centennial State's Spanish heritage provided inspiration. Less obviously, at the University of Colorado in Boulder, the inspiration for new campus projects came from the hill towns of Tuscany, built with stone walls and tile roofs.

The Arts and Crafts movement was girded by several values that encouraged the American people's fascination with the Mountain States and guided that region's architecture.[2] Above all else was a reverence for nature. It was central to the movement, and it contributed to the desire of urban Americans to see this part of the country. As was the case with destinations in the American South, many travelers went west to unwind from demanding city jobs. Others made the trip to recover their health, hoping to recuperate in the dry air. The sheer drama of the Rockies also was enticing, a sight that offered visitors the sort of sublime experience described by philosopher Edmund Burke in the eighteenth century and embraced by the British in the nineteenth century. This attraction to untamed nature carried into the Arts and Crafts movement and crossed the Atlantic to the United States, where an appreciation for the American wilderness took hold. Buildings designed for such settings frequently had expansive porches, connecting people with nearby forests, wildlife, and views of distant peaks. Visitors could enjoy rustic compounds that included clusters of log cabins and a communal lounge. In designing for remote places, architects adopted the Arts and Crafts principle of choosing indigenous materials, using native stone and timber. The Arts and Crafts call for simplicity was readily applied to the rustic architecture of the mountains. Yet even

FIGURE 7.1. A. A. Anderson, Pahaska Tepee, Cody, Wyoming, 1903–5.

among architects designing in revival styles, simplicity prevailed, with professionals favoring restraint for buildings based on precedents drawn from the past.

ADVENTURERS AND SIGHTSEERS

In northwestern Wyoming, William F. Cody seized an opportunity to capitalize on Americans' curiosity about the frontier, an interest he promoted in touring with his Wild West shows. Renowned as Buffalo Bill, he was as talented as an entrepreneur as he was as a scout. Realizing that the region could benefit from a center with lodging and services catering to visitors, Cody and investors founded the town of Cody in 1896. Ensuring its success, he persuaded the Chicago, Burlington, and Quincy Railroad to run a spur to the new community, and he advised the government on creating a wagon route that would link Cody to Yellowstone National Park. He also built an in-town hotel, an inn on the mountain road, and a lodge that was just two miles east of the park entrance.[3]

The lodge, Pahaska Tepee, was his favorite project—to his mind "the gem of the Rockies" (fig. 7.1).[4] The word *Pahaska* came from the name that Cody's Lakota friends had given him, which translated as "long hair of the head," a reference to his flowing locks. When selecting the site, on leased land in the Shoshone National Forest, Cody understood that the lodge would appeal to adventurers embarking on fishing and hunting expeditions as well as sightseers traveling into the Yellowstone park. During the offseason, he would host personal guests. In 1903, after the road was finished, construction of the lodge began. It opened a year later and was completed in 1905. The designer was A. A. Anderson (1846–1940), a painter, rancher, and conservationist.

At its essence, the building is like vernacular log cabins in the Mountain West.[5] Constructed with logs of native lodgepole pines, the structure has a traditional front-facing gable. Pahaska Tepee, however, is much larger than a cabin. It rises to two stories in height, and it is especially wide. Logs on the second story were notched to hold logs for interior walls. Often vernacular cabins had a roof that cantilevered beyond the front wall to create outdoor living space and protect a door from winter snows. In Anderson's design for Pahaska Tepee, the front gable projected outward, but unlike humble cabins, the second-story space was enclosed to contain a private suite for Cody. Below the suite, on the ground level, is a porch that wraps around three sides of the building. There, guests can relax and look over the valley and the north fork of the Shoshone River. Visitors pass through a double door, a touch of grandeur that's also welcoming. In the lobby, they encounter a hall dominated by a freestanding fireplace built of local stone. To one side is a staircase of logs that rises to a balcony and guestrooms. Within a few years, Cody expanded his operation, erecting two-room log cabins, a log dance pavilion, a rifle range, and tennis and croquet courts.

For the famed frontiersman, Anderson was an excellent collaborator, someone who appreciated the attributes of the region. Born to a wealthy New Jersey family, Anderson divided his time among homes in New York City and Paris and at Palette Ranch near Meeteetse, thirty miles south of Cody. In 1890 he built a traditional log cabin, gable-fronted and set into a hill.[6] There he painted and managed his herds of cattle. On the main level of the cabin were two small rooms, one for sleeping and another for working, and below was a kitchen nestled into the sloping land. The roof extended beyond the log walls in the usual way, but in this case it covered porches on two levels, and the upper porch functioned as a studio. Content as Anderson was with his rustic retreat, between 1900 and 1901 he built Bryant Park Studios in Manhattan, where he worked when he was in New York City. Yet he continued to care deeply about Wyoming. The timberlands he knew well were being desecrated by deliberate burning and grazing, despite their designation as the country's first national forest, and at the end of 1901, he joined a campaign to protest the abuses. In the year that followed, President Theodore Roosevelt appointed him Special Superintendent of Forest Reserves, an administrative position that Anderson ran from his little cabin-cum-studio.

NEAR THE OLD FAITHFUL GEYSER

Conservation initiatives were in keeping with the Arts and Crafts movement, and a milestone in American history was reached in 1872 when Congress created Yellowstone National Park, the first such park in the country.[7] Tourists, however, didn't think that Yellowstone was all that attractive. To begin with, its peculiar thermal features, steaming and spewing, made people uneasy. Visiting in 1888, Rudyard Kipling complained, "Today I am in the Yellowstone Park, and I wish I were dead."[8] Entirely unlike the serene gardens of England, the park was "a howling wilderness" that was "full of all imaginable freaks of a fiery nature."[9] Decent accommodations also were lacking. To meet the demand, in the 1880s the government granted concession rights to the Northern Pacific Railroad, which stood to reap a profit if it could entice more tourists to the park. Managing the operation turned out to be a struggle, however, and at the end of the next decade, the railroad turned the challenge over to a subsidiary, led by Montana businessman Harry Child.[10]

In 1902 plans were prepared for accommodations near the Old Faithful geyser, and laborers began cutting logs to build lodging in a rustic style. Then in January 1903, when Child was wintering in San Diego, he had second thoughts. He sought out architect Robert C. Reamer (1873–1938) and recruited him to work at Yellowstone.[11] Reamer proposed building a hotel in the Upper Geyser Basin that was rustic yet far more grandiose than the earlier plan—to be called Old Faithful Inn (fig. 7.2). Work started in the spring, and the building opened in 1904.

Dating from the same years, Reamer's inn and Anderson's hunting lodge for Cody are similar in several respects. Both were constructed with logs and rock harvested nearby so that they are at one with their natural settings. Both have large porches, places that delighted guests, with double doors opening to spacious lobbies where people could socialize. Massive freestanding fireplaces are part of the magic of these halls, and they rise past balconies of logs to open-timber roofs. Yet Anderson's scheme for Pahaska Tepee owes more to the vernacular mountain cabin in its construction, aligning it with the Arts and Crafts value of employing regional building traditions; Reamer's Old Faithful Inn was a modern fantasy.

What Reamer created is a hotel that is rustic in appearance, artfully conceived to impress well-heeled tourists.[12] When guests first spotted the inn, they saw flags fluttering at the top of an oversize, steeply sloping roof. Alighting from stagecoaches under the protection of a porte cochere, they entered a lobby that soars to seven stories, its balconies supported by weighty logs and twisted branches. In the evenings, guests were entertained by musicians who climbed a series of open staircases to a platform where they performed near the peak of the roof. Reamer had masterminded a spectacle.[13] The architect also was attuned to the appeal of handicraft. A native of

FIGURE 7.2. Robert C. Reamer, Old Faithful Inn, lobby, Yellowstone National Park, Wyoming, 1903–4.

FIGURE 7.3. George Colpitts and workshop, lobby clock, Old Faithful Inn.

Ohio, he had worked in Chicago in the early 1890s and would have witnessed the Arts and Crafts movement coalescing there.[14] For Old Faithful Inn, he devised all sorts of iron ornaments and accoutrements, from door hardware to a huge windup clock (fig. 7.3) to a giant popcorn popper, all crafted by Montana blacksmith George Colpitts (1855–1937) and his workshop.[15] Like any quality hotel, Old Faithful Inn was served by plumbing, electricity, and steam heat. It was not a lodge for hunting, which was outlawed at Yellowstone in 1894. Reamer's design was log cabin-ish, built with saddle-notched logs at ground level and with logs and more logs inside. But the upper stories of the building were conventionally framed, and most of its exterior was clad in wood shingles.[16]

A NEW TYPE OF AMERICAN VACATION

By the 1920s, American tourists, especially from the East, were intrigued by the idea of trying something new by spending a week or two in an authentic log cabin. Entrepreneurs in the Mountain States, including Montana, Wyoming, and Colorado, responded by erecting dude ranches—compounds with a structure for dining and socializing, cabins, and support buildings.[17] Marketing was handled by the railroads through brochures that they distributed around the country. In 1926 the Dude Ranchers' Association was founded, furthering the interest in this new type of vacation destination. The phenomenon of the dude ranch can be considered an outgrowth of the Arts and Crafts movement, which emerged as a rejection of the industrial economy and urban living. Dude ranches were defined by simple, moderately scaled buildings that were rustic in appearance, constructed with indigenous materials and vernacular methods. Visitors participated in wholesome activities, especially horseback riding. They also might try fishing or twirling a rope. Evening entertainment revolved around games and dancing in the lounge. Nevertheless, unlike the communities that were founded with an Arts and Crafts mission, dude ranches were not built for any lofty purpose—social or artistic. Indeed, most dude ranches weren't even ranches. Rather, they were exclusively tourist destinations. Moreover, not everyone was welcome. Brochures assured potential guests that they would find themselves in the company of "desirable" people, and references were often required.[18]

Several dude ranches opened along the road between Cody and the Yellowstone park, including Elephant Head Lodge, named for the shape of a nearby rock formation.[19] It was built and managed by Josephine Goodman Thurston (1876–1961) after she and her husband, Harry W. Thurston, received a permit at the end of 1926 to lease land in the Shoshone Forest.[20] Bolstering her decision to undertake this project was the example set by her mother, Julia Cody Goodman, who managed the Irma Hotel in Cody for her younger brother, the showman Buffalo Bill.[21] The site that Josie Thurston chose for Elephant Head Lodge was one she knew well. There her husband, the first ranger in the Wapiti district, had received permission in 1920 to build a log cabin that would shelter the couple during the summers.[22] In the usual manner, the cabin had a front-facing gable and projecting roof over an outdoor living area.

When Josie Thurston oversaw construction of the dude ranch compound in 1927, she retained the ranger's cabin. For the building that would serve as a lounge, she wanted a rustic design that was sunny by day and commodious for evening activities (fig. 7.4).[23] She settled upon a one-story log structure with saddle-notched corners that was side-gabled, with a low-pitched roof that continued as a shed roof over a center front door, but not over the windows on either side.[24] Rejecting the idea of the wraparound porch, Thurston prioritized bringing light into the lounge. Inside it was open to the roof, with exposed log walls, beams, and purlins, and a fireplace of native stone at one end.

Two years later, a travel magazine published an article about Elephant Head Lodge, describing it as "a hobby with Mrs. Thurston."[25] Is that what she told the writer? If so, one can only guess why she thought readers would look favorably upon this assertion. Perhaps she thought potential guests would imagine that a woman who was running a dude ranch as a hobby, and not as a serious source of income, would be more hospitable. Or perhaps she felt that if she presented her work as a hobby, she would be regarded as a woman who was respectably middle class—sharing the status of her guests.

A MOUNTAIN GETAWAY

Of course, a hard-nosed, moneymaking man didn't face this problem. A man who became wealthy, such as Charles Boettcher, knew what he was doing. Born in Germany, he arrived as a teenager in Cheyenne, Wyoming, in 1869 to join his brothers in business, moved to Colorado at the end of the next decade, and settled in Denver in 1890, amassing a fortune along the way through the sale of hardware, Portland cement, cattle, and sugar beets. In 1915 he bought sixty-two acres in nearby Golden, where he erected a mountain getaway.[26]

Between 1870 and 1890, Denver had grown from a town of less than five thousand residents to more than one hundred thousand, making it the second-largest city in the West, after San Francisco. In the opening years of the new century, the city's leaders debated how to control development, especially the heights of steel-framed office buildings.[27] At the end of 1908, the local government enacted a height limit of twelve stories. Buffalo Bill Cody observed ruefully, "I cannot but think of the time when a view of the foothills could have been obtained—and a good one, too—from any point in the city."[28] Boettcher financed several such big buildings, but when it came to his retreat, it would be sited to offer sweeping views in three directions.

Boettcher's Lorraine Lodge was designed by leading Denver architects, brothers William Ellsworth Fisher (1871–1937) and Arthur Addison Fisher (1878–1965), and built in 1917 (fig. 7.5).[29] Located at the top of Lookout Mountain, the rustic two-story house is integrated with a terrain of rocky outcroppings and ponderosa pines. The main elevation is constructed of native fieldstone and fronts on a terrace rimmed by low stone walls. On its other sides, the house is somewhat English in its references, with a profusion of jerkinhead gables and Tudor half-timbering of peeled logs with stucco infill. Upon passing through a small vestibule, guests found themselves in a "great hall," similar to the halls of Arts and Crafts houses in the English countryside. The walls are stone and rise to a vaulted ceiling with visible framing, which features timbers accented by carved animal heads. On one of the long walls is a large recessed fireplace that was flanked by oak settle benches, while wrought-iron and glass lanterns illuminated the room.[30]

FIGURE 7.4. Josephine Goodman Thurston, Elephant Head Lodge, featuring Harry and Josephine Goodman Thurston with their grandchildren, Shoshone National Forest, Wyoming, 1927.

FIGURE 7.5. Fisher and Fisher, Lorraine Lodge, Golden, Colorado, 1917.

The Fishers were born in Canada and came to Denver with their parents when they were young.[31] Both trained in offices, including stints in New York City, before returning home. In 1915 William Fisher served as president of the Colorado chapter of the American Institute of Architects. When Denver established a Planning Commission in 1929, Arthur sat on the Executive Committee.[32] For the next two decades, the commission held the line on the city's twelve-story height restriction to ensure that Denver would be "a city of spacious beauty."[33]

DRY AIR IN COLORADO SPRINGS

Seventy miles to the south of Denver, Colorado Springs was another place of beauty—a place where ailing people came to breathe dry air and recuperate from tuberculosis. Artus Van Briggle was one of the suffering who traveled there, making his first trip in 1899.[34] An Ohio native, he began his career as a decorator for the Rookwood Pottery in Cincinnati and later studied in Paris, where he met artist Anne Lawrence Gregory. In 1902 they obtained backers to open the Van Briggle Pottery, and they also married. Two years later, Artus died, and Anne became president of the company. Under her leadership, a large new pottery, designed by Nicolaas van den Arend (1870–1940), was built (fig. 7.6). Construction began in 1907 and was finished in the following year.[35] The Dutch architect was a new arrival to Colorado Springs, having relocated there in 1904, shortly after his wife contracted tuberculosis. With Anne's active participation, Van den Arend created a brick building that was unusual and whimsical, conceived to attract tourists who would purchase Van Briggle wares. Elements of the building recalled Flemish farmhouses, which were low and picturesque, with multiple gables and dormers. Although unrelated to the architecture of Colorado, as Arts and Crafts theory would prefer, the allusion to Flanders honored the ancestry of Artus. In other ways, the pottery building was expressive of the Arts and Crafts activity that would take place inside. Anne personally designed the tile and molded ornament that was embedded in the building. At the end of one wing, customers walking toward the entrance would see a ceramic sundial and a crowing rooster. Van Briggle products, characterized by a matte glaze, were highly successful. At the 1907 exhibition in Boston of the Society of Arts and Crafts, Van Briggle ceramics were selected for display alongside those of Henry Chapman Mercer and Adelaide Alsop Robineau.[36]

Architects coming from the East were well-received in Colorado, and several who were sympathetic to the Arts and Crafts movement were invited to oversee major projects. In Colorado Springs, George E. Barton (1871–1923) planned the Myron Stratton Home in 1911 for the region's destitute children, many of whom were orphans, and the elderly poor.[37] Rather than one large structure, Barton envisioned thirteen buildings on a landscaped campus, which spread over more than one hundred acres. The work was completed by Maurice B. Biscoe (1871–1953) between 1913 and 1914. Funding came through the six-million-dollar bequest of Winfield Scott Stratton, a prospector who struck gold on a slope of nearby Pikes Peak.

Barton came from Boston and began his career as a draftsman for Henry Vaughan, a protégé of George F. Bodley, and then joined the office of Cram, Wentworth, and Goodhue.[38] On a trip to England, likely in 1895, Barton spent time with William Morris. Back in Boston, the young architect became a charter member of the Society of Arts and Crafts and was elected its secretary. Journeying again to England in 1899, he visited the model worker village of Port Sunlight, established by Lever Brothers near Birkenhead, and wrote about it for the *Architectural Review*.[39] Barton's career was taking off, and in 1902 R. Clipston Sturgis invited him to become his partner, an association that lasted seven years. Through much of this period, Barton was suffering with tuberculosis, and he finally went west to get better.

Landing in Colorado Springs, Barton responded well to the dry air and treatment, and by 1911 he was busy working out his ideas for the Myron Stratton Home. In a report, he described how it would provide industrial training for the young of both genders, enabling them to become independent, self-sufficient adults.[40] The children would be prepared for traditional roles—the boys would be taught shop and farm skills, and the girls would be taught sewing, cooking, and rudimentary nursing skills.[41] The elderly would be given housing and care. As the project moved forward, Barton was laid low once more, this time after one of his feet was frozen in the winter cold and he became partially paralyzed.[42] Biscoe, a colleague in Denver, took over. Like Barton, he had spent the first years of his career in Boston. As a onetime a partner of H. Langford Warren, president of the Society of Arts and Crafts, Biscoe appreciated the movement's objectives.[43]

FIGURE 7.6. Nicolaas van den Arend, Van Briggle Pottery Building, Colorado Springs, Colorado, 1907–8.

FIGURE 7.7. George E. Barton with Maurice B. Biscoe, Independence Hall, Myron Stratton Home, Colorado Springs, Colorado, 1911–14.

After the Stratton Home opened, Barton eventually recovered. In 1917 he helped found and became president of what is now the American Occupational Therapy Association, shaped by Arts and Crafts thinking.

When imagining the buildings for the Stratton Home, Barton and Biscoe approached the task in a scholarly manner, reflecting their training. They designed a superintendent's house, group houses for boys and girls, and cottages for the elderly, all in a style that referred to the Spanish presence in Colorado. The structures had roofs with red barrel tiles, deep eaves, and stuccoed walls. Independence Hall, for the boys, is a two-story building that has three curved parapet gables on the front façade, its middle gable ornamented by a star window, a mark of the Mission Revival (fig. 7.7). Washington Hall, for the girls, is two stories in height and has two curved parapet gables and an arcade across the main level—the arcade also associated with the Mission Revival.

A UNIVERSITY OF COLORADO STYLE

In 1918 the University of Colorado hired Charles Z. Klauder to prepare a plan that would guide development and bring coherence to a hodgepodge of buildings on the Boulder campus.[44] The architect had been practicing in Philadelphia with Frank Miles Day, and they were renowned for their academic commissions, especially at Princeton and Wellesley. Embracing an Arts and Crafts perspective, they created Collegiate Gothic buildings that were exemplary, including Klauder's Gothic Cathedral of Learning for the University of Pittsburgh, designed in the mid-1920s (see fig. 3.18). For the University of Colorado, Klauder's first impulse was to work in a medieval vein, but he concluded that it wasn't the right choice if new buildings were to be constructed with the region's pink sandstone. His thoughts turned to his travels in rural Tuscany, where he admired vernacular buildings of stone with red-tiled roofs and picturesque chimneys, and they

FIGURE 7.8. Charles Z. Klauder, Liberal Arts Building (Hellems Arts and Sciences Building), main entrance, University of Colorado, Boulder, 1919–21.

became the basis for what he would call the University of Colorado style.

The campus in Boulder was established on a windswept hill with a view of great sandstone outcroppings to the west and the foothills of the Rocky Mountains in the distance. When Klauder finished his development plan in 1919, he proposed demolishing the Victorian buildings, which dated to the founding of the university in 1876. The Arts and Crafts respect for history didn't apply to structures of this vintage. Writing in *College Architecture in America,* a book published in 1929, Klauder and co-author Herbert C. Wise observed that such buildings were "monumental annoyances," quite different from the survivors of the colonial and federal periods on eastern campuses.[45] Employing favorite words of the Arts and Crafts movement, they explained that these buildings in the East were revered for their "simplicity, dignity, truthfulness, and restraint."[46] Nevertheless, Colorado's Victorian halls were spared, mainly because they were needed as enrollment grew.

Klauder and Wise argued that the architectural conception of a campus should find "its own footing in its own locale."[47] For the buildings at Boulder, pink sandstone, quarried north of the city, was rough-cut in blocks and laid to create a jagged surface, harmonizing with the natural environment. As in rural Tuscan villages, roofs sloped gently and were covered with barrel tiles of terracotta. Klauder designed his campus buildings with discrete masses pressed against each other, capturing the additive, rambling effect of the buildings that he sketched in Italy. Valuing simplicity, Klauder used ornament sparingly. It was carved from Indiana limestone and in the language of the Italian Renaissance.

The Liberal Arts Building, renamed the Hellems Arts and Sciences Building (1919–21), established Klauder's University of Colorado style (fig. 7.8).[48] A long two-story rectangular mass runs into a pavilion at each gable end that rises abruptly to three stories, and each of those is buttressed by a two-story block with a shed roof. The textures of the red barrel tiles and variegated pinks of the sandstone are visible from afar, but at close range, one appreciates a classical limestone door surround, carved roundels of the seals of the state and university, and cartouches on the wall near the roof. In the conclusion of their book, Klauder and Wise urge builders of campus architecture to erect "monuments of good craftsmanship" reared with "bricks and stones of honesty and truth."[49] Thus Arts and Crafts ideals, indebted to John Ruskin and Morris, offered a rationale for a style that Klauder envisioned to unify a growing university campus set against a mountain backdrop—a style that would respond to the natural beauty of Colorado.

Buildings in the Mountain States could be rustic or refined. Or a little of both. The movement's emphasis on nature, native materials, and simplicity led logically to erecting Old Faithful Inn and Lorraine Lodge. On the other hand, architects from the East, instilled with a scholarly orientation, such as Barton and Klauder, believed their job was to identify historic sources that would be suitable for the settings where they were hired to work. An Arts and Crafts philosophy could lead designers up and along several different trails when they embarked upon new commissions in the high, tree-covered mountains.

EIN
E.L. BLUMENSCHEIN
HOME & MUSEUM
Taos Historic Museums

8 Texas and the Southwest: Spanish and Native

For people living in Texas and the Southwest who were drawn to Arts and Crafts ideals, the way forward wasn't at all clear. The challenge for architects and others in sympathy with an Arts and Crafts outlook was how to design buildings that would respond to the distinctive heritage and characteristics of their regions. When hired to design a new campus in Houston, architects Cram, Goodhue, and Ferguson of Boston and New York City concluded that the architecture of the Mediterranean world would provide a solid jumping-off point. El Paso architect Henry C. Trost, who spent eight years in Chicago, embraced Prairie School ideas when he built a house for himself. After all, the Prairie School theorists believed they were advancing an approach to residential design that could be construed as American.

Yet as the first decade of the twentieth century passed into the second, the view took hold that Spanish Colonial history and the legacy of the region's Indigenous peoples provided the best sources for new buildings. In Santa Fe, the city encouraged features of Spanish and Pueblo architecture. At the same time, in keeping with the Arts and Crafts movement's long involvement with historic preservation, architects and residents in the Southwest supported and directed the preservation of early Spanish and Native American structures. Then, too, rustic styles, another facet of American Arts and Crafts architecture, were popular in the Southwest, well-suited to its untamed landscapes.

UNDER THE TEXAS SUN

In 1909 the president and trustees of the Rice Institute were ready to build a new campus.[1] They didn't have a faculty or students, but they had land, located about four miles southwest of downtown Houston, and they had the necessary funding. William M. Rice, murdered in a scandal in 1900, had bequeathed a substantial sum to found an institution of higher education in the city where he had made his millions. His gift was well-intended, although to a limited extent. In his will, he wrote that the school should admit only white students, a barrier that did not fall until 1965.

To discuss the commission, the new president, Edgar Odell Lovett, journeyed to Boston to meet with Ralph Adams Cram, whose firm, Cram, Goodhue, and Ferguson, was highly regarded for campus work.[2] Both Cram and his partner, Bertram Goodhue, were

FIGURE 8.1. Cram, Goodhue, and Ferguson, administration building (Lovett Hall), Rice University, Houston, 1911–12.

committed to Arts and Crafts principles and were members of Boston's Society of Arts and Crafts. The buildings for Rice University, as the institute is now known, would be embellished by talented artists and artisans. But first the question arose: What style would be suitable for a campus on a barren prairie under the Texas sun?

In his autobiography, Cram recalled thinking that Gothic would have been "out of place," while noting, "Wild horses would not have driven us to use the 'Mission Style,'" a revival that he viewed with distaste.[3] As for "Spanish-Indian-Baroque," he rejected it as irrelevant to the locale. "Manifestly the only thing to do was to invent something approaching a new style," he explained.[4] That style would reflect the Houston climate and draw upon the architecture of Mediterranean lands, in particular the richly decorated, polychromatic buildings of Byzantine Italy. Goodhue delivered a general plan for the campus, governed by an axis that starts at a main gate, continues along a drive flanked by live oaks, and brings visitors to an administration building.[5] Later renamed Lovett Hall, it was designed by Cram and built between 1911 and 1912 (fig. 8.1). A long, expansive structure, it's organized around a four-story central tower penetrated by a monumental arch that opens onto a court bordered by academic halls.

The administration building introduced the materials that would unify the campus.[6] Rose-hued brick was made from clay obtained locally along the Buffalo Bayou, granite was quarried near Austin, and marble was brought in from Oklahoma. Columns of imported marble of different hues and a frieze of turquoise and green tile added colorful accents. Round arches and stone horizontal bands contributed to the Byzantine effect. Also derived from Byzantine monuments are the column capitals, drilled and undercut in a manner that was employed in the work of Henry Hobson Richardson.[7] To animate the carving, the architects favored original, even droll, animals and human visages, including corbels with heads of students (fig. 8.2). Oswald J. Lassig (1873–1935), an Austrian immigrant recruited from Chicago, was responsible for the sculpture.[8] On the side of the hall that faces the academic court are plaques representing science and art modeled by New York City artist C. Percival Dietsch and carved by Lassig.[9] Henry Chapman Mercer and the Moravian Pottery and Tile Works, of Doylestown, Pennsylvania, supplied customized designs in ceramics that were set into the walls and made tile for the flooring.[10] Hardware and furnishings also were designed by the architects. Entirely original, Cram's "new style" depended upon the same high level of craftsmanship and artistry that characterized English and East Coast Arts and Crafts architecture.

FIGURE 8.2. Oswald J. Lassig and workshop, corbel of a freshman, Rice University administration building.

PRAIRIE SCHOOL NEAR THE RIO GRANDE

El Paso architect Henry C. Trost (1860–1933) was every bit as committed to obtaining fine craftsmanship and artistry for the house he built for himself in the Sunset Heights district of his adopted city, almost 750 miles west of Houston.[11] What makes it noteworthy is the degree to which it resembles Prairie School houses and the fact that it's contemporaneous with them (fig. 8.3). Although Trost was capable of working in many styles, including the Mission Revival, when he was his own client, he chose a progressive image. By 1906 he had bought a corner lot, offering views of the Rio Grande River and Mexico, and began sketching. In 1909 the dwelling was completed.

Born and raised in Toledo, Ohio, Trost trained as a draftsman and practiced in Colorado, Texas, Louisiana, and Kansas before ending his wanderings in Chicago, where he resided between 1888 and 1896.[12] As a member of the Chicago Architectural Club, he encountered the novel design ideas that were circulating in the city—ideas that would contribute to Chicago's Arts and Crafts movement and the Prairie School.[13] Trost specialized as a designer of ornamental metalwork, and in 1889 he and architect Emil Henry Seeman opened an art metal business, which they operated for about a year. Seeman was then hired by Adler and Sullivan. Although it's not known where Trost next found employment, he kept a close watch on new work by Sullivan as well as by Frank Lloyd Wright. Leaving Chicago for short stints in Colorado and Arizona, Trost then joined a brother, Gustavus Adolphus Trost, in El Paso in 1903, and they formed a partnership. The two were compatible, and Henry finally put down roots.

In several respects, the Trost House resembles Wright's Susan Lawrence Dana House (1902–4) in Springfield, Illinois (see fig. 5.5). Both have gabled roofs with deep overhanging eaves, weighty corner piers that stop well below the roof, and walled terraces. Both are built of Roman brick with raked horizontal joints. Trost also adopted the round arch at the entrance to the Dana House for the entrance to his home. Sullivan influenced Trost, too, as may be seen in the pattern sculpted in the frieze near the roof, while Robert Spencer's influence shows in the application of flat boards and plaster, based on half-timbering, above the brick.

Responding to the way in which the Prairie School architects pursued the Arts and Crafts concept of coordinating interior decoration and furnishings, Trost oversaw

FIGURE 8.3. Henry C. Trost, Trost House, El Paso, Texas, 1906–9.

the decoration of his house to create a unified whole.[14] He designed the woodwork, art glass, stenciling, and furniture. His color choices, from yellow ochers to brownish reds, reflect the native landscape, a palette that also happened to be preferred in Arts and Crafts decorating. His ornamental motifs are reminiscent of local flora, including cacti, which he conventionalized. For a stenciled frieze in the public rooms, Trost used curving, intertwining elements in the spirit of Sullivan. On the other hand, his art glass designs are angular, more like the glass in buildings by Wright. To execute his ideas, Trost arranged for a decorator from the Chicago firm of Mitchell and Halbach to come to El Paso, and it's likely he contracted with the firm for the art glass.[15] The woodwork and furniture were handled by a local craftsman, J. P. Paulson of El Paso, representing the Brunswick-Balke-Collender Company.

THE SANTA FE STYLE

In New Mexico, the first Planning Board of Santa Fe established a vision that would guide development for the entire city—a vision that has been supported to this day. New construction was to be designed in the "Santa Fe style," which the board defined in 1912 based on a study of surviving Pueblo and Spanish Colonial adobe buildings.[16] At the beginning of the century, the city was losing population and struggling economically; however, it benefited from a dry climate, brilliant sunlight, and an intriguing past. Tourism could turn things around. By this time, a fascination with New Mexico's history was catching on. The Historical Society of New Mexico had been founded in 1859, and although it went dormant at the onset of the Civil War, it was revived in 1881 and encouraged sensibilities that would nurture the Planning Board's work of 1912. The people who produced the city's development plan and the Santa Fe style were men of varied talents. None of them were architects, yet they shared an appreciation for the ancient neglected buildings of their region and determined that these examples could inspire new buildings to differentiate Santa Fe from other cities and attract visitors from around the country.

One of the city's most effective boosters was Harry Howard Dorman (1872–1960). Appointed by the mayor to chair the Planning Board, Dorman marshaled support from the business community.[17] Born and raised in New York City, he descended from old New England stock, which may have contributed to his fondness for history. As a young man, he was stricken with tuberculosis, and in 1901 he moved to Santa Fe to regain his health. He got his footing selling insurance and building houses. For the quality of his projects, he was judged as having "the eye of an architect, the hand of a master builder, and the soul of an artist."[18] The opportunity to influence the future of Santa Fe was a challenge that Dorman took seriously. He solicited comprehensive plans from major American cities as well as one from Germany, and he sought advice from Frederick Law Olmsted, Jr., and John Nolen. Through the planning process, Dorman ensured that the local chamber of commerce was involved. The board's report, issued at the end of 1912, broke new ground for American city plans by calling for the preservation of Santa Fe's historic buildings and designated streets. It also recommended that "no building permits be issued" until assurance was given that "the architecture will conform exteriorally with the Santa Fe style."[19] Although the city didn't enact a design ordinance until 1957, the new style was generally followed.

Planning Board member Sylvanus Morley (1883–1948), an archaeologist who would become a noted scholar of the Maya, had the training to identify the style's salient characteristics.[20] A 1907 graduate of Harvard College, he was associated with the School of American Archaeology in Santa Fe. He and his colleagues on the board distanced themselves from the Mission style architecture of California, with its sloping tile roofs and curved parapet gables. The old buildings of Santa Fe, made of adobe, had flat roofs, protruding beams called *vigas,* thick walls, porches called *portales,* and wood posts capped by flat, shaped corbels called *zapatas.* Embellished by carving and painting, the buildings appealed to those with an Arts and Crafts mindset. Yet the pervasive view in Santa Fe was that its Pueblo and Spanish buildings were dusty and worn. To encourage popular interest in them, Morley proposed holding an event. Organizers obtained photographs, drawings, and models of historic buildings as well as original designs to present a "New-Old Santa Fe" exhibition. With tourism on his mind, Dorman wanted a sketch of a hotel in the Santa Fe style to display and show how such a building might look.[21] He sent architect Isaac Rapp (1854–1933) photographs of Taos Pueblo, suggesting that it might offer ideas for a design. Although Rapp couldn't meet the exhibition deadline, the concept stuck, and Rapp's firm built La Fonda Hotel from 1921 to 1922 in the Santa Fe style (fig. 8.4).

Other Planning Board members who were integral to the initiative were Edgar Hewett, director of the Museum of New Mexico and the School of American Archaeology, and Bronson Cutting, who, like Dorman, was a native of New York City and recovering from tuberculosis.[22]
A gifted student in his youth, Cutting graduated from Harvard in 1910 before heading southwest. Two years later, he bought the local newspaper, the *Santa Fe New Mexican,* and it became a platform to promote the Santa Fe style and the cause of preservation. When the plan was adopted by the city council in December of 1912, it rejected grandiose Beaux-Arts planning and classical styles of the day while it expanded on Arts and Crafts

FIGURE 8.4. Isaac Rapp, La Fonda Hotel, Santa Fe, 1921–22.

FIGURE 8.5. Mary and Ernest Blumenschein, Blumenschein House (Blumenschein Museum), Taos, New Mexico, 1919–20 and 1931.

principles that valued historic streets and buildings, native materials, and craftsmanship.

A SPRAWLING ADOBE HOME

As in the East, the ways in which New Mexico's historic buildings were preserved ran the gamut. Some admirers of these survivors made substantial changes to them without hesitation, whereas others endeavored to secure and restore them. In Taos, about one hundred miles northeast of Santa Fe, artists Mary and Ernest Blumenschein altered several small adobe buildings that they incorporated into a sprawling home (fig. 8.5).[23] Mary Shepard Greene (1869–1958) and Ernest L. Blumenschein (1874–1960) met in Paris in 1903 and married two years later. Ernest had already discovered Taos, and a few years after he and Mary wed, he traveled there each summer. In 1915 he became a founding member of the Taos Society of Artists.[24] One of its objectives was "to preserve and promote the native art."[25] Near the end of the decade, Mary came into a large inheritance, and the couple decided to make Taos their home. Respectful of both the Indigenous and Hispanic peoples, they appreciated the historic adobe buildings.

In 1919 the Blumenscheins bought a four-room adobe house from W. Herbert "Buck" Dunton, another founder of the Taos Society of Artists. Dating from 1797, the one-story dwelling was part of the original fortification of Taos—a cluster of buildings, constructed by Spanish colonists, connected to each other around a central plaza. Across the front of the house was a traditional porch with wooden posts and *zapatas.* Dunton and then the Blumenscheins modified the historic building to serve their purposes. In a room that became his studio, Dunton inserted large windows. When the Blumenscheins took over, Mary directed most of the work and made further changes. To create a spacious dining room, she combined two historic rooms. She also opened an exterior wall to insert three windows grouped together, a typical arrangement among Arts and Crafts houses. At the same time, she valued the original ponderosa pine *vigas* and saw to it that they were preserved. Many of the projects inside the house were executed by Star Road, a Pueblo Indian, baptized as Geronimo Gomez, who also worked as Ernest's model.[26] Star Road handled cabinetry and carpentry, and he mixed a Venetian red paint for the library. In 1920 the Blumenscheins and their daughter moved in. Purchases of adjacent property followed in 1931, enabling the couple to enlarge their home. On one parcel was a building dating from 1825. Covering its ceiling were adzed pine boards—handwork that the Blumenscheins prized and chose to retain.

During the period from 1924 through 1929, the mission church of San Estévan del Rey at Acoma Pueblo was restored in a manner that was more closely aligned with the preservation philosophy of William Morris and Philip Webb.[27] Located fifty-five miles west of Albuquerque, the mission was founded by Spanish Franciscans on a remote and rocky mesa. Although the friars directed the construction of the church, erected between 1629 and 1644, it was the Acomas who built it. A massive structure enclosing an uninterrupted nave, choir loft, and altar, it dominates the site, measuring 145 by 44 feet. Its load-bearing walls were literally handmade, constructed of adobe brick and plastered by hand, and its flat roof was supported by ponderosa pine *vigas* and covered with adobe. Over the centuries, the Acomas maintained the building, annually repairing the walls and applying new adobe plaster. Nevertheless, deterioration set in.

In 1922 a campaign to preserve New Mexico's mission churches began. The person driving the endeavor was Anne Evans of Denver, a socially prominent artist who raised the funds and recruited volunteers for what became known as the Committee for the Preservation and Restoration of New Mexico Mission Churches.[28] A key recruit was the young architect John Gaw Meem (1894–1983).[29] After contracting tuberculosis, he came to Santa Fe in 1920. Meem had been educated for a career in civil engineering, but during his recovery, he shifted his professional interest to architecture. He accepted an opportunity to train in Denver with Fisher and Fisher. Back in Santa Fe, while launching his practice, he agreed to assist—unpaid—with the restoration of the church at Acoma Pueblo (fig. 8.6).

The project was accomplished in phases, beginning with rebuilding and repairing the roof, then continuing with repairs to the walls and the reconstruction of two bell towers over the front elevation. Day-to-day work at the site was managed by project supervisors Lewis Riley in 1924 and B. A. Reuter from 1926 to 1929. Labor was provided by the tribe, and building materials came from tribal lands. The Acomas, Franciscans, and

FIGURE 8.6. John Gaw Meem, restoration of San Estévan del Rey, Acoma Pueblo, New Mexico, 1924–29.

Anglo-Americans all had a voice in the decision-making in a remarkable and sustained collaboration. They shared a commitment to stabilize the church edifice, consistent with what had become enlightened views in England and the eastern United States about preservation. Yet unlike the restoration of an English or East Coast building of stone, brick, or even wood, the restoration of an adobe building would result in an entirely new exterior. Surviving fabric would be plastered over completely. Even so, as Meem reported to Evans in November 1926, "None of the new work looks at all rigid. There is the same informal look to the walls that the ancient walls have."[30] Much thought was given to the vulnerability of adobe and the demands of maintaining an edifice of such size. Protecting the building was a top priority, and therefore stone was chosen for the copings on the parapet and for the base of the walls. More challenging were questions about the appropriateness of reconstruction. When workmen discovered vestiges of a circular staircase in one of the church towers, the Acomas and Franciscans were eager to see it rebuilt. Recognizing their rightful interests, Meem wrote to the committee that "since they were all so keen about it, I feel it was the wise thing to do."[31] Another decision was reached to replace the incongruous belfries, dating from 1902 to 1911, with belfries that were compatible with the rest of the monument. When the restoration of the Acoma church came to a close, its exterior was new, yet traditional building methods and local materials were used to secure it in as authentic a way as possible.

In the 1920s the craftsmanship of the Pueblos and the early Spanish residents of New Mexico attracted the attention of people who related it to Arts and Crafts values. In 1925 the Society for the Revival of Spanish Colonial Arts was founded in Santa Fe to conserve and promote works of art and handicraft, from religious paintings to carved wooden doors to woven blankets and rugs.[32] The society also sought to preserve neighboring village churches, including one at Cordova. As a member of the organization, Meem provided guidance.[33] A California painter and printmaker, Pedro J. de Lemos, appreciated the talents of the Pueblos as builders and artisans. While employed as director of the Museum and Art Gallery at Stanford University, he visited New Mexico and subsequently published an article in 1928 called "Marvelous Acoma and Its Craftsmen."[34]

MEEM AND THE SPANISH-PUEBLO REVIVAL

In his architectural practice, Meem produced some of New Mexico's finest buildings in the Spanish-Pueblo Revival style. Distinguished by their ornament, they represent the long duration of the Arts and Crafts movement in American architecture.[35] His artistry is admired at the University of New Mexico campus, located in Albuquerque, where he designed all of the buildings from 1934 to 1959.[36] In 1936 he started work on the University Library, later named the Zimmerman Library, which opened in 1938 (fig. 8.7).[37] Funded through the federal Public Works Administration as a New Deal program, it benefited from the government's desire to give jobs to artisans. With flat roofs and battered walls covered in concrete stucco, the massing of the library was inspired by the buildings of the Taos Indian pueblo. The original main entrance alludes to the Spanish colonial era and is approached through a broad porch with posts and *zapatas*. Years later, Meem explained that he wanted "to recall by means of a conventionalized symbolic form the heritage of ancient buildings, or the characteristic shapes of the landscape," demonstrating his adherence to an Arts and Crafts outlook, even for a building constructed with reinforced concrete and steel.[38]

The most memorable spaces of the library are a great hall, originally the book delivery room, and two connecting reading rooms, each 192 feet long. Handcraftsmanship is visible everywhere, from adzed boards to sawn wooden corbels to carved and decorated wooden doors and bookcases.[39] The wood carving was done by Daniel Murabel of Taos Pueblo, Faustin Talachi of San Juan Pueblo, and Justin Yazzie, a Navajo descendant. Meem and members of his office also designed light fixtures that were fashioned in tin and hand-punched, honoring a folk craft that originated in New Mexico in the nineteenth century. Their fabrication was handled locally by Native and Hispanic artisans working for Walter B. Gilbert in Albuquerque.

When the occasion demanded it, Meem could envision a building that was rustic in style. Such was the situation when the Los Alamos Ranch School, located northwest of Santa Fe, hired him to design a multipurpose building for its camp-like setting.[40] Fuller Lodge, erected in 1928, included a dining hall and other rooms to serve the boys' boarding school. A rustic "Big House," already on the grounds, established a look for the lodge. Like that building, Fuller Lodge was constructed with vertically

FIGURE 8.7. John Gaw Meem, University Library (Zimmerman Library), University of New Mexico, Albuquerque, 1936–38.

installed pine logs, selected from nearby land. Columns of pine supported a two-story porch that ran across the width of the entrance. Reflecting his commitment to craftsmanship, Meem designed iron lanterns that employed the school emblem of a boy on horseback, an image created by Santa Fe artist Gustave Baumann.

A RUSTIC DOUBLE HOUSE

For two brothers and their wives living in Flagstaff, Arizona, the region's abundance of ponderosa pines inspired them to build a double house that was rustic in style.[41] Timothy and Michael J. Riordan came from Chicago to Flagstaff to join a half-brother in the lumber business, and eventually the siblings took it over and prospered. The brothers had married sisters, and with their new wealth they decided to erect two residences that were connected. Linking the two-story homes was a large one-story recreation room. The duplex, called Kinlichi Knoll, was built in 1904 and designed by Charles F. Whittlesey (1867–1941).

Michael Riordan proposed treating the exterior of the mansion in a rustic style, utilizing timber from the stands that were the source of the family money. Modern frame construction was clad with peeled log slabs, shiplap, and hand-split shakes. Locally quarried volcanic rock was selected for the foundation and set in round arches at two separate entrances. The recreation room also is rustic in appearance, its walls covered in pine planks. Peeled log beams tie together a space that is open to the rafters, while a fireplace of irregular volcanic rock anchors one side of the room. On the opposite side are windows that incorporate glass panes bonded to transparencies illustrating the Arizona landscape and Native Americans, photographed by John K. Hillers.

Whittlesey, the architect, spent the early years of his career in Chicago with Addison and Fiedler, worked for Louis Sullivan, and practiced on his own. Hired in 1900 by the Atchison, Topeka, and Santa Fe Railway as chief architect, he moved to Albuquerque.[42] When commissioned by the Riordans, Whittlesey was designing El

Tovar Hotel (1903–5), which would be erected at the South Rim of the Grand Canyon.[43] His choices for El Tovar, including peeled logs, log slabs, and boulders with round arches, appear in the Riordan commission. At the same time, Sullivan's influence on Whittlesey is apparent in the Riordan houses' stained glass windows, which are enlivened by abstract floral motifs. Built-in cabinets, inglenooks, and custom-made furniture are additional Arts and Crafts features of the interiors (fig. 8.8). To further unify the decoration, the Riordans bought oak furniture from Gustav Stickley's United Crafts and pieces from L. and J. G. Stickley.[44]

Many individuals were involved with the design of Hopi House (1901–5), situated near El Tovar at the Grand Canyon (fig. 8.9).[45] An early example of Pueblo Revival architecture, it was planned for a museum and gift shop to be run by the Fred Harvey Company, which operated Santa Fe Railway concessions. In June 1901 William H. Mohr (1860–1946), a staff architect in the railroad's Los Angeles office, created a perspective drawing and elevations for a "Proposed Hopi Building."[46] What he represented was quite similar to what would be built: a three-story stone structure, terraced with flat roofs, stepped buttresses, projecting *vigas,* small windows, and ladders, reminiscent of the historic Hopi village of Old Oraibi. Two years later, Whittlesey took the plans and specifications for the project and showed them to Fred Harvey officials. This was a project with potential. Striving for authenticity, they hired Heinrich Richert Voth (1855–1931), a Kansas-based ethnologist and missionary, who had lived with the Hopis and was an expert on their culture. From the fall of 1904 until the end of the year, Voth oversaw construction of Hopi House. With the goal of accuracy in mind, he arranged for Hopis to leave their reservation and assist with the work, building fireplaces and installing storage bins—elements one might see in the rooms of their pueblo. Finally, prior to Christmas, Mary Colter (1869–1958), a freehand drawing teacher in St. Paul, arrived with her sister to decorate the salesroom and arrange the displays of Native American crafts.[47] Hopi House opened on January 1, 1905. Not only did it purvey textiles, pottery, and jewelry of Native peoples. Hopis lived in the upstairs rooms, and during the day they demonstrated weaving and other craft skills.

FIGURE 8.8. Charles F. Whittlesey, Kinlichi Knoll, dining room in the home of the Timothy Riordan family, Flagstaff, Arizona, 1904.

FIGURE 8.9. Charles F. Whittlesey with William H. Mohr, Heinrich Richert Voth, and Mary Colter, Hopi House, Grand Canyon National Park, Arizona, 1901–5.

Like a medieval cathedral, Hopi House was the product of a collective effort. But who came up with the germ of the idea that Mohr pictured in his 1901 drawings? He was a capable and creative architect, as can be seen in his design of Santa Fe Railway depots, one example being the delightful 1924 Spanish Colonial Revival station in Claremont, California.[48] Nevertheless, as chief architect for the Santa Fe, Whittlesey would have been a more probable source.[49] It's also possible that a member of the Fred Harvey family proposed the concept. In 1901, recognizing an opportunity to sell Native handiwork to tourists, the company launched an Indian Department.[50] A year later, when the Alvarado Hotel opened in Albuquerque, it included a place to market the department's wares. Regardless of who came up with the idea of a pueblo-styled building at the Grand Canyon, the Harveys clearly liked it. Hopi House, a museum as well as a shop, would be an authentic representation of the Southwest's most historic architecture. And just as Harry Dorman provided photographs of Taos Pueblo that led to the design of La Fonda Hotel in Santa Fe, we may guess that someone sent pictures of the Old Oraibi pueblo to Mohr in Los Angeles. Thus Arts and Crafts ideals, valuing local culture and craft, were subverted—directed toward marketing and making a profit.

On the other hand, altruism motivated Tucson's Isabella Greenway in her activities. In 1927 she founded Arizona Hut, a workshop that created jobs for disabled veterans of World War I.[51] The company became known for the high-quality furniture that the men made. In providing needy people with satisfying as well as remunerative labor, Greenway joined a long line of Arts and Crafts adherents, in the United States and England, with the same goal. Business declined, however, with the onset of the Great Depression. Committed to the veterans, the wealthy and widowed Greenway began buying the Hut's furniture and warehoused it. Deciding to do something with it, she built the Arizona Inn (1930–31), a small resort on fourteen acres at the edge of the city (fig. 8.10). Tucson architect Merritt H. Starkweather (1891–1972), a

FIGURE 8.10. Merritt H. Starkweather, Arizona Inn, guest cottages, Tucson, 1930–31.

Wisconsin native who spent several years with Spokane's Cutter and Malmgren, helped bring her dream to life.[52] The resort was a rambling compound of buildings, deliberately designed to be simple and homelike, but not rustic. Boxy in massing, the structures were one to two stories in height, stuccoed and bright pink, with deep-blue shutters and trim. Most roofs were flat, although some had tiled shed roofs. Spanish Colonial in appearance, the buildings alluded to the region's architectural heritage. Intrigued by the regional landscape, Greenway planted a garden of cacti and other native plants.[53] For a focal point, Starkweather designed a fountain that Gladding, McBean in Los Angeles custom-made in concrete.[54] The unstoppable Greenway also was involved in politics, and in 1933 she ran for Arizona's congressional seat, vacated midterm, which she won. A year later, she was reelected and served a full term.

In Texas and the Southwest, the history, landscapes, and even local climate contributed to an architecture of the early twentieth century that reflected Arts and Crafts thinking. At the Rice Institute, the hot, humid climate supplied a rationale for a Byzantine Revival style. Sometimes architects and clients embraced rustic styles that blended with the natural surroundings. Oftentimes, an Arts and Crafts philosophy encouraged designs that echoed Spanish Colonial and Native American buildings, while the movement also supported an emulation of Spanish and Native craftsmanship. During the first two, even three, decades of the twentieth century, Americans in these sparsely settled states appreciated an informal approach to life. Far from major cities, architects and their clients were predisposed to accept the Arts and Crafts value of simplicity.

9 Pioneer Spirit in the Pacific Northwest

In 1905 a full century had passed since Meriwether Lewis and William Clark led the Corps of Discovery westward, trudging between peaks of the Cascade Range, navigating the churning Columbia River, and penetrating damp and fog to reach the Pacific Ocean. Washington and Oregon were now connected by rail and steamship to the rest of the United States, and their cities were expanding. The urban centers of the Pacific Northwest weren't large by eastern standards—in 1900 Seattle's population was about eighty thousand residents, and Portland had reached a population of ninety thousand. But their citizens were aware of the Arts and Crafts movement, and they rallied behind organizations that supported it.[1] Recent settlers in the West, they were endowed with an adventurous, pioneer spirit.

In Seattle, members of the Women's Century Club gathered in 1903 to hear papers about John Ruskin, William Morris, and Elbert Hubbard. Two years later, the women sponsored an art exposition in which works of handicraft also were displayed. Shortly thereafter, architects united with people involved with the applied arts. In 1908 the Washington state chapter of the American Institute of Architects joined the Washington State Art Association at the Seattle Public Library to mount an exhibition on architecture that included woodcarving and decorative tile. Across the state, the Spokane Art League demonstrated its interest in the movement by offering classes in the applied arts, and in a 1903 exhibition, it presented handcrafted products alongside works of fine art.[2]

In Oregon, the Portland Architectural Club was established with a mission to promote not only architecture but also the "allied arts and crafts."[3] Founded in 1906, the club held an exhibition two years later and included handcrafted decorative work such as stained glass.[4] The movement gained momentum in 1907 when the Arts and Crafts Society of Portland was organized.[5] Encouraged by relations with the Society of Arts and Crafts in Boston, the Portland society sponsored its first exhibition in 1908 and opened the Shop of Fine Arts and Industries. A year later, the Arts and Crafts Society of Portland heard from C. R. Ashbee, traveling in the Northwest on a lecture tour that also stopped in Eugene and Seattle.[6]

EVOCATIONS OF ENGLAND

The influence of the English Arts and Crafts movement on the architecture of Seattle ran more deeply than in

Portland, especially in residential design.[7] At the close of the nineteenth century, a larger number of Seattle architects had trained in England or Germany than in France, and interest in classical styles was relatively weak. It was the Tudor Revival, evoking images of England, that affluent Seattle residents desired when they built substantial homes. Charles Douglas and Harriet Stimson set a precedent for the style when they retained Spokane architect Kirtland Kelsey Cutter (1860–1939) to design their mansion on First Hill, northeast of the city's commercial center.[8] C. D., as Charles Stimson was known, had become rich as a lumberman, and Cutter's reputation was growing. Cutter was raised in a suburb of Cleveland and aspired to be an illustrator. After studying at the Art Students League in New York City and continuing his studies in Europe, he realized he would prefer the career of an architect and moved to Spokane in 1886. Although he lacked professional training, he had a gift for visual drama. His rustic Idaho State Building, constructed of basalt and logs for the 1893 World's Columbian Exposition in Chicago, piqued interest and admiration.

The C. D. Stimson House, built between 1898 and 1901, is a handsome example of the Tudor Revival, although it would have been regarded as relatively conventional in the East or Chicago by this time. It has a first story of brick, while its second and attic stories are stucco and half-timbered. The façade is asymmetrical, with two small dormers in the roof balancing a broad, front-facing gable to the right. Windows are grouped and diamond-paned, and the oak front door is Gothic. Adzed timbers have rough, textured surfaces that tell that the wood was hand-hewn.

Upon entering the house, the visitor is drawn into a compelling sequence of spaces, extending from an entry hall painted with rampant lions, through a deep round arch, across a stair hall, to the dining room with a frieze that focuses on a banqueting king and court (fig. 9.1). The English medievalism in the public rooms is reminiscent of interiors by Richard Norman Shaw. Cutter designed and managed the decorating, including oak and sycamore woodwork, furniture, and textiles—an ideal opportunity for any Arts and Crafts architect.[9] Yet a reception room is purely French, with Empire plasterwork and furniture, exuding imperial pretentiousness that breaks with the Arts and Crafts ethos. Cutter strayed from the movement's ethos in another respect. To adhere to a true Arts and Crafts approach, he would have identified local craft workers with whom to collaborate. Instead, he turned to a trusted company in Cleveland for cabinetry and engaged a craft worker in New York City for dragon andirons. Nevertheless, he thought the Western Mill Factory in Seattle delivered satisfactory results when he relied on it for carved scrolling vines to finish the dining room mantelpiece.[10] On the whole, the Stimson House captures the spirit of the Arts and Crafts movement, although the richness of its embellishment was conservative. Architects and their clients soon developed a taste for greater simplicity—a shift that had become prevalent in England and much of the United States.

Houses that represent the more modern and restrained versions of the Tudor Revival can be seen on Seattle's Capitol Hill, a streetcar suburb to the north of First Hill.[11] One such residence is a sizable house designed by Cutter and his partner, Karl Gunnar Malmgren, built in 1906–7 for Charles J. Smith on a large lot with vistas to the west.[12] Red brick with stone trimmings, it's a picturesque two-and-a-half-story dwelling with a prominent gable, dormers, and a crenellated parapet. A pointed-arch front door is modest in scale, and mullioned windows are filled with small panes, intimate features that typified the English country house.

Seattle architect Arthur L. Loveless (1873–1971) designed Tudor-inspired houses throughout his career.[13] A native of Michigan, he studied architecture at Columbia University until he ran out of money. When he left the program, he was hired by one of his professors, William Adams Delano of Delano and Aldrich, a distinguished New York City firm. Around 1907 Loveless moved to Seattle and promptly landed commissions. Both he and his clients appreciated the abstract qualities of English Arts and Crafts architecture, as is evident in his design of a stucco house for John A. Porter (1922) in Mount Baker Park, southeast of downtown Seattle.[14] Two large gables, one with a catslide roof, characterize the entry elevation, which is indebted to the work of C. F. A. Voysey and is similar to Howard Van Doren Shaw's Ragdale (1897–98) in Lake Forest, Illinois (see fig. 5.3). Writing in 1933, Loveless explained how an architect in the Northwest should treat residential work. "New forms in architecture should logically grow out of and be a development of the forms which have preceded them, rather than be created out of thin air," he asserted, subscribing to a widely held Arts and Crafts view.[15]

Loveless employed a Tudor vocabulary for his own cottage-like office building, erected in 1925 on Capitol

FIGURE 9.1. Kirtland Kelsey Cutter, Stimson House, dining room, Seattle, 1898–1901.

Hill.[16] After a few years passed, he had it moved and incorporated it into a rectangular block of shops and apartments. Called the Studio Building, it dates from 1930 to 1933 and was designed with an associate, Lester P. Fey (fig. 9.2).[17] Planned around an interior courtyard, the story-and-a-half structure has a roofscape of gables and dormers. Walls are wood-framed, faced on the two commercial sides with cinder blocks of mixed sizes that were painted and sprayed with marble dust and sand to simulate stone. Ruskin's call for honesty went unheeded. Nevertheless, the building conveys an Arts and Crafts charm, with hand-split cedar shake roofing, leaded glass windows, and sandstone trim. At the street level under one gable are three Gothic arches, each decorated at its springing by a capital of carved fleurons, while under a second gable is a wide drip mold that's also ornamented with floral motifs. A passage between shops leads to the courtyard, lushly planted by landscape architect Otto E. Holmdahl,

FIGURE 9.2. Arthur L. Loveless with Lester P. Fey, Studio Building, Seattle, 1930–33.

for the apartment residents to enjoy. At one corner is a polygonal stair tower topped by a lead weathervane of a horse and buggy, designed by artist Frank Hall-Edmands.

PRAIRIE SCHOOL IN SEATTLE

The bold ideas advanced by Chicago's Prairie School architects were introduced in Seattle by architects Andrew P. Willatsen (1876–1974) and Barry Byrne (1883–1967), who met in Frank Lloyd Wright's Oak Park, Illinois, studio.[18] Both started as apprentices in 1902 and contributed to significant Wright projects—Willatsen to the Darwin D. Martin House and Byrne to Unity Temple (see figs. 2.12 and 5.11). Willatsen subsequently worked for Prairie School architects Robert C. Spencer, Jr., and Irving and Allen Pond.[19] In 1907 he left Chicago for the Pacific Northwest. Spokane's Cutter and Malmgren took him on and sent him to Seattle. Willatsen encouraged Byrne to join him there, and in 1909 they formed the partnership of Willatsen and Byrne.

A house that the firm designed on Seattle's Queen Anne hill for George and Irene Matzen (1910–11) gave Willatsen the chance to build a Prairie School residence that would be unified in its architecture and interior decoration (fig. 9.3).[20] Finished on the exterior with stucco and trimmed with dark wood, it's sheltered by the Prairie School's characteristic shallow hipped roof with deep overhanging eaves. Stretching across the first story is a wide porch on a high podium, while across the second story are four pairs of casement windows grouped in a horizontal band. Inside, the stair hall, living room, and dining room flow together, connected by large openings. Friezes and walls are accented by strips of wood, while art glass decorates a lamp on a staircase newel post and the doors of built-in bookcases and china cabinets. In the living room is a fireplace of Roman brick, and in the second-floor master bedroom is a fireplace with Grueby tile. The effect of the interiors is one of harmony, illustrating the Prairie School architects' desire to emphasize simplicity, building materials, and craftsmanship, consistent with Arts and Crafts priorities.

Another transplant from Chicago was Ellsworth Storey (1879–1960), who arrived in Seattle in 1903.[21] He absorbed design elements from his native city as well as Europe to generate a distinctive approach to residential architecture that responded to the conditions of the Puget Sound region. In his early teens, Storey decided that he would become an architect. As he matured through the 1890s, he was well-situated to learn about ideas that theorists and activists in Chicago were advancing on topics relating to artistic and social reform. He entered the University of Illinois in 1898 and graduated five years later with a degree in architecture. During that time, he spent a year abroad, visiting Europe and the Middle East. Of particular interest to him were the chalets of Switzerland and vernacular dwellings of other countries that evolved in response to their natural surroundings.[22]

Ready to embark on his career, Storey moved to Seattle. In 1903 he designed a house for his parents on land in Denny-Blaine, northeast of downtown and above Lake Washington. Two years later, he built an adjacent house for himself and his wife, linking the two dwellings with a breezeway.[23] Constructed with standard milled lumber and clad in shingles, the houses are simple in design, reflecting an Arts and Crafts preference. At the same time, in their emphasis on wood and in the low pitch of their roofs, they evoke the Swiss chalets that Storey admired. The influence of the Prairie School can be seen in the houses' deep eaves and ribbons of banked windows. While devoid of historical ornament, the dwellings are animated by patterns of horizontals, verticals, and diagonals, most noticeable in the window muntins.

As was often the case among forward-looking architects of the period, Storey didn't make a clean break with history in all of his projects. For example, when designing a chapel for the Episcopal Church of the Epiphany (1910–11), in the neighborhood of Madrona, he produced a simplified interpretation of the Tudor Revival, with a tower, pointed arches, and half-timbering (fig. 9.4).[24] Such references to England's parish churches would have been appreciated by members of the congregation. But in its

FIGURE 9.3. Willatsen and Byrne, Matzen House, Seattle, 1910–11.

FIGURE 9.4. Ellsworth Storey, Church of the Epiphany, Seattle, 1910–11.

bold massing, the squat proportions of the tower, and its rough textures, the chapel has modern qualities that bring to mind William R. Lethaby's All Saints' Church, Brockhampton (1901–2), in Gloucestershire.

Around this time, Storey was devoting more thought to the question of how to design houses that would be suited to the locale where he had settled. Between 1912 and 1915, he built a cluster of cottages in Mount Baker, in southeast Seattle, on property overlooking Lake Washington (fig. 9.5).[25] They were conceived as inexpensive rentals that Storey and his family would retain and manage. Their cost was determined by what Storey could afford, but he also appears to have been motivated by the desire, shared by English and American Arts and Crafts architects, to provide attractive housing for people of moderate means. The parcels he acquired were located on a steep site, covered with firs, madronas, and maples.

At first he erected four cottages on a plateau; these were followed by a group of eight cottages further down the slope. To control costs, he employed rectangular footprints for buildings of a single story. Each cottage had a front porch that extended across the house's full width, two bedrooms, a large living-dining room, a kitchen, and a bath.[26] When Storey erected the first four cottages, he gave them roofs that were almost flat, but for the second group, he returned to the chalet-type roof with a front-facing gable, the ridge running longitudinally over the house. Tongue-and-groove boards of native fir were installed between the studs, all left exposed, giving emphasis to the local material and structure of the cottages. For visual interest, Storey called for porch railings of wide and narrow slats to be installed vertically in an alternating pattern. As an enhancement, Storey invested in custom-made windows and doors incorporating geometric designs that were similar to those that he used in the houses for his parents and himself.

In 1960 Seattle architect Victor Steinbrueck published an article about Storey's cottages in *Pacific Architect and*

Builder. He described the "honesty and simplicity of the architecture" and identified "restraint" as one of the main qualities of the buildings.[27] In closing his essay, he encouraged a study of Storey's work, saying that it would inspire an architecture "appropriate to this area and climate."[28] Notably, midway through the twentieth century, the cottages elicited words and comments indebted to Arts and Crafts values, while their design also presented a new direction for modern residential architecture in the Pacific Northwest.

The inexpensive house also interested Seattle's Jud Yoho (1882–1968), who grasped the potential of the bungalow market.[29] As owner of the Craftsman Bungalow Company, he built and sold the modestly sized dwellings from 1911 to 1918. He also sold plan books, called *Craftsman Bungalows,* that he pitched to working- and middle-class buyers. Promotion was Yoho's talent, and in 1912 he began publishing *Bungalow Magazine,* a monthly that competed with Gustav Stickley's *The Craftsman.* While both Yoho and Stickley were entrepreneurial, Yoho was all business, lacking an Arts and Crafts commitment to high-caliber architecture, handicraft, and social improvement, ideals that Stickley endorsed through his periodical. In 1915 Yoho and a few associates started the Take-Down Manufacturing Company to sell prefabricated houses and garages—a business that purveyed factory-made buildings as commodities. Moreover, the company employees worked as laborers, not "craftsmen," despite Yoho's appropriation of the word.[30]

RUSTIC LODGING AT MOUNT RAINIER

About ninety miles south of Seattle, in a meadow at Mount Rainier National Park, is a rustic lodge of stone and timber, both materials obtained a short distance away. For

FIGURE 9.5. Ellsworth Storey, cottage (in "Storey Cottages" enclave), Seattle, 1912–15.

FIGURE 9.6. Heath and Gove, Paradise Inn, Mount Rainier National Park, Washington, 1916–17.

visitors, the primary attraction is glacier-capped Mount Rainier, the highest peak in the Cascade Range. The lodge, Paradise Inn, was built in Paradise Valley between 1916 and 1917 (fig. 9.6). Marked by a ruggedness that harmonizes with the natural setting, it follows the exemplar of Yellowstone's Old Faithful Inn (1903–4; see fig. 7.2).[31]

The park that contains Mount Rainier came into being by stages through the 1890s. In 1893 President Benjamin Harrison authorized the preservation of forty square miles around the mountain, which became the Pacific Forest Reserve. Four years later, Congress expanded the protected area, naming it the Mount Rainier Forest Reserve. Finally, in 1899 Congress established the Mount Rainier National Park, encompassing 369 square miles. The effort to preserve the region's natural assets during the century's closing decade coincided with the solidifying interest in the Arts and Crafts movement and the value its supporters placed on natural settings. At a time when the populations of Seattle and Portland were rapidly increasing, urban and suburban residents were good candidates to explore the new national park. They needed accommodations. In 1915 a vision for a lodge was outlined by Stephen T. Mather, assistant to the U.S. Secretary of the Interior; two years later, he became the first director of the National Park Service. At Mather's encouragement, Tacoma businessmen formed the Rainier National Park Company and built the inn, its design prepared by Tacoma architect Frederick Heath (1861–1953) of Heath and Gove.

The most memorable feature of Paradise Inn is its long gabled roof. Steeply pitched, it drops to cover two-thirds of the building's height. Because the structure is buried in snow every winter, the roof had to withstand and shed exceptional loads. Both the foundation and chimneys were constructed with stone, whereas most of the building was framed and braced with logs and clad with cedar shingles. The shingles on the walls soon weathered to a silvery gray, contrasting with the shingles on the roof, which were painted green. The look of weathered logs was considered desirable, and it happened that such logs were readily available. A stand of Alaska cedars in the park had survived a fire in the 1880s, and they were felled for the project. The entrance to the lodge is barely noticeable, discreetly positioned in the long, low wall of the front elevation. Inside the inn, the log beams and trusses of the soaring lobby produce a stunning impression. By 1925 a mezzanine level was added around the room's perimeter to reinforce the structure. From the lobby, visitors pass through French doors to be welcomed into a dining room that presents visible log framing.

The furnishing of Paradise Inn complements the rusticity of the building and reflects an Arts and Crafts attitude. Chandeliers were fashioned from short logs into triangles that carry light bulbs and are suspended on chains. A German-born carpenter, Hans Fraehnke (1861–1958), used Alaska cedar to craft weighty tables, two pairs of oversize chairs, and other pieces, some made at the site and others at his shop in Fife, near Tacoma.[32] Beginning in March 1916, more than a year before the inn opened, he worked on the assignment, which continued for seven seasons. His showstoppers are a fourteen-foot-tall grandfather clock and an upright piano, encased with log pieces and cedar panels (fig. 9.7). Augmenting Fraehnke's marvels were rustic chairs, tables, and settees sold by Old Hickory Chair Company of Martinsville, Indiana.

In the 1930s, an Arts and Crafts philosophy continued to inspire the embellishment of the inn. The cedar posts of the lobby and dining room were painted with abstractions of evergreen trees and flowers, folklike in execution. For the ample fireplace in the lobby, a blacksmith made wrought-iron andirons, shaping their ends to resemble Alaska cedars. Also during this period, local women and wives of park employees painted parchment shades for light fixtures with the imagery of native wild flowers.[33] The involvement of women in the decoration of buildings had become a commonplace practice in the Arts and Crafts movement.

FIGURE 9.7. Hans Fraehnke, piano for Paradise Inn.

ALLIED ARTS IN OREGON

One of the most influential architects in early twentieth-century Oregon, Ellis F. Lawrence (1879–1946), encouraged an Arts and Crafts perspective.[34] Born in Malden, Massachusetts, near Boston, he entered the Massachusetts Institute of Technology in 1897, just months after the Society of Arts and Crafts, Boston, was chartered. After completing an undergraduate degree in architecture, he continued his studies to pursue a master's degree, granted in 1902. Even while he was preparing for his career, enrolled in a program modeled after the École des Beaux-Arts, Lawrence could observe how Boston architects were advocating for Arts and Crafts interests—organizing exhibitions, sponsoring workshops, and overseeing a salesroom.[35]

Upon finishing his education, Lawrence worked for a few years in Boston and then left for an extended tour of England and the Continent. In 1906 he settled in Portland, joining an MIT classmate, E. B. MacNaughton, in the partnership of MacNaughton, Raymond, and Lawrence. Lawrence participated with MacNaughton in founding the Portland Architectural Club. When the club presented its first exhibition in 1908, Lawrence was its chairman.[36] Included in the show were submissions representing the allied arts, an approach that may be traced to his exposure to the Arts and Crafts exhibitions held in Boston when he lived there. In 1910 Lawrence was elected the Portland Architectural Club's third president, and the following year he was elected the first president of the Oregon chapter of the American Institute of Architects. After leaving his partnership with MacNaughton, he practiced briefly on his own and then entered a long-term partnership with another MIT friend, William Holford.[37]

In 1914 Lawrence was invited to launch an architecture school at the University of Oregon, located in Eugene.[38] It became the first such program in the state, and he would serve as its dean for nearly thirty-two years. The program that Lawrence started, called the School of Architecture and Fine Arts, was conceived to bring together students in architecture and art. Apparently the name troubled him, and between 1916 and 1917 the program was rechristened the School of Architecture and the Allied Arts.[39] Did "Fine Arts" sound too much like the name of the French school? Perhaps not coincidentally, in 1914 Lawrence's alma mater, MIT, had appointed a prominent figure in the American Arts and Crafts movement, Ralph Adams Cram, as head of its Department of Architecture. Lawrence also must have paid attention to the architecture program at Harvard, founded in 1893 and led by H. Langford Warren. As longtime president of Boston's Society of Arts and Crafts, Warren encouraged the alliance among architects, artists, and craftsmen.[40] For Lawrence, a School of Architecture and the Allied Arts struck a better note, more in tune with his objectives. There also was the matter of curriculum. Like Warren, Lawrence taught Oregon's required sequence of architectural history courses.[41] He subscribed to the view that imparting a knowledge of Western architectural styles was essential in training an architect.

As a practicing architect, Lawrence designed buildings that were characterized by a regard for history, craftsmanship, and restraint. Among the most admired of his early institutional projects was Westminster Presbyterian Church in the northeast Portland neighborhood of Irvington (fig. 9.8).[42] Dating from 1912–14, the new edifice would serve his own congregation. What he created was a building based on English Perpendicular parish churches, in line with the late Gothic type that Cram introduced in Boston in the 1890s. Westminster's façade is asymmetrical, with a square tower to the left of the main body of the building, which is dominated by a gable over a large pointed-arch window. When entering the church, worshippers file through an arched portal in the tower. Carving is minimal and located for the greatest effect. The name of the church is framed and located over Gothic doors, and a row of shields is positioned under the main window. To create aesthetic interest, Lawrence called for the walls to be constructed with random ashlar jasper, quarried from Rocky Butte in western Oregon. Trimmings are a light sandstone from Tenino, Washington, north of Portland.[43] In choosing stone from the region, Lawrence followed the Arts and Crafts preference. As with the church's exterior, the interior is not extravagantly decorated, its beauty mainly derived from geometrically patterned stained glass windows made by Edward Bruns, who was working at the time in Portland.[44] Congregants seated in the pews gaze at a window that illuminates the flat end of the chancel, and upon leaving, they can view the window of the front elevation, visible behind the choir loft.

Westminster Presbyterian Church was well-received by the architectural community. Credited to the firm of Lawrence and Holford, it was illustrated in *American Architect* in July 1918.[45] In 1919 it was selected by a jury as

FIGURE 9.8. Lawrence and Holford, Westminster Presbyterian Church, Portland, Oregon, 1912–14.

one of ten "most notable buildings" in Portland, the only church building to be so honored.[46] That year, the *Architect and Engineer of California* published photographs, the plan, and jury notes about the church. Readers were told that the stonework was "good in both color and treatment." The design, continued the commentary, "has the sort of sincerity and self-restraint which we Americans believe to be a trait of our best art." Thus the building was admired in terms of Arts and Crafts values: "sincerity and self-restraint."[47] These were familiar words. Three months later, the Boston-based *Architectural Review* covered the Portland competition and included an illustration of the church.[48] The author of the article was C. Howard Walker, a prominent Boston architect and the design critic for the city's Society of Arts and Crafts.[49] Lawrence had successfully interpreted the Arts and Crafts church type that originated in Massachusetts with Cram and Goodhue.

In Lawrence's residential work, he favored Arts and Crafts designs, although he also served clients who commissioned Colonial Revival styles.[50] Shortly after moving to Portland, he built himself an Arts and Crafts house in Irvington.[51] Dating from 1906, it was planned as a duplex where his family would live on one side and his mother and sister on the other. It is asymmetrical, with multiple gables and dormers. Eaves project and windows are grouped. Clad in shingles, the house has settle benches flanking the front door and double-hung sash windows, features of Arts and Crafts houses in New England. In Portland, the house was a bit different.[52]

On a much more ambitious scale, Lawrence designed a stuccoed and half-timbered house for Thomas A. and Edna Livesley in Salem, south of Portland (fig. 9.9).[53] Built between 1923 and 1924, the primary residential block is rectangular, while a service wing is attached at an angle to one side, a common configuration among country houses of the period. Sheltering the house is a high hipped roof, broken by small dormer windows, while a tower with a conical roof rises next to the service wing. The portico entrance has a flat arch of cast stone, and the second floor projects in a jetty over the first, supported by brackets. Artisans provided leaded casement windows, wrought iron, and a family crest over the entrance. Arriving in the foyer, visitors admire oak woodwork, including beams and a screen of three Tudor arches. Off the main hall, a spacious reception room once had a hooded fireplace of cast stone. The room also contained a built-in pipe organ with a console that Lawrence's firm designed. Soon after moving into the house, Livesley was elected mayor of Salem, and he then was elected as a state representative. During these years, his wife hosted charitable events. Consistent with Livesley's public persona, the stuccoed house was a sociable place.

Another Portland architect who embraced Arts and Crafts ideas was Wade Hampton Pipes (1877–1961).[54] Born and raised in the Willamette Valley, he left Oregon for England and professional training. From 1907 to 1911, he studied in London at the Central School of Arts and Crafts under William R. Lethaby, principal of the program. What Lethaby sought was to bring future designers and artisans together and offer a curriculum that would give them a comprehensive understanding of building. While abroad, Pipes traveled the countryside, paying particular attention to vernacular houses from the Middle Ages and modern domestic work by Voysey and Edwin Lutyens.

Back in Oregon, Pipes attracted clients who commissioned houses that captured the qualities of the English architects. Minimally ornamented, his houses have a simplicity about them that emphasizes their geometric forms and the textures of their building materials. In conceptualizing the Maurice Crumpacker House (1922–23), for a lot in a suburb of Portland, Pipes started with a rectangular mass covered by a high pyramidal roof with lower front-facing gables (fig. 9.10).[55] A service wing extends to the left, connecting to a perpendicular wing where the garage is located. Like many Voysey houses, the Crumpacker House has a roof that flares at the outer edges and exterior walls that are finished in stucco. Borrowing from Voysey's Hollymount (1904–7) in Buckinghamshire, Pipes gave the Crumpacker House a round-headed door with a circular window and protected the entrance with a semicircular hood. Inside the house, Pipes repeated the round arches, and he called for stuccoed plaster. Consistent with the exterior, the interior is sparingly decorated. The fireplace, for example, is edged with cast stone that simply defines the firebox, and a plain oak shelf projects above it.

FIGURE 9.9. Ellis F. Lawrence, Livesley House, Salem, Oregon, 1923–24.

FIGURE 9.10. Wade Hampton Pipes, Crumpacker House, Dunthorpe, Oregon, 1922–23.

Like Thomas Livesley, Crumpacker served in government, beginning in 1924 when he was elected a U.S. congressman. The house that Pipes designed for him reached a level of restraint that went beyond that of the typical Tudor. Even so, Crumpacker's new home was located in a neighborhood that was clearly for the well-to-do—Dunthorpe, south of downtown Portland, on the west side of the Willamette River. Construction on the parcels was tightly controlled, with a minimum cost required for each dwelling and commercial development prohibited. Residents were not to be of "African or Mongolian descent" unless they were household help.[56] Far across the American continent, racism was accepted, and a house designed in a manner to embody numerous virtues was built with this understanding. The moral considerations of the Arts and Crafts movement could only go so far, even in the Eden of the Pacific Northwest.

Distant as the citizens were, living far from the East Coast and England, residents of the Northwest's major cities sponsored exhibitions, ran a shop, and welcomed lecturers to promote an Arts and Crafts ethos. Architects designed residential and ecclesiastic projects that were inspired by English Arts and Crafts styles. The movement's concerns for values such as honesty and simplicity also were influential, expressed by the cottages of Seattle's Ellsworth Storey. His architecture was especially innovative, and it pointed toward a stylistic direction that architects in the region would pursue by responding to the landscape and the climate.

10 California: Fresh Air, Fresh Thinking

Many of the prominent figures in California who encouraged Arts and Crafts ideals had come from somewhere else. Whether they were living in the northern or southern part of the state, these advocates had much in common with other newcomers who arrived in the late nineteenth century—newcomers in pursuit of places that hadn't been sullied by sooty factories or darkened by tenements, the blights of cities in the East and Chicago. In California one could breathe fresh air and live close to nature, near mountains and ocean, in environments that were dewy and green in the Bay Area or dry and golden in the Southland.

San Francisco was the destination that attracted the most residents, gloriously situated on a hilly peninsula between the Pacific Ocean and an enormous bay. By 1890 the seaport city ranked as the largest municipality on the West Coast. Home to three hundred thousand inhabitants, it was far more populous than Los Angeles, where fifty thousand people lived. Over the next ten years, both cities added about fifty thousand residents. Sophisticated in its culture, San Francisco appealed to architects and artists, and in 1894 several of them organized the Guild of Arts and Crafts, inspired by the English movement. The story in Los Angeles was different, reflecting the fact that settlement there was spread out. Nevertheless, Arts and Crafts ideas gained a foothold and increasingly influenced the region's buildings. Pasadena residents were especially interested in an Arts and Crafts perspective, while in Santa Barbara, Riverside, and San Diego, architects adopted principles of the Arts and Crafts movement as the basis for buildings in original and distinctive styles.[1]

As in other parts of the nation, California's Arts and Crafts architects responded to regional landscapes and cultural history, leading to fresh thinking about what would be built. In the north, houses and churches were designed to take advantage of wood shingles and rough boards from native timberlands, whereas in the south, designs reflected the region's Spanish-Mexican past. Simplicity also suited Californians. This Arts and Crafts preference meshed with the easygoing ways of the West. The Arts and Crafts interest in visible methods of construction, harking back to John Ruskin, led California architects to create dwellings modeled on the Swiss chalet and the Japanese temple, which exposed their framing. Tudor Revival houses, associated with the movement in England, found favor, too. By the second decade of the

FIGURE 10.1. Willis J. Polk, Polk-Williams House, San Francisco, 1892.

twentieth century, Spanish Baroque buildings captured the imagination of designers in the Southland, two of them highly esteemed architects who began their careers in the East.

AGITATING IN SAN FRANCISCO

Flamboyant and outspoken, Willis J. Polk (1867–1924) arrived in San Francisco in 1889.[2] Already an adherent of Arts and Crafts ideas, he started agitating for better architecture. Born and raised in the Midwest, he trained in Kansas City, Missouri, with Henry Van Brunt and audited classes in New York City with William Robert Ware at Columbia College, now a part of Columbia University. Through the 1860s and 1870s, these mentors had been partners in Boston, attaining prominence as interpreters of Ruskinian Gothic architecture and incipient Arts and Crafts principles. While in New York, Polk was hired by A. Page Brown. When Brown moved to San Francisco, he urged his former employee to join him.

After spending a little more than a year in Brown's office, Polk established an independent practice. Brimming with energy, he launched an upstart monthly journal, *Architectural News,* in November 1890; however, he could only keep it going through January.[3] Like progressive architects in the East and in England, he urged architects to take a scholarly approach to precedent while also urging them to strive for originality. In September 1894 Polk was in the thick of an effort to organize the Guild of Arts and Crafts, modeled upon the London-based Arts and Crafts Exhibition Society, whose members presented their first show in 1888.[4] As with the English society, the San Francisco endeavor brought together architects, artists, and artisans. To their credit, they succeeded in mounting two exhibitions, both in 1896, before breaking up a year later.[5] Their initiative was precocious, but the Guild of Arts and Crafts didn't garner much attention beyond the Bay Area.[6]

For Polk, theories merged with practice when he designed a duplex built in 1892.[7] The Polk-Williams House is located on Russian Hill, a neighborhood northwest of San Francisco's commercial center, across the street from a group of modest shingled houses (fig. 10.1). One side of the duplex would shelter the Polk family, and the other would become the home of artist Dora Norton Williams. The question for Polk was how to respond to the rusticity of the neighboring houses while grounding his design in precedents from the Western tradition. After he decided that he would clad the house with shingles, he looked to the late medieval dwellings in the towns of England and northern France. On the main elevation are two steeply pitched gables of different sizes, the larger containing a Gothic-arched window. Casement windows on the first and second stories reflect the same Northern European sources. In this distillation of late medieval domestic architecture, Polk was inspired by the work of C. F. A. Voysey. He also reworked ideas from the Shingle style, fashionable in the East, although there this style was usually employed in suburban and country settings. Inside his San Francisco house, Polk mixed the rustic and the refined, finishing rooms with redwood boards and classical ornament. While informed by history, the result was unlike anything from the past.

The idea of the rustic city house also attracted Polk's friend and fellow architect Ernest Coxhead (1863–1933). Coxhead was English born and bred, and through office training and formal academic study in London, he became accomplished as a designer working in the Gothic Revival and the classical tradition.[8] At the end of 1886 he moved to Los Angeles, relocating four years later to San Francisco, where he and Polk began spending time together. When the Guild of Arts and Crafts was organized, he became a member.[9]

FIGURE 10.2. Ernest Coxhead, Waybur House, San Francisco, 1901.

In 1893 Coxhead designed a shingled house for himself and his brother in Pacific Heights on a north-facing lot overlooking San Francisco Bay. His familiarity with English Arts and Crafts architecture is evident, while he also proved to be adept as an interpreter of the American Shingle style. His house has a steeply peaked roof, tall chimneys, and banked casement windows. Managing a modest budget, Coxhead avoided the expense of decorative components.[10]

The design was spare, but that treatment didn't represent some sort of conviction held by Coxhead. For clients with deeper pockets, he willingly included ornament, based on his academic experience. His shingled house for James P. Ferguson (1896–97), also in Pacific Heights, blends the picturesque qualities of medieval dwellings with an elegant classical entryway. While the entry elevation features a pair of sharp gables, under them at ground level is a door framed by Corinthian columns carrying a broken entablature. Drawing on his mastery of precedents in European architecture, Coxhead created a novel design that fit the San Francisco setting.

The architect continued to be intrigued by the possibilities of starting with a rustic house and applying references to it from the European past. In 1901 Julian and Margaret Waybur built a shingled house, designed by Coxhead, on a site at the southeastern corner of the city's Presidio.[11] Simple and boxy in its massing, the Waybur House is symmetrically organized with double-hung wood windows positioned on either side of the main façade. At its center, however, Coxhead used familiar architectural forms and dealt with them imaginatively. Three windows on the top story defy expectations. In the middle is a round-arched window, and on either side are tall, narrow windows. In combination, the arrangement suggests a Palladian window, but the three openings are detached from each other. Moreover, a decorative balcony under the center window has a base that's not horizontal, but steps down to the right. Under this grouping is the front entrance, positioned to the left of center (fig. 10.2). Even though it's not where one might expect it, the location works in that it balances the rightward movement of the balcony base. The design of the entrance is unusual, too. Surmounting the front door is an enormous rounded and broken pediment supported by oversized scrolled brackets with garlands, mannerist and assertive. Framing the entrance are leaded panes of glass, set in a diamond pattern, which also fill the tympanum of the pediment. They're relatively small, vaguely

FIGURE 10.3. A. Page Brown with Bernard Maybeck, Church of the New Jerusalem, sanctuary, San Francisco, 1894–95.

medieval, charming, and engaging. Next door, Coxhead designed a house for Margaret Waybur's brother, the artist Bruce Porter, but the effect is bland and without verve.

A SWEDENBORGIAN CHURCH

In the mid-1890s, the new stylistic direction in Bay Area houses could be seen in religious architecture, too, starting with the Church of the New Jerusalem (1894–95), built in Pacific Heights for a Swedenborgian congregation.[12] It embodied the values of its minister, Joseph Worcester, a native of Boston and graduate of Harvard, environments where he was exposed to Ruskinian ideals and Arts and Crafts thinking. As a young man, he was impressed by Henry Hobson Richardson's Trinity Church (1872–77), an early example of a collaboration between the architect and artists, and he saved articles about it.[13] Nevertheless, the building that Worcester wanted was completely different from the churches designed by the Boston architects who followed Richardson and promoted the Arts and Crafts movement, such as Cram, Wentworth, and Goodhue and H. Langford Warren. These architects' churches alluded to the Perpendicular parish churches of England, whereas in San Francisco, Worcester envisioned a design that was simple, Mediterranean in certain aspects, and reflective of nature.

A. Page Brown (1859–1896) was the building's architect of record, and Bernard Maybeck (1862–1957) was the primary draftsman and probably contributed ideas.[14] The actual place of worship is set back from the street. One must first pass through a loggia with pebble-dash stucco and a red tile roof and stroll through a garden before reaching the church, its brick walls interspersed with misshapen clinkers. The form of the bell tower derives from towers of Italian village churches—an allusion that seemed appropriate in light of the comparable climate and hilly terrain of San Francisco. Consistent with the church's exterior, the sanctuary is rustic and unassuming, with a welcoming fireplace that suggests a domestic interior (fig. 10.3). The structure of the roof is exposed, carried by madrone logs harvested from the Santa Cruz Mountains and installed unpeeled. Redwood boards cover the ceiling, while Douglas fir is used for wainscoting. Like the city's early shingled houses, the materials of the church evoke the California landscape. This regional manifestation of the Arts and Crafts movement has become known as the First Bay Tradition.[15]

Although the Swedenborgian church is stylistically different from the Gothic churches most often erected by Arts and Crafts advocates, in the manner of those churches, artists and artisans collaborated to embellish it. William Keith painted pastoral scenes, Bruce Porter was responsible for two stained glass windows, and artist Mary Curtis Richardson designed the pulpit and communion table. Mission-style chairs with rush seats were probably conceptualized by Maybeck and A. J. Forbes; they were designed under Brown and made by Forbes.[16] Within a few years, the church and the minister became known for their roles in establishing a new regional trend. In 1905 author Charles Keeler told readers of Gustav Stickley's *The Craftsman* about the "art spirit" that arose in the city due to Worcester, "a certain quiet and retiring minister," under whose direction the picturesque church was built.[17]

MAYBECK'S HOUSE FOR THE KEELERS

Maybeck had arrived in San Francisco in 1890. A New York City native, he had studied at the École des Beaux-Arts and trained in the atelier of Louis-Jules André. Once he was back in California, he took jobs with other architects, including Brown, but he was ready to open his own practice. On a ferry ride from Berkeley to San Francisco, he met Charles Keeler, and the men discovered that they were like-minded souls, drawn to the ideas of Ruskin and William Morris. By 1893 Maybeck landed his first clients—the newly married Charles and Louise Keeler.[18]

On a hillside lot in Berkeley, just north of the University of California campus, the Keeler House was erected between 1894 and 1895 (fig. 10.4). At the outset of his career, Keeler worked as a naturalist, and the shingled house reflected this sympathy, conceived as it was to mirror the natural setting. It was constructed of native redwood inside and out, with everything left unpainted, unlike most houses of the era. Another unconventional feature of the dwelling was its deck-like sleeping porch, open to the sky, which minimized the barrier between the occupants and nature.[19]

As Maybeck saw it, the house was Gothic in principles. It was picturesque in its silhouette, crowned by pitched

FIGURE 10.4. Bernard Maybeck, Keeler House, Berkeley, California, 1894–95.

roofs combined with smaller pyramidal roofs that flared at their ends. Under the eaves, the Keeler House had bands of casement windows, often seen in medieval dwellings. In its massing, the house appeared to have grown over time. On the lower end of the property, the house was just one story high, containing the family's "living room library."[20] It was a chapel-like space, distinguished by exposed posts and rafters. Connecting to that room was a two-story block that contained the rest of the house.

Several theorists and practitioners influenced the design. The visible expression of structure responds to the ideas of Eugène Viollet-le-Duc and Ruskin while also reflecting Maybeck's knowledge of French and German medieval dwellings. Sharing Keeler's interest in fine craftsmanship, Maybeck sketched wrought-iron strap hinges that were hand-hammered to enhance the front door.[21] After the house was finished, Keeler organized a Ruskin reading club, and when he wrote *The Simple Home,* a short book published in 1904, he advanced Ruskinian ideas.[22] Richardson was another likely influence on the house. Maybeck would have followed Richardson's career, knowing that the renowned architect had preceded him in the atelier of André.[23] Maybeck surely admired Richardson's picturesque rooflines, use of natural shingles, and emphasis on craftsmanship. Worcester, too, should be credited for contributing to the Arts and Crafts views held by Maybeck and Keeler, which they applied to the new dwelling.

Redwood shingles, weathered naturally to brown, were soon chosen for other types of buildings in the Berkeley hills. For example, Berkeley's First Unitarian Church (1897–98), by Albert Cicero Schweinfurth (1863–1900), was enveloped by shingles on its roof and walls, resulting in an effect that was simple and rustic (fig. 10.5).[24] As a teenager, Schweinfurth left his birthplace in Upstate New York for Boston, where he trained under Peabody and Stearns. He then relocated to New York City, where he worked for Brown, moved to San Francisco to work for Brown again, and began his independent practice in 1894.[25] When envisioning the Berkeley church, Schweinfurth drew upon his East Coast years and observation of the Shingle style. Also reflecting his familiarity with buildings in the East was his adoption of an expansive front-facing roof gable, in particular the example of McKim, Mead & White's William Low House (1886–87), in Bristol, Rhode Island. At the same time, the landscape of Berkeley inspired Schweinfurth, and he took his church design to another level by investing it

FIGURE 10.5. Albert Cicero Schweinfurth, First Unitarian Church, Berkeley, California, 1897–98.

FIGURE 10.6. Julia Morgan, Saratoga Foothill Club, Saratoga, California, 1915.

with a primordial character. In porches under each end of the gable are trunks of redwood trees, their bark left on. Geometric shapes, often pronounced in Arts and Crafts architecture, here are emphatic, with a triangle defined by the gable and a large circle of a window under the gable's peak. When the church was finished, it became the meeting place for the Hillside Club, an organization that local women started in 1898 to campaign for development that would respect the area's natural beauty. In 1902 the club was reorganized to include men, and shortly thereafter Keeler became president, serving from 1903 to 1905.

A simple shingled building also appealed to the women of the Saratoga Foothill Club when they decided to erect a clubhouse in what was then the village of Saratoga, southwest of San Jose. In 1915 architect Julia Morgan (1872–1957) was asked to create the group's permanent home.[26] She provided four options, and the club chose a low-slung design covered with redwood shakes on the roof and walls (fig. 10.6). At the top of the façade is a wide gable that embraces a rose window, features also seen in Schweinfurth's Berkeley church. Morgan would have known that building; however, she gave her rustic clubhouse a few refined details. This juxtaposition is especially apparent at the entrance, positioned to the left of the gabled assembly hall. There, above paired doors, is a wood panel with the club's name carved in Roman capital letters flanked by carved ribbons and wreaths of cornucopias with bellflowers. Although not elaborate, the classical motifs reflect Morgan's training at the École des Beaux-Arts. In 1898 she became the first woman admitted to its architecture program, and in 1902 she was awarded the graduation certificate. Like Maybeck, her friend and onetime teacher, she benefited from Paris training, but once she opened her San Francisco practice, she was comfortable working in several styles, depending on the setting and the preferences of the client. The First Bay Tradition was just one of several possibilities that she successfully pursued.

FIGURE 10.7. Bernard Maybeck, First Church of Christ, Scientist, sanctuary, Berkeley, California, 1909–11.

ECLECTIC AND MODERN

For Maybeck, the son of a woodcarver, a building's craftsmanship was of paramount importance, and the Arts and Crafts movement and its English theorists reinforced this perspective. That said, he was closely tied to France, where he maintained contacts and met new colleagues, and to Germany, the country of his forebears.[27] His half-timbered house for Leon L. Roos (1909), in San Francisco, may have been inspired by French or German medieval houses. Yet this project also resembled America's English Tudors and was in line with his Arts and Crafts sympathies.

Maybeck's masterpiece, the First Church of Christ, Scientist (1909–11), in Berkeley, is indebted to many sources.[28] An altogether original response to the Arts and Crafts movement, Maybeck justifiably considered it modern in style.[29] When surveying the building, set close to the street, one sees broad gables and pergolas, elements associated with Craftsman houses and the First Bay Tradition. Both the entrance portico and the pergolas incorporate fluted piers with figural capitals, based on precedents from Romanesque Provence. For roofing, Maybeck chose red clay tile, reminiscent of Mediterranean architecture. In the sanctuary, four great wooden trusses, pierced with a Gothic motif, span a central-planned space (fig. 10.7). Tracery in the windows also is Gothic, as is the organ screen behind the reading desk. Above the worshippers, the trusses define a flattened dome, while stenciling creates shimmering patterns of red, blue, green, and gold that are Byzantine in spirit.

Maybeck was explicit in acknowledging the extent of Viollet-le-Duc's influence, which was evident in his emphasis on structural elements such as the pergolas and the trusses of the auditorium.[30] Yet the interest that Maybeck shared with Keeler in the writings of Ruskin was important, too. When the architect agreed to design the church, he told the building committee that it would be conceived to express "sincerity and honesty," employing the moral language of Ruskin, Morris, and the Arts and Crafts movement.[31] Completing the church would require artists and artisans to sculpt models for the capitals, apply the stenciling, and fabricate the metal light fixtures with trefoil cutouts.

Like many of his contemporaries, Maybeck saw no inconsistency in experimenting with innovative materials. The new building was constructed with cast concrete, concrete asbestos panels, and steel-framed windows. Moreover, from the time he was hired, he was clear that the concrete would be visible inside and out, exposed "without sham or hypocrisy," as he said.[32] Although it was a bold move, designing a church with exposed concrete did not break new ground in 1909; Frank Lloyd Wright's Unity Temple in Oak Park, near Chicago, had been finished in this way in 1908 (see fig. 5.11). Well before that, the French architect Anatole de Baudot deployed concrete at Saint-Jean de Montmartre, a modern Gothic church in Paris that Maybeck must have known.[33] After work began in Paris in 1894, a flap was raised over the safety of the design. Authorities ultimately issued their approval, and the building was completed in 1904.[34] In addition to appreciating concrete's structural advantages, de Baudot and Maybeck would have seen how concrete's characteristics were suited to the Gothic vocabulary. They liked that when the material is in its liquid state, it can be molded readily into pierced components such as tracery—supporting the principle that forms should reflect the character of a given material.[35]

SPANISH IN THE BAY AREA

In the early 1890s, Bay Area architects with Arts and Crafts affinities joined others in California who were intrigued by the state's Spanish heritage.[36] Of particular interest were the ancient missions, moldering yet evocative, similar to medieval landmarks in England. Built with adobe brick, local timber, and clay tile, the missions were indigenous and handcrafted. In 1890 Polk ran an article about them in his short-lived *Architectural News,* widely considered the first essay on the topic in a professional publication.[37] A year later, Brown and his firm designed the California Building in the Mission style for the 1893 World's Columbian Exposition in Chicago.[38] Something of a mishmash, it incorporated heavy plastered walls, domed towers, arcades, curved parapet gables, and star windows. The Mission Revival took off. Its popularity, however, was far greater in the Southland than the Bay Area, where few buildings from the Spanish colonial past were to be found.

San Francisco's Chinatown might have provided a spark for a new regional style, but that never happened. In fact, developers floated plans to destroy the district, adjacent to the city's business center. Keeler, generally progressive in his views, described the demolition proposal with enthusiasm, euphemistically terming it a "conversion."[39] Writing in *The Craftsman* in 1905, he conceded that Chinatown was "a picturesque quarter" with displays of "gorgeous" wares, but he argued that its presence wasn't in "the best civic interests of the city."[40] He backed a scheme to replace it with a model business district and entice the Chinese residents to move beyond the city limits, where a new town would be built for them. It would be designed "to emphasize the picturesque features of old China," which the project's advocates hoped would mollify the displaced residents.[41] Despite the fact that immigrants from China had been living in San Francisco since the mid-nineteenth century, neither Keeler nor San Francisco's architects valued the Chinese presence as part of a shared local history.

On the other hand, Bay Area architects, Polk among them, adopted references to Spanish buildings for their projects.[42] Moreover, while rejecting the Mission style, Polk continued to admire California's historic missions. These buildings were worthy of preservation. In 1917 he was hired by San Francisco's Roman Catholic archdiocese to restore the Mission Dolores, a survivor of the 1906 earthquake.[43] Erected by Franciscans and Indigenous peoples between 1782 and 1791 as the Mission San Francisco de Asís, it was roofed with tile and had columns around an arched entry. Like other American architects who advanced an Arts and Crafts ideology, Polk pragmatically accepted the use of steel, and he specified the installation of steel beams to strengthen the church roof. Work on the building was completed in 1920.

In the next decades, the regional interest in the Arts and Crafts movement was extended through the activities of Pedro J. de Lemos (1882–1954), an artist, educator, author, and architectural designer. He arrived in Palo Alto in 1917 to direct the Stanford University Museum and Art Gallery, and two years later he began editing *School Arts* magazine, reaching thousands of art teachers across the country.[44] Devoted to design and the applied arts, he and his wife, Reta, helped found the Allied Arts Guild in

FIGURE 10.8. Pedro J. de Lemos, de Lemos House, view from the entry into the courtyard, Palo Alto, California, 1931–41.

nearby Menlo Park in 1928. Through these various pursuits, de Lemos brought attention to the arts of Native Americans and Hispanic people.

His most ambitious creation is his Palo Alto home, constructed from 1931 to 1941.[45] Connected blocks of the *hacienda* vary in height, from one to two stories, and enclose a courtyard (fig. 10.8). The house feels Spanish, with barrel roof tiles, plastered walls, a loggia, and balconies. Handicraft is evident everywhere, including carved wooden door panels, decorative iron, and tile made by Pedro and Reta, his students, and artisans from San Jose. When traveling to Mexico and Mediterranean countries, de Lemos collected more tiles that he added to his regularly expanding home. He also arranged for wood flooring to be laid in different patterns, signed by the workers. Art and craft and scholarship were thus integrated into a unique and highly personal residence.

ON A BANK OF THE ARROYO SECO

Art, craft, and scholarship also came together in the creation of the Los Angeles home of Charles Fletcher Lummis (1859–1928), located northeast of the city center in present-day Highland Park on a bank of the Arroyo Seco (fig. 10.9).[46] He named the house El Alisal, local Spanish for "place of the sycamore." Like de Lemos, Lummis erected the dwelling in stages over several years, constructing it between 1898 and 1910. Lummis was a serious student of the Spanish in the Americas and the Indigenous peoples of the Southwest, subjects he focused on in his writing, photography, and musical recordings made on wax cylinders. Striking in his green corduroy suit, he was often disheveled.[47]

Born near Boston, Lummis entered Harvard in 1877 and studied with Charles Eliot Norton, esteemed professor of fine arts and friend of Ruskin.[48] In 1879 Norton founded the Archaeological Institute of America, serving as its first president; almost two decades later, he was elected president of the Society of Arts and Crafts, Boston. The rambunctious Lummis was far from a model student, but his mind, like Norton's, was receptive to investigations of diverse cultures and his temperament led him to become an outspoken advocate for historic preservation.

FIGURE 10.9. Charles Fletcher Lummis, El Alisal, Los Angeles, 1898–1910.

In 1903 the Archaeological Institute asked Lummis to organize a regional chapter, which he did, an effort that led to his establishing the Southwest Museum in Los Angeles in 1907.[49] That year, when Lummis addressed the institute, the elderly Norton was in attendance and was pleased by his former student's "zeal and energy."[50]

The appearance of El Alisal is rustic, its walls faced with boulders from the riverbed and its doors, each different, adzed by Lummis. Wrought-iron hinges and ornament were crafted by the Fruhling Brothers of Los Angeles.[51] Lummis's love of California's missions, which he campaigned to restore, is evident in the building's curved parapet and bell. Pueblo round towers inspired a tower to the left of the entrance. Eventually the dwelling acquired an L-shaped plan. Evoking a Spanish ranch house, its interior veranda opened onto a patio where an ancient sycamore spread its branches. The center of El Alisal is a combination social hall and museum where Lummis displayed Native American carpets and pottery. On a large window, he surrounded three clear panes with glass transparencies of the people and places he had photographed. Lummis's house was very much in accord with Arts and Crafts ideals—built with native materials, crafted by hand, and designed with forms that responded to regional history. It was all about Southern California.

But building one's own house, adding to it in stages and using materials from the property, was not a realistic option for most newcomers to the Southland. The domestic building type that they aspired to buy was the bungalow.[52] Through the 1890s, demand for this sort of house took off, its appeal coinciding with a deepening interest in the Arts and Crafts movement and its values. Of paramount importance, the one- to one-and-a-half-story bungalow harmonized with nature, hugging the ground and connecting indoors to outdoors with a broad front porch. It was simple and humble. Many people, notably Stickley, considered it artistic. Featured in plan books and magazine articles, bungalows were erected in every part of the country.[53] Despite this success, not everyone was wild about the cozy little houses. Chicago architect Robert C. Spencer, Jr., observed that "the name has been a God-send to many who a few years ago would not have dared to

FIGURE 10.10. Greene and Greene, Gamble House, Pasadena, California, 1907–9.

build such cheap dwellings in good middle-class suburban neighborhoods."[54]

Cheap versions notwithstanding, the bungalow aesthetic attracted architects and even well-heeled clients who liked its image. For architects Charles Greene (1868–1957) and Henry Greene (1870–1954), the concept of the bungalow led to a commission for an extravagant version of the type when they were asked to build a house for David and Mary Gamble in Pasadena, northeast of Los Angeles.[55] Designed and erected between 1907 and 1909, the Gamble House, like El Alisal, was sited along the scenic Arroyo Seco (fig. 10.10). In keeping with the basic bungalow, the dwelling's massing is low and horizontal, even though it rises a full two stories. On its front elevation, the house integrates two bungalow designs, the left side defined by a large gable and the right side by a front-sloping roof and long dormer.[56] Walls are clad with stained redwood shakes, contributing to a natural and informal effect. Ends of beams, rafters, and purlins are visible, and eaves extend well beyond the exterior walls.

FIGURE 10.11. Emil Lange, stained glass set in the front door to the entrance hall, Gamble House, 1907–9.

Inside, the first floor is finished with wood paneling and built-ins, including cabinets and an inglenook, as found in better bungalows. In plan, however, the Gamble House is more akin to an English country house, with a large hall running front-to-back, terminating at glazed double doors that open to the outside.[57] The humble bungalow's front porch is gone, and the space for socializing has been transferred to the rear of the house, where private terraces and a garden present views of the arroyo. Original as it is, the Gamble House reflects the academic approach instilled in the brothers when they studied architecture in Boston at MIT. As mature architects practicing in Southern California, they looked to many precedents, including the Swiss chalet and the Japanese temple, which were both references for the Gamble House.

After MIT, the brothers apprenticed with Boston architects who had worked for Richardson and were later involved with the Arts and Crafts movement, most notably Warren.[58] With the Gambles as clients, Charles, the main designer of the house, was able to pursue an Arts and Crafts emphasis on fine craftsmanship. Woodworkers led by Peter Hall were asked to round and finish the ends of the Gamble House's exposed structural components. The front entrance is enhanced by doors with leaded stained glass, designed by Charles and made by Emil Lange (1866–1934) to represent a California live oak (fig. 10.11). The living room is crowned by a frieze of panels with scenes of nature, carved by John Hall, Peter's brother. As was the case with other ideal Arts and Crafts commissions, in England and the United States, the

FIGURE 10.12. Ernest A. Batchelder, Batchelder House, Pasadena, California, 1909 and 1912–13.

architects also designed furnishings for the public rooms, to achieve a unified whole.

In September 1909, a mile and a half south of the Gamble House, Ernest A. Batchelder (1875–1957), a Pasadena art and design instructor, bought land near the bottom of the arroyo to erect a more conventionally sized bungalow of six rooms for himself.[59] Prior to the start of construction that year, his plans for the one-story dwelling expanded to include a second-floor bedroom and a sleeping porch. Small though it was, the bungalow was handsomely embellished, resulting in a jewel of the Arts and Crafts movement (fig. 10.12).

At the beginning of 1909, Batchelder left his position as director of art at Pasadena's Throop Polytechnic Institute, predecessor of the California Institute of Technology. A New Hampshire native, he had earned his degree from Massachusetts Normal Art School in Boston and worked for Denman W. Ross, a design theorist, at the Harvard professor's summer school.[60] Batchelder was stimulated by Ross's ideas, leading him to publish two books on design.[61] After arriving at Throop, Batchelder directed his own summer program for the Handicraft Guild of Minneapolis from 1905 through 1909. He also spent time in the English Cotswold village of Chipping Campden, observing the experiment of C. R. Ashbee's Guild of Handicraft.

Once Batchelder felt settled in his new bungalow, he erected a shop in the backyard, installed a kiln, and began making hand-pressed tiles, inspired by Henry Chapman Mercer of Doylestown, Pennsylvania. Batchelder's tiles immediately attracted a following and were commercially successful. But the soot from his kiln made for unhappy neighbors and soon ended the idyll under the olive trees. In 1912 he moved his operation to an industrial site in Pasadena. With further success, he relocated to a factory in Los Angeles, where he eventually employed 175 workers. Hit hard by the Great Depression, he was forced to close the business in 1932.

Batchelder's bungalow is of the Swiss chalet type, its low gable spreading over the living room. Dark shingles cover the walls, enlivened by a chimney built with misshapen clinker bricks and stone from the arroyo. Visitors are welcomed by a Mercer tile on the front door and copper hardware and a matching mailbox crafted by Douglas Donaldson. The metalworker also made light fixtures for the bungalow's paneled living room and dining room.[62] Open to the rafters, the living room has a large fireplace and chimney. Upon his marriage in 1912, Batchelder faced the fireplace completely with tiles made by him and by Mercer. Two tiles represent lions holding shields—one shield decorated with a rabbit sketching, an emblem of

Batchelder, and the second shield decorated with a harp, an emblem of his musical wife.

SAVING THE MISSIONS

Early in the American preservation movement, a group of Californians organized to save the decaying missions of the Southland. Led by Charles Lummis, the Landmarks Club of Southern California was launched in 1895, with architects Sumner P. Hunt (1865–1938) and Arthur B. Benton (1858–1927) supplying professional assistance.[63] Lummis was predisposed to carry the banner, given his New England origins and the influence of Harvard's Norton—a background that exposed him to a preservation ethos that, in turn, was encouraged by Ruskin, Morris, and Philip Webb. Yet unlike the Yankees and the English who sought to safeguard buildings that had been erected by individuals of their own ethnic heritage, Lummis and fellow club members banded together to preserve monuments erected by Spanish Franciscans and Native Americans, both of whom were regarded as unrelated to the new arrivals. Proceeding quickly, the Landmarks Club raised the money and undertook the restoration of missions at San Juan Capistrano, San Fernando, San Diego, and San Luis Rey. At the club's behest, San Diego architect Irving J. Gill and a partner stabilized the San Diego mission.[64]

Within a few years, California's legislators were on board with the campaign to preserve the Spanish landmarks, passing an act in 1905 to acquire the Sonoma mission in the north. Reporting on the accomplishment, the *Architect and Engineer of California* told readers in 1908 that "no other State in the Union can boast of a history more interesting, more picturesque, or more romantic."[65] Worthy of preservation, the mission buildings had become "monuments to those self-sacrificing padres who labored unceasingly for the betterment of the Indians."[66] The argument for preservation reflected an evolving view about the Franciscans, who a few decades earlier had been seen as foreign. By this time, the hoary old buildings told a story of benevolent European missionaries and fortunate Native peoples; the reality of the padres aggressively coercing the Indigenous men and women into hard work and religious conversion was suppressed.[67]

Adobe houses from the Spanish and Mexican periods became preservation projects, too. In San Diego, Hazel Wood Waterman (1865–1948), a Gill protégé, oversaw the restoration of the Casa de Estudillo between 1908 and 1910 (fig. 10.13).[68] The house, dating from 1827 to 1829,

FIGURE 10.13. Hazel Wood Waterman, restoration of Casa de Estudillo, San Diego, 1908–10.

FIGURE 10.14. James Osborne Craig, completed by Carleton M. Winslow, El Paseo, Santa Barbara, California, 1921–24.

was marketed as a tourist destination associated with "Ramona's Marriage Place," a location described in a widely read nineteenth-century novel by Helen Hunt Jackson. Despite the hype, Waterman took her job seriously, studying historic manuscripts, photographs, and sites in order to repair and reconstruct the landmark in an authentic manner. With an Arts and Crafts frame of mind, she sought out Mexican workers who could make tile and adobe brick by hand.[69]

Around the same time, the Casa de la Guerra, recognized as the finest Spanish house in Santa Barbara, underwent a restoration. Work on the early nineteenth-century dwelling took place between 1910 and 1914 and was managed by Francis T. Underhill (1863–1929), whose wife descended from the man for whom it was built.[70] Afterward, relatives occupied one wing, while other rooms were devoted to gift shops and a tea room. Planned in a U shape that defined a courtyard, the distinguishing feature of the building is a veranda with substantial piers of adobe.

In the fall of 1921 a scheme was unveiled to turn the Casa de la Guerra into the nucleus of a commercial, office, and residential complex, the new buildings designed in a Spanish style. The development was envisioned by Santa Barbara architect James Osborne Craig (1888–1922). After Craig died in 1922, architect Carleton M. Winslow (1876–1946) saw the project to completion, adhering to the original designs.[71] It opened in 1924 and was branded as El Paseo (fig. 10.14).[72] Patrons explored shops and reached a patio café by wending their way through an interior pedestrian corridor that suggested a "street in Spain." Ancient and modern were sympathetically integrated, and the new buildings were treated with restraint, ornamented sparingly with tile, iron grilles, and iron light fixtures. But the thinking about historic preservation had changed, reflecting changed values. In 1925 the *Pacific Coast Architect* lauded El Paseo for keeping alive "California's golden traditions of romance and beauty."[73] Supporters of preservation work now encouraged it to provide "romance" rather than framing it in the moral terms that had been fundamental to the movement.

If the Arts and Crafts principle of designing buildings that affirm a region's heritage raise important questions about architecture across the United States, more questions than usual arise about the stylistic reference chosen for El Paseo. By alluding to a Spanish streetscape, Craig cast the development as European, which would have been accepted by patrons of European descent. Design sources from Mexico were not acknowledged. Nevertheless, Craig realized that Mexico's imagery was useful, in one case finding inspiration in a photograph published a few years earlier of an arcade in Cuernavaca.[74] As for the people making their homes in the immediate neighborhood, their heritage wasn't considered at all. Immediately behind El Paseo, on Canon Perdido, lived struggling Chinese fishermen and shopkeepers.[75] Over time, the success and expansion of El Paseo led to investment in the area, including a new theater and a post office. With additional commercial development, hastened by an earthquake in 1925, the Chinese were displaced, and their history in the neighborhood, never embraced, was ultimately erased.

STARK AND WHITE

The stark white buildings of San Diego architect Irving J. Gill (1870–1936), inspired by the missions, represent some of the most forward-looking designs of the early twentieth century.[76] Although severe in form, they derive from Gill's training in Chicago during the early 1890s when he absorbed many ideas from the Arts and Crafts movement. As a resident of Southern California, he sought to respond to the region's history by suggesting its Spanish architecture; he planned his buildings to connect with their natural settings; and he advocated for simplicity in design.[77] While striving for simplicity, however, he was more adventurous than his colleagues. Despite the fact that he spent two years in Louis Sullivan's office, where great quantities of ornament were generated, Gill minimized the use of ornament in his mature projects. In Chicago, Gill also was exposed to daring attitudes toward modern materials and construction. In San Diego, he was creative and experimental in his use of concrete.

One of Gill's most innovative buildings is the La Jolla Woman's Club (1912–14), located in the coastal town northwest of San Diego (fig. 10.15).[78] The commission came through Ellen Browning Scripps, who funded it and was a prominent club member.[79] Early in life, she assisted her brother James in his Detroit newspaper business, and when she joined half-brother E. W. in establishing the

FIGURE 10.15. Irving J. Gill, La Jolla Woman's Club, La Jolla, California, 1912–14.

Scripps newspaper chain, she grew wealthy. In 1890 Ellen moved to California. Through the early years of the twentieth century, her interest in the Arts and Crafts movement and in architecture was likely heightened when she heard about developments with family in Detroit. In 1906 George Booth, James's son-in-law, was elected the first president of the Detroit Society of Arts and Crafts, and a year later Booth and his wife, James's daughter, began construction of Cranbrook, their Tudor Revival home in Bloomfield Hills (see fig. 6.2). Both Ellen Scripps and the La Jolla club women supported progressive causes, and choosing Gill to design their permanent home was consistent with their open-minded inclinations.

Across the long front elevation of the clubhouse is an arcade with round arches, reminiscent of Spanish missions and dwellings, while white painted walls evoke traditional plastered surfaces. At the building's front and sides are doorways that link it to lawns and gardens, and both sides are flanked by pergolas covered with vines. For the exterior walls, Gill employed a "tilt-slab" method of concrete construction, which required the contractors to build enormous tray-like forms, laid out on the site, into which the mixture was poured and left to harden. The walls were then jacked up and set into place.[80] The structure is pure form, without moldings or a cornice. Reductive in its design, it corresponds to the austere Arts and Crafts architecture of Voysey and M. H. Baillie Scott. At the same time, the work of an artisan is noticeable in iron scrolls set into the glass of the front doors.

REVIVING THE BAROQUE

In the second decade of the twentieth century, a new category of Spanish Revival architecture coalesced. This was the revival of the Baroque architecture of eighteenth-century Spain and Mexico, called Churrigueresque. Bertram Grosvenor Goodhue and Myron Hunt (1868–1952) each made contributions to popularizing the style in the Southland. Goodhue led the way when he published a design for a Churrigueresque church in Havana, Cuba, in 1907, which included an ebulliently decorated tower and entry portal. Although never built, it offered an alternative to the Mission style.[81] It was surely seen by Hunt. During the 1890s, the two architects were starting out in Boston and traveled in the same circles. After studying architecture at MIT, Hunt worked in Boston firms, leaving to join the Chicago office of Shepley, Rutan, and Coolidge.[82] At the end of the decade, both architects signed on with Arts and Crafts societies—Goodhue in Boston and Hunt in Chicago.[83] In 1897 Hunt and his wife participated in founding the Chicago Arts and Crafts Society, along with other Prairie School architects.[84] When his wife contracted tuberculosis, the couple left the cold for Pasadena.

In 1910 Hunt and a partner, Elmer Grey, won a competition to design a new edifice for the First Congregational Church of Riverside with a proposal in the Mission style.[85] Later that year, the partners dissolved their relationship and Hunt took over, modifying the design to feature a Churrigueresque tower, entrance, and window surround (fig. 10.16). Mastering what was then a novel vocabulary, he called for rich embellishments, including estipite pilasters shaped like upside-down obelisks. Hunt was scholarly in his method, diverging with the Prairie School architects of Chicago. Instead, he grounded his work in history, like Arts and Crafts architects in the Northeast who were studying the Gothic and Anglo-Colonial past. The problem was how to design a church building that reflected the heritage of the Congregationalists as well as the heritage of old California. With this stated goal, a 125-foot tower was erected to capture "the spirit of New England towers," while its Spanish Baroque style was chosen to fit the locale.[86]

Hunt was committed to Arts and Crafts workmanship, and the ornament that he sketched was modeled by artisans, then cast in concrete. For the roof, he specified a terra-cotta tile supplied by Atholl McBean of Gladding, McBean in San Francisco.[87] Not the company's standard product, it had been introduced by McBean as "a labor of love" to repair the old missions of California.[88] Writing in 1918, architect Dwight James Baum observed that ancient tile roofs were one of "the most romantic touches of old Spain and Mexico."[89] The "romantic" barrel tile of the Riverside church was as important to its character as the ornament.

Before the house of worship was finished in 1913, plans were moving forward in San Diego for the Panama-California Exposition, which would open at Balboa Park in 1915.[90] Goodhue, by this time based in New York City, was the architect in charge, and he determined that the unifying design for the fair would draw upon the region's Spanish colonial period.[91] The Mission style was too plain for Goodhue and too plain for organizers of the fair. On the other hand, Goodhue was something of an expert on the architecture of early Mexico, having traveled there in 1892 and 1899 and written about it.[92] Mexico's Baroque

FIGURE 10.16. Myron Hunt, First Congregational Church of Riverside, California, 1910–13.

churches were ideal as a source for exposition buildings that should dazzle the fairgoers.

Passing under an arched gate, visitors entered the Plaza de California, anchored by Goodhue's domed California Building (fig. 10.17).[93] Stylistically, it's Churrigueresque, entirely different from the Gothic architecture for which Goodhue was renowned. But in the caliber of its craftsmanship, it reflects the same concerns that informed Goodhue's medieval work. He personally designed the building's blue, green, and yellow patterned roof tiles, made by employees of Walter Nordhoff at California China Products in National City, outside San Diego, based on historic Spanish and Moorish ceramics. The building's profusely embellished entrance includes sculptures of royalty, conquistadors, and religious figures, modeled by Furio and Attilio Piccirilli of New York City. Other ornament was modeled by their brothers Horatio and Thomas and cast in concrete by Tracy Brick and Art Stone in San Diego.[94] Intended as a permanent structure, the California Building was constructed of reinforced concrete and hollow tile skimmed in gray stucco. The hall did indeed dazzle visitors, and it produced a wave of Churrigueresque designs throughout Southern California. Little did it matter that buildings of this lavishness had never been part of the colonial landscape.

FIGURE 10.17. Bertram Grosvenor Goodhue, California Building, San Diego, 1911–15.

INTO THE TWENTIES

With the prosperity of the twenties and an influx of residents, architects in Southern California were in demand. Through these years, when hiring professionals to build their homes, clients preferred styles that seemed "appropriate" in some way—adopting an Arts and Crafts principle that in fact was quite puzzling. Some clients wanted Tudor houses, subscribing to the idea that Americans are basically English, while others wanted Spanish or Mediterranean houses, in keeping with the Spanish history and dry climate of the region. The values of simplicity and restraint faded. At the same time, for clients with the resources, handcrafted decoration was as desirable as ever.

In 1922 African American architect Paul R. Williams (1894–1980) opened his practice in Los Angeles with commissions for Tudor and Spanish Colonial Revival houses. He had overcome extraordinary hurdles relating to financial need and racism.[95] Orphaned by the age of four, he studied engineering at the University of Southern California, took art and architecture classes elsewhere, and trained under several prominent area architects. In 1920 he was appointed by the mayor of Los Angeles to serve on the newly established City Planning Commission. The first project for which he was hired was a sprawling Tudor Revival house for Louis and Virginia Cass (1921–22) in the wealthy development of La Cañada Flintridge, northwest of Pasadena.[96] Picturesquely massed and stuccoed, it includes adzed half-timbering and casement windows.

Also early in his career, Williams was hired to design houses in the Los Angeles neighborhood of Hancock Park, northwest of downtown, some for the upper-middle class and others for people of great wealth. The Frederick and Esther Leistikow House (1923) and the Philip Rothman House (1926) are brick Tudors in the Arts and Crafts tradition, embellished with leaded glass casement windows, sculpted mantelpieces, wood paneling, and stenciling (fig. 10.18).[97] Walter S. and Juliet Bachman

FIGURE 10.18. Paul R. Williams, Rothman House, Los Angeles, 1926.

FIGURE 10.19. George Washington Smith, Casa del Herrero, Montecito, California, 1922–25.

preferred the Spanish Colonial Revival for their Hancock Park house, built in 1927.[98] Williams enhanced it with a Churrigueresque hood over the front door. By this time, he had become the first Black member of the American Institute of Architects, elected in 1923. In 1957 he would become the organization's first African American Fellow. As his career blossomed, he designed houses and commercial buildings in a range of styles. Over the decades, his talent in visualizing ornament, whatever the vocabulary, impressed his clients.

In Santa Barbara and its environs, George Washington Smith (1876–1930) produced some of the most admired Spanish Colonial houses of the 1920s.[99] Reared in Philadelphia, he entered Harvard's architecture program, run through the Lawrence Scientific School, in 1895. There he studied under Warren at a time when the Arts and Crafts movement was emerging. After Smith's second year, his family's financial reversals compelled him to leave, and he pivoted to a career selling bonds. By 1912 he was able to retire and head to Paris to work as an artist. World War I put an end to the dream, and in 1917 he and his wife settled in Montecito, five miles east of Santa Barbara. The houses he erected for his family, the first from 1918 and a second from 1920, based on farmhouses of Andalusia, were so well regarded that he abandoned art for architecture.

In 1922 a St. Louis industrialist, George F. Steedman, commissioned Smith to design a winter retreat in Montecito.[100] Like Smith, Steedman was a Harvard man. When he and his wife built a home on Westmoreland Place, the finest address in St. Louis, he hired architect John Lawrence Mauran, who had been an usher at his wedding.[101] For the Montecito house, Steedman and Smith collaborated closely, planning an informal assemblage of low masses, covered in red tile and painted white (fig. 10.19). For the most part, the house seems Spanish, yet it also has Italian sources, especially on the garden façade that has a large pair of arches and deep loggia. Finished in 1925, Casa del Herrero was understood to be "Spanish only in essence," an American original.[102]

A distinction of the house is the extent to which it incorporates antique Spanish architectural components. In 1923, as construction proceeded, Steedman and New York City authors Arthur Byne and Mildred Stapley Byne traveled to Spain to buy museum-worthy salvage for Steedman's residence.[103] They bought wrought-iron grilles for windows and a fifteenth-century painted wooden ceiling for the entry vestibule. They also purchased a small amount of antique tile, but the quantity was insufficient. At Smith's suggestion, Byne traveled to Tunis to locate Jacob Chemla, whose pottery could meet the standard of the old tile and satisfy Byne, Smith, and his client.[104]

The Casa del Herrero became a year-round house when Steedman retired. In making this transition, he went to Boston in 1927 to study silversmithing with George C. Gebelein, a master craftsman with the Society of Arts and Crafts.[105] Returning to Montecito, Steedman spent his last years hammering and shaping silver, like Frances Glessner in her basement in Chicago. Finding joy in his work, Steedman was a contented California craftsman living out his last years in a Spanish Colonial Arts and Crafts house.

Architects and clients influenced by Arts and Crafts ideals readily engaged with California's landscapes and history to inspire their buildings. Californians erected shingled structures, which they liked for the way they reflected nature, and bungalows, respected for their simplicity. Craftsmanship, too, was encouraged and nurtured—by Keeler, Maybeck, and de Lemos in the north and by the brothers Greene, Batchelder, and Smith in the south. Missions and Spanish Colonial houses came to be admired by Californians who applied the concept of historic preservation from the East and England to their own ancient buildings. In California, an Arts and Crafts ethos provided the rationale for shingled houses by Polk and Coxhead, a Churrigueresque church by Hunt, and a Tudor house by Williams. It also gave rise to an innovative concrete clubhouse by Gill. Arts and Crafts thinking guided all of them.

Conclusion

Last Gleaming

Beginning in the 1890s, American men and women founded Arts and Crafts societies, and, as in England, architects were in the thick of the organizational efforts. Indeed, the architects often dominated these groups. Traveling by train, they met with clients and spread their vision. Carrying notebooks and sketchbooks, they journeyed from Boston to Houston, from New York City to San Diego, from Philadelphia to Boulder, and from Chicago to Buffalo. Connected to their colleagues through architectural associations, exhibitions, and publications, they encouraged Arts and Crafts principles that would shape new development. Ralph Adams Cram, Bertram Goodhue, Charles Z. Klauder, and Frank Lloyd Wright ranked among the nation's most influential designers. Other architects, such as Leila Ross Wilburn, John Gaw Meem, and Ellis F. Lawrence, were influential in the regions where they lived.

An appreciation for nature, springing from European Romanticism, was at the heart of the movement, and Americans readily embraced this value. Increasingly they came to prize their own natural landscapes, whether woods, timberlands, or prairies, while architects responded by designing buildings that used native materials, from granite to sandstone, from ponderosa pine logs to redwood shingles. Nature often provided the inspiration for architectural enhancements, such as stained glass that abstracted sumac leaves on the prairie or cacti on the desert. Arts and Crafts houses were planned with porches and banked windows to connect indoor rooms with gardens and scenic vistas. Massing a building in an irregular manner, picturesque in effect, was considered a natural approach, equated with organic growth over time.

Simplicity was a byword of the movement, reflecting a shift away from the overwrought aspects of Victorian architecture. Modest bungalows were considered artistic. Rustic houses, lodges, and inns were judged to be simple and artistic, too, even when they were grandiose. In aiming for simplicity, some of the architects reduced their designs to basic geometric forms with unbroken expanses of wall, covered in shingles or stucco.

To the minds of many architects with an Arts and Crafts inclination, a building should express its structure clearly. Respectful of John Ruskin's exhortations, they created Gothic Revival churches with visible wood trusses and masonry vaults. Tudor Revival houses were characterized by half-timbering, which was supposedly structural, although as often as not, the wooden boards were just applied decoration.

Architects who were active in Arts and Crafts societies took a concerted interest in encouraging artisans and artists who could embellish their buildings. Architectural exhibitions and periodicals showcased the creations of these collaborators. Sculptors included John Evans, Lee Lawrie, and Richard Bock. Samuel Yellin was renowned for his shop's ironwork. Stained glass was made by Charles J. Connick. Among the most successful tile producers were Grueby, Henry Chapman Mercer, Pewabic Pottery, and Ernest Batchelder.

Of the various Arts and Crafts tenets, the most challenging was surely the conviction that architecture should affirm a people's own heritage. While the English, going back to Augustus W. N. Pugin, understood this concept to mean eschewing the classical tradition in favor of native Gothic forms, Americans struggled with defining themselves. What ensued were assertions about who Americans are and the essence of American identity. Given the vastness of the United States, architects and their clients recognized that the country encompassed regions with significant differences, and they determined that regional distinctions ought to be seen in a positive light.

With rigor, architects turned to local history and studied vernacular buildings. A deepening knowledge of architectural history came about through the expansion of architectural programs among institutions of higher education, an increasing array of professional periodicals, and greater opportunities for travel. Based upon their investigations and expertise, the architects proposed design solutions that were well-reasoned and persuasive.

In the Northeast, architects who were invested in the Arts and Crafts movement identified their heritage as English. This self-image was especially strong in Boston and Philadelphia, and it was reinforced by the architects' contact with colleagues in England. As a result, at an early date, the architects of these regions designed English Perpendicular churches and Tudor Revival houses. They also employed a distilled Gothic style that was advanced by M. H. Baillie Scott and C. F. A. Voysey.

In other parts of the United States, English styles were also considered American—in places as diverse as Atlanta, Chicago, Seattle, and Los Angeles. In San Francisco, when planning was underway for the Panama-Pacific Exposition, which would be held there in 1915, the *Architect and Engineer of California* published an appeal from a local architect who argued that the fair buildings should be English Gothic. Envisioning such an ensemble, the writer declared, "How grandly it would grace this farthest western frontier of the civilization of the Anglo-Saxon, where it faces its antitype, the oriental!"[1] Coincidentally, in the same issue, the frontispiece illustrated a telephone exchange building in San Francisco's Chinatown, erected in 1909 after the earthquake, fashioned after a Chinese pagoda with a tiered roof.[2] It was an oddity, however, serving a neighborhood of citizens who were perceived as foreigners.

As the medieval styles of the English Arts and Crafts movement became popular, American architects began theorizing that other styles could be embraced as native and put to use. Depending on the region's history, these professionals felt that Anglo-Colonial and Spanish Colonial styles offered imagery for new buildings, while in the Southwest and California, the adobe buildings erected by Indigenous peoples could provide the basis for Mission and Pueblo styles. From today's vantage point, we note issues when we analyze which historic sources were revived. For example, the range of styles that the architects employed excluded the ancestral traditions of many of the country's racial and ethnic groups. They were not seen. On the other hand, in recent decades, historians have written critically about the Mission style, recognizing that it can't very well be divorced from the abuse inflicted by the white invaders, especially the padres, on Indigenous peoples.

By contrast, styles that responded to local landscapes and climates continue to be admired for the ways in which they harmonize with their sites. In Asheville, North Carolina, the granite rocks of the Grove Park Inn blend with the resort's rustic setting. In Springfield, Illinois, the low masses of the Dana House speak of the flat prairie. In Houston, the original brick buildings of the Rice University campus, Byzantine Revival in style, relate to a sunny, sultry climate. In Seattle, a cluster of wooden cottages constructed with native fir sits snugly on a tree-covered hillside.

From the urban centers where architects adopted Arts and Crafts ideas and introduced a variety of styles, the concepts spread, reaching new American territories. Hawaii, annexed by the United States in 1898, became home to architect Hart Wood (1880–1957) after he gained experience in the Bay Area.[3] In his practice, he created buildings with sheltering hipped roofs that he believed would reflect the Hawaiian culture and environment. Two

FIGURE 11.1. Antonin Nechodoma, Casa Roig, Humacao, Puerto Rico, 1920.

years before the Alaska Territory was established in 1912, New York City–based partners William Orr Ludlow (1870–1954) and Charles S. Peabody (1880–1935) designed the campus of the Sheldon Jackson School, a missionary boarding school in Sitka for Alaska Natives.[4] Its Craftsman-style beauty is still enjoyed, even as its purpose to assimilate the children into Western culture has been repudiated. In Puerto Rico, an American territory as of 1917, architect Antonin Nechodoma (1877–1928) introduced Prairie School designs that drew upon his experiences in Chicago (fig. 11.1).[5] Another island resident, Pedro Adolfo de Castro Besosa (1895–1936), pursued the scholarly direction of American Arts and Crafts architects. Upon completing his degree at Syracuse University in 1918, he became the first Puerto Rican graduate of an American architectural school. When he launched his practice, he adopted elements of Spanish architecture for his projects to link them to the territory's history.[6]

The Arts and Crafts call to affirm a people's past was intertwined with historic preservation. England's John Ruskin, William Morris, and Philip Webb all felt a deep affection for their country's medieval churches and houses and became advocates to protect them. In the United States, the same attitude was absorbed—with the preservation of a historic log cabin at Pinehurst, North Carolina; the adobe church of San Estévan del Rey, Acoma Pueblo, in New Mexico; and the missions along the coast of California. Ideas about what buildings should be preserved continue to evolve. Indeed, the Arts and Crafts buildings of the last century have themselves become a part of the American heritage. They have been surveyed and documented by government agencies, turned into museums and tourist attractions, and valued as a legacy that provides us with lessons both sobering and inspiring.

Across the American nation, architects, craft workers, and writers transmitted Arts and Crafts principles, resulting in buildings that vary widely in appearance—a physical, visible inheritance for us all. These buildings are Gothic, Prairie School, Pueblo, and Spanish Colonial, incorporating fieldstone, brick, *vigas,* and clay tile. They embody a myriad of responses to a question that was once all-important: What native materials, landscapes, and histories will serve us when we build, to suit the special places where we live, in the United States of America?

Notes

INTRODUCTION

1. "The Last Spike," *Los Angeles Evening Express,* September 6, 1876.
2. David Frazer Lewis, *A. W. N. Pugin* (Liverpool: Liverpool University Press, 2021); Rosemary Hill, *God's Architect: Pugin and the Building of Romantic Britain* (2007; repr., New Haven, CT: Yale University Press, 2009); Paul Atterbury, ed., *A. W. N. Pugin: Master of Gothic Revival,* exh. cat. (New York: Bard Graduate Center; New Haven, CT: Yale University Press, 1995).
3. A. W. N. Pugin, *Contrasts: Or, a Parallel between the Noble Edifices of the Fourteenth and Fifteenth Centuries, and Similar Buildings of the Present Day, Shewing the Present Decay of Taste* (London: The author, 1836); Pugin, *The True Principles of Pointed or Christian Architecture* (London: J. Weale, 1841).
4. John Ruskin, *The Seven Lamps of Architecture* (London: Smith Elder, 1849). See also Michael Brooks, *John Ruskin and Victorian Architecture* (1987; repr., London: Thames and Hudson, 1989).
5. John Ruskin, "The Nature of Gothic," in *The Stones of Venice,* vol. 2 (London: Smith Elder, 1853), 151–231.
6. Fiona MacCarthy, *William Morris: A Life for Our Time* (New York: Knopf, 1995).
7. Tessa Wild, *William Morris and His Palace of Art* (London: Philip Wilson, 2018).
8. Peter Stansky, *Redesigning the World: William Morris, the 1880s, and the Arts and Crafts* (1985; repr., Palo Alto, CA: Society for the Promotion of Science and Scholarship, 1996).
9. William Morris, "The Prospects of Architecture in Civilisation," in *William Morris on Architecture,* ed. Chris Miele (Sheffield, UK: Sheffield Academic, 1996), 64. Delivered in 1881, the talk was published in William Morris, *Hopes and Fears for Art* (London: Ellis and White, 1882).
10. William Morris, "Gothic Architecture," in Miele, *William Morris on Architecture,* 156. The lecture was delivered before the Arts and Crafts Exhibition Society in 1889. It was published by Morris in *Gothic Architecture* (London: Kelmscott, 1893).
11. On Arts and Crafts architecture in Britain, see Peter Davey, *Arts and Crafts Architecture* (1980; repr., London: Phaidon, 1995); and Elizabeth Cumming, "Architecture in Britain," in *The Arts and Crafts Movement,* by Elizabeth Cumming and Wendy Kaplan, rev. ed. (London: Thames and Hudson, 2002), 31–65. On webs of relationships and influential offices, see Margaret Richardson, *The Craft Architects* (New York: Rizzoli, in association with the Royal Institute of British Architects, 1983), 23–57.
12. Caroline Dakers, *Clouds: The Biography of a Country House* (New Haven, CT: Yale University Press, 1993); Sheila Kirk, *Philip Webb: Pioneer of Arts and Crafts Architecture* (Chichester, West Sussex, UK: Wiley-Academy, 2005).
13. Andrew Saint, *Richard Norman Shaw* (New Haven, CT: Yale University Press, 1976).
14. Michael Hall, *George Frederick Bodley and the Later Gothic Revival in Britain and America* (New Haven, CT: Yale University Press, 2014).
15. Godfrey Rubens, *William Richard Lethaby, His Life and Work* (London: Architectural Press, 1986); Davey, *Arts and Crafts Architecture,* 65–77; Stansky, *Redesigning the World,* 132–40.
16. Fiona MacCarthy, *The Simple Life: C. R. Ashbee in the Cotswolds* (London: Lund Humphries, 1981); Alan Crawford, *C. R. Ashbee: Architect, Designer, and Romantic Socialist* (New Haven, CT: Yale University Press, 1985).
17. Karen Livingstone, *C. F. A. Voysey: Arts and Crafts Designer* (London: V&A, 2016); Wendy Hitchmough, *C. F. A. Voysey* (London: Phaidon, 1995).
18. Diane Haigh, *Baillie Scott: The Artistic House* (London: Academy, 1995); James D. Kornwolf, *M. H. Baillie Scott and the Arts and Crafts Movement: Pioneers of Modern Design* (Baltimore: Johns Hopkins Press, 1972).
19. Davey, *Arts and Crafts Architecture,* 140–41; Cumming, "Architecture in Britain," 55.
20. Davey, *Arts and Crafts Architecture,* 105–7.
21. For a national perspective, see Wayne Craven, *Marble Halls: Beaux-Arts Classicism and Civic Architecture in the Gilded Age* (Newark: University of Delaware Press, 2017). For a much narrower but informative study, see Elizabeth Macaulay-Lewis, *Antiquity in Gotham: The Ancient Architecture of New York City* (New York: Fordham University Press, 2021).
22. Robert Judson Clark, ed., *The Arts and Crafts Movement in America, 1876–1916,* exh. cat. (Princeton, NJ: Princeton University Press, 1972). See also Gillian Naylor, *The Arts and Crafts Movement: A Study of Its Sources, Ideals and Influence on Design Theory* (Cambridge, MA: MIT Press, 1971); Isabelle Anscombe and Charlotte Gere, *Arts and Crafts in Britain and America* (New York: Van Nostrand Reinhold, 1978).
23. Davey, *Arts and Crafts Architecture.*
24. Richard Guy Wilson, "American Arts and Crafts Architecture: Radical Though Dedicated to the Cause Conservative," in *"The Art That Is Life": The Arts and Crafts Movement in America, 1875–1920,* exh. cat.,

ed. Wendy Kaplan (Boston: Museum of Fine Arts, 1987), 101–31. Other important catalogues accompanying exhibitions on the Arts and Crafts movement include Wendy Kaplan, *The Arts and Crafts Movement in Europe and America: Design for the Modern World,* exh. cat. (Los Angeles: Los Angeles County Museum of Art, 2004); Karen Livingstone and Linda Parry, *International Arts and Crafts,* exh. cat. (London: V&A, 2005); and Monica Penick and Christopher Long, eds., *The Rise of Everyday Design: The Arts and Crafts Movement in Britain and America,* exh. cat. (New Haven, CT: Yale University Press, 2019).

25. Wendy Kaplan, "Regionalism in American Architecture," in Cumming and Kaplan, *Arts and Crafts Movement,* 107–42.
26. James Massey and Shirley Maxwell, *Arts and Crafts Design in America: A State-by-State Guide* (San Francisco: Chronicle, 1998).

CHAPTER 1. ENGLISH IN NEW ENGLAND

1. The most comprehensive study of architecture and the Arts and Crafts movement in New England is Maureen Meister, *Arts and Crafts Architecture: History and Heritage in New England* (Hanover, NH: University Press of New England, 2014). See also Beverly K. Brandt, *The Craftsman and the Critic: Defining Usefulness and Beauty in Arts and Crafts-Era Boston* (Amherst: University of Massachusetts Press, 2009). Also informative, although not about architecture, is Marilee Boyd Meyer, consulting curator, *Inspiring Reform: Boston's Arts and Crafts Movement,* exh. cat. (Wellesley, MA: Davis Museum and Cultural Center, Wellesley College, 1997).
2. On Norton's relationship with England's Arts and Crafts theorists, see Meister, *Arts and Crafts Architecture,* 74–77, 80–84. For general studies about Norton, see Kermit Vanderbilt, *Charles Eliot Norton: Apostle of Culture in a Democracy* (Cambridge, MA: Belknap Press of Harvard University Press, 1959); James Turner, *The Liberal Education of Charles Eliot Norton* (Baltimore: Johns Hopkins University Press, 1999); and Linda Dowling, *Charles Eliot Norton: The Art of Reform in Nineteenth-Century America* (Hanover, NH: University of New Hampshire Press, 2007).
3. Charles Eliot Norton, *Notes of Travel and Study in Italy* (Boston: Ticknor and Fields, 1859).
4. Norton, *Notes of Travel and Study,* 192.
5. See Norton's letters to Ruskin of February 10, 1874, and March 18, 1874, in Sara Norton and M. A. DeWolfe Howe, eds., *Letters of Charles Eliot Norton,* vol. 2 (Boston: Houghton Mifflin, 1913), 34–35, 40.
6. James F. O'Gorman, *Living Architecture: A Biography of H. H. Richardson* (New York: Simon and Schuster, 1997), 137–39.
7. Maureen Meister, "From Architecture to Occupational Therapy: George Barton—Morris Disciple and Arts and Crafts Advocate," *Useful and Beautiful* (Summer/Fall 2019): 3–7 (published by the William Morris Society in the United States).
8. See editors' note in Frank C. Sharp and Jan Marsh, eds., *Collected Letters of Jane Morris* (Woodbridge, UK: Boydell, 2012), 251n1, citing William Morris's Day Diary, May 19, 1896, British Library.
9. Some sources identify Goodhue as a founder of the Society of Arts and Crafts, but the organization's earliest surviving records indicate that this was not the case. See Meister, *Arts and Crafts Architecture,* 233n9.
10. Annie Robinson, *Peabody and Stearns: Country Houses and Seaside Cottages* (New York: W. W. Norton, 2010), 24–27.
11. Maureen Meister, *Architecture and the Arts and Crafts Movement in Boston: Harvard's H. Langford Warren* (Hanover, NH: University Press of New England, 2003), 8–9.
12. On Dawes and his career, see "A Biographical Dictionary of the Architects of Greater Manchester, 1800–1940," Architects of Greater Manchester, 1800–1940, https://manchestervictorianarchitects.org.uk/ (a website of the Victorian Society [UK]).
13. Meister, *Arts and Crafts Architecture,* 30.
14. Robert W. Edis, *Decoration and Furniture of Town Houses* (London: C. K. Paul, 1881). It also was published in New York by Scribner and Welford (1881).
15. Meister, *Arts and Crafts Architecture,* 111–14.
16. *Boston Sunday Globe,* March 21, 1897.
17. Meister, *Arts and Crafts Architecture,* 10–15, 53 (on other early Arts and Crafts initiatives in the United States).
18. May R. Spain, *The Society of Arts and Crafts, 1897–1924* (Boston: Society of Arts and Crafts, 1924), 11–12. She identifies Norton as the author.
19. William Morris, "The Prospects of Architecture in Civilisation," in *Hopes and Fears for Art,* 169.
20. Meister, *Arts and Crafts Architecture,* 89.
21. Meister, *Arts and Crafts Architecture,* 65–72.
22. Papers of the Society of Arts and Crafts, Boston, Archives of American Art, Smithsonian Institution, microfilm reel 300, frame 628.
23. "Mr. John Evans, Modeler and Carver," *Architectural Record,* Great American Architects series, no. 3 (July 1896): 116–17.
24. Meister, *Arts and Crafts Architecture,* 99; Robinson, *Peabody and Stearns,* 50–53. Glass from the Burne-Jones window is in the collection of the Delaware Art Museum.
25. Robinson, *Peabody and Stearns,* 82–83. Peabody and Stearns took a similar approach with their design of the Moses Williams House (1885), in Brookline, Massachusetts. It was illustrated as "House at Brookline, Mass." (fig. 35) in "Peabody and Stearns," *Architectural Record,* Great American Architects series, no. 3 (July 1896): 87. See also "Williams, Moses-Hunt House," Massachusetts Historical Commission, BKL.1207, October 1977, rev. August 1979, prepared by L. Larkin, W. Frontiero, and S. Ofenstein.
26. Vincent J. Scully, Jr., *The Shingle Style and the Stick Style,* rev. ed. (New Haven, CT: Yale University Press, 1971). He did not discuss the John Charles Phillips House nor the Moses Williams House.
27. The Thayer House was illustrated in *American Architect and Building News* 24, no. 659 (August 11, 1888) (imperial edition): n.p. It also appeared in Edward Everett Hale, "Picturesque Massachusetts," in *Picturesque and Architectural New England,* vol. 2 (Boston: D. H. Hurd, 1899), 91–92.
28. Photographs of the house are held by Historic New England, Library and Archives, Boston, Soule Art Company collection. See also Meister, *Arts and Crafts Architecture,* 138–39.
29. The Museum of Fine Arts, Boston, was then located on Copley Square in a building designed by Sturgis and Brigham, dating from 1876. Because Walker was training at the firm during the mid-1870s, he may have met Robinson through his work.
30. See *American Architect and Building News* 39, no. 898 (March 11, 1893): n.p., with an illustration.
31. James L. Yarnall, *Newport through Its Architecture* (Hanover, NH: University Press of New England, 2005), 124–27. See also Margaret Stavridi, *Master of Glass: Charles Eamer Kempe, 1837–1907* (Hatfield, UK: John Taylor for the Kempe Society, 1988).
32. Robinson, *Peabody and Stearns,* 60–63.
33. Ralph Adams Cram, *Church Building: A Study of the Principles of Architecture in Their Relation to the Church* (Boston: Small, Maynard, 1901), 220.
34. On Vaughan, see William Morgan, *The Almighty Wall: The Architecture of Henry Vaughan* (New York: Architectural History

Foundation; Cambridge, MA: MIT Press, 1983). Morgan discusses the chapel (89–100).

35. For a discussion of church design and the craft workers involved, see Meister, *Arts and Crafts Architecture,* 122–25. See also *American Architect and Building News* 37, no. 868 (August 13, 1892): n.p.; and Douglass Shand-Tucci, *Built in Boston: City and Suburb, 1800–2000,* rev. ed. (Amherst: University of Massachusetts Press, 1999), 155–81.
36. Meister, *Arts and Crafts Architecture,* 96–98; Scully, *Shingle Style,* 19–33. Brandt also discusses the relationship between the Colonial Revival and Boston's Arts and Crafts movement.
37. Meister, *Arts and Crafts Architecture,* 154–56. See also Margaret Henderson Floyd, *Architecture after Richardson: Regionalism before Modernism—Longfellow, Alden, and Harlow in Boston and Pittsburgh* (Chicago: University of Chicago Press, with Pittsburgh History and Landmarks Foundation, 1994), 103–9.
38. The John C. Schwab House was published in *American Architect and Building News* 53, no. 1080 (September 5, 1896): n.p.
39. Sturgis delivered a paper titled "Our Wooden Suburbs." See William D. Austin, "A History of the Boston Society of Architects in the 19th Century," 3 vols., manuscript, 1942, Boston Athenaeum, vol. 3, ch. 17, p. 4.
40. *American Architect and Building News* 63, no. 1212 (March 18, 1899): 88. See also illustrations in *American Architect* 66, no. 1243 (October 21, 1899): n.p.
41. See entry by Maureen Meister on the Thomas Dreier House, Snug Gables and Enclosing Fence, in *Drawing toward Home: Designs for Domestic Architecture from Historic New England,* ed. James F. O'Gorman (Boston: Historic New England, 2010), 172–73, 231. Construction drawings for the house and garden are held by Historic New England, Library and Archives.
42. Frank Chouteau Brown, "A House for Work and Play," *Country Life* 44, no. 4 (August 1923): 40–42.
43. Frank Chouteau Brown, *Modern English Country Houses* (Cleveland: J. H. Jansen, 1923).
44. Brown's membership in the Society of Arts and Crafts is first listed in the 1899 exhibition catalogue and continues in annual reports through 1908, all held by Boston Public Library, Fine Arts Department, Society of Arts and Crafts Archives, Early Documents, 1897–1927, box 1.
45. On Warren's Harvard lectures, see Meister, *Architecture and the Arts and Crafts Movement,* 74. See also Ralph Adams Cram, *Church Building;* Cram, *English Country Churches* (Boston: Bates and Guild, 1898); Cram, *The Ruined Abbeys of Great Britain* (New York: J. Pott, 1905); C. Howard Walker, *Parish Churches of England* (Boston: Rogers and Monson, 1905).
46. Frank Chouteau Brown, *Modern English Churches* (Cleveland: J. H. Jansen, 1923).
47. For more extensive discussion on the chapel, see Meister, *Architecture and the Arts and Crafts Movement,* 110–15; and Meister, *Arts and Crafts Architecture,* 127–29. When published, it was attributed to Warren, Smith, and Biscoe. See, for example, *American Architect and Building News* 65, no. 1231 (July 29, 1899): n.p. Payment records for the chapel are held by Historic New England, Library and Archives, "Architecture—Building accounts, bills, etc.," box 1.
48. On Cram, see Douglass Shand-Tucci, *Boston Bohemia 1881–1900: Ralph Adams Cram, Life and Architecture* (Amherst: University of Massachusetts Press, 1995); Shand-Tucci, *Ralph Adams Cram: An Architect's Four Quests* (Amherst: University of Massachusetts Press, 2005).
49. Economy Manufacturing Company's work at St. James, Woodstock, Vermont, is noted in an advertisement in *Christian Art* 4, no. 2 (November 1908): iv. See also *Some Examples of the Recent Use of Concrete Stone* (New Haven, CT: Economy Manufacturing, 1907), n.p., which identifies work by Lee Lawrie.
50. John G. Doll, *Heart of the Hilltop* (Newport, RI: St. George's School, 2003); Shand-Tucci, *Ralph Adams Cram,* 235–37; Meister, *Arts and Crafts Architecture,* 136–37.
51. Alan Priest, introduction to *The Sculpture of Joseph Coletti* (New York: Macmillan, 1968).
52. Transcript titled "Oral history interview with Andrew Dreselly," June 26, 1981 (updated March 28, 2013), Archives of American Art, Smithsonian Institution.
53. See Sturgis's tribute to John Stewardson, *Twenty-Fifth Anniversary Report of the Secretary of the Class of 1881 of Harvard College* (Cambridge, MA: Riverside, 1906), 203–4; Ralph Adams Cram, "American University Architecture," in *The Ministry of Art* (Boston: Houghton Mifflin, 1914), 193.
54. David R. Dunigan, *A History of Boston College* (Milwaukee: Bruce, 1947); Donna M. Cassidy, "The Collegiate Gothic Designs of Maginnis and Walsh," *Studies in Medievalism* 3, no. 2 (Fall 1990): 153–85; "The Recitation Building of Boston College, Newton, Mass.," *American Architect* 105, no. 1986 (January 14, 1914): 12–14.
55. John Evans Collection, Fine Arts Department, Boston Public Library, "Sketchbook/Record Book 1910–14," May 10, 1911; Dunigan, *History of Boston College,* 199.
56. This subject is discussed further in Meister, *Arts and Crafts Architecture,* 147–53.
57. See Vera Kreilkamp, ed., *The Irish Arts and Crafts Movement: Making It Irish,* exh. cat. (Chestnut Hill, MA: McMullen Museum of Art, Boston College, 2016), 73–151.
58. For more on the relationship between the Arts and Crafts movement based in Boston and the Colonial Revival, see Meister, *Arts and Crafts Architecture,* 154–78.
59. "Dedication of William Fogg Memorial Library at Eliot—Address by Ex-Mayor Baxter of Portland," *Portland Press,* May 23, 1907; Gail Willis Libby, "The History of Libraries in Eliot," unpublished manuscript, 1957, both William Fogg Library, Eliot, Maine, History of the Fogg Library collection, binder 7.
60. See "Beech Hill Summer Home District," National Register of Historic Places, NR 86003079, listed January 14, 1988, prepared by Lucinda A. Brockway. See also Institute Archives and Special Collections, MIT, Cambridge, Massachusetts, Howe, Manning, and Almy Papers, box 9.
61. Doris Cole and Karen C. Taylor discuss the house briefly in *The Lady Architects: Lois Lilley Howe, Eleanor Manning, and Mary Almy: 1893–1937* (New York: Midmarch Arts, 1990), 35.
62. *Bulletin of the Society for the Preservation of New England Antiquities* 4, no. 1 (August 1913): 33–36. The society is known today as Historic New England.
63. *Bulletin of the Society for the Preservation of New England Antiquities* 3, no. 1 (March 1912): 9–11.
64. On the firm's work at Proctor Academy, see Meister, *Architecture and the Arts and Crafts Movement,* 136–39. See also *Proctor Academy Catalogue* (1909–10), held by Proctor Academy, Andover, New Hampshire. Early photographs of work by Warren and Smith at Proctor Academy are held by Historic New England, Library and Archives. The Slocumb name was spelled Slocomb when the project was undertaken.
65. For the Warren House, see Meister, *Architecture and the Arts and Crafts Movement,* 122–28. Photographs of the house are held by Historic New England, Library and Archives.

66. See "Maginnis, Charles Donagh House," Massachusetts Historical Commission, BKL.1006, April 1980, prepared by Carla Benka.
67. Elizabeth Maginnis, daughter of the architect, identified the maker of the iron to the current owners of the house. Irving and Casson provided the woodwork.

CHAPTER 2. EMPIRE STATEMENTS

1. The interest in French Beaux-Arts architecture is described in *A History of Real Estate, Building, and Architecture in New York City during the Last Quarter of a Century* (New York: Record and Guide, 1898). Within this, see "A Review of Architecture," 612, which reports that since 1893, new buildings had reflected "the importation of the Academic Beaux-Arts manner, which is now the latest mode in architecture."
2. Amelia Peck and Carol Irish, *Candace Wheeler: The Art and Enterprise of American Design, 1875–1900,* exh. cat. (New York: Metropolitan Museum of Art, 2001).
3. Max West, "Revival of Handicrafts in America," ed. Carroll D. Wright, *Bulletin of the Bureau of Labor,* no. 54 (September 1904): 1606–7.
4. Florence N. Levy, ed., *American Art Annual,* vol. 11 (New York: American Federation of Arts, 1914), 246–47.
5. Levy, *American Art Annual,* 205.
6. *Catalogue of the Third Annual Exhibition of the Architectural League of New York* (New York: Architectural League of New York, 1887), 20 (on entries lent by Norton).
7. *The Architectural League of New York Illustrated Catalogue of the Twelfth Annual Exhibition* (New York: Knickerbocker, 1897).
8. "Pioneer of the Overall Industry Dies," *Clothing Designer and Manufacturer* 12, no. 1 (October 1917): 73, 85.
9. Suzanne Stephens, "The Formative Years," *Architectural Record* 204, no. 1 (January 1, 2016): 44–45.
10. A Classic [Montgomery Schuyler], "A Long-Felt Want," *Architectural Record* 7, no. 1 (September 1897): 118–20.
11. *Architectural Record* 12 (May–December 1902).
12. Harry W. Desmond and Herbert Croly, *The Stately Homes in America from Colonial Times to the Present Day* (New York: D. Appleton, 1903), 241.
13. Elmer Grey, "The Architect and the 'Arts and Crafts,'" *Architectural Record* 21, no. 8 (February 1907): 131–34.
14. See, for example, the index to *Architectural Record* 32 (July–December 1912).
15. For an authoritative survey of the city's architecture, see Andrew S. Dolkart and Matthew A. Postal, *Guide to New York City Landmarks,* 4th ed., ed. Matthew A. Postal (New York: New York Landmarks Preservation Commission, 2009).
16. Sandra Bloodworth and William Ayres, *New York's Underground Art Museum: MTA Arts and Design* (New York: Metropolitan Transit Authority and Monacelli, 2014), 13–15.
17. Janet Adams, "Heins and La Farge," in *Grove Encyclopedia American Art,* ed. Joan M. Marter, vol. 2 (New York: Oxford University Press, 2011), 486.
18. See the Grueby and Rookwood advertisements in *Sweet's Indexed Catalogue of Building Construction* (New York: Architectural Record, 1906), 363, 368–70; and *Sweet's Indexed Catalogue of Building Construction* (New York: Architectural Record, 1909), 115, 128.
19. One early example is a brick manufacturing building at 168 Duane Street (1886–87), designed by Stephen Decatur Hatch, mentioned in Dolkart and Postal, *Guide to New York City Landmarks,* 21. For a relevant study, but not on architecture, see Kathleen Eagen Johnson, "Frans Hals to Windmills: The Arts and Crafts Fascination with the Culture of the Low Countries," in *The Substance of Style: Perspectives on the American Arts and Crafts Movement,* ed. Bert Denker (Winterthur, DE: Henry Francis du Pont Winterthur Museum, 1996), 47–67.
20. See Dolkart and Postal, *Guide to New York City Landmarks,* 283 (for Fire Engine Company 253 [originally 53], Bensonhurst) and 275 (Fire Engine Company 252 [originally 52], Bushwick).
21. On Cram and St. Thomas, see Shand-Tucci, *Ralph Adams Cram,* 84–89. On Goodhue, see Richard Oliver, *Bertram Grosvenor Goodhue* (New York: Architectural History Foundation; Cambridge, MA: MIT Press, 1983), 61–75.
22. Ralph Adams Cram, *My Life in Architecture* (Boston: Little Brown, 1936), 115, 114–17 (on St. Thomas). See also Shand-Tucci, *Ralph Adams Cram,* 83–89.
23. Cram, *My Life in Architecture,* 116.
24. Montgomery Schuyler, "The Works of Cram, Goodhue, and Ferguson," *Architectural Record* 29, no. 1 (January 1911): 72.
25. Schuyler, "Works of Cram, Goodhue, and Ferguson," 46.
26. See the annual reports for the Society of Arts and Crafts, Boston, held by the Boston Public Library. Goodhue is listed as a member through the 1917 report.
27. "St. Thomas' Church," *Architecture and Building* 52, no. 4 (April 1920): 44, plates 40, 41.
28. Julie L. Sloan, *The Windows of St. Thomas Church* (North Adams, MA: n.p., 2018).
29. For a discussion of these two traditions and the country house, see Mark Alan Hewitt, *The Architect and the American Country House* (New Haven, CT: Yale University Press, 1990).
30. On Lindeberg, see Peter Pennoyer and Anne Walker, *Harrie T. Lindeberg and the American Country House* (New York: Monacelli, 2017). See also Royal T. Cortissoz, introduction to H. T. Lindeberg, *Domestic Architecture of H. T. Lindeberg,* with new introduction by Mark Alan Hewitt (1940; repr., New York: Acanthus, 1996).
31. "A Thatched Palace: An Estate at Pocantico Hills," *Architectural Record* 28, no. 5 (November 1910): 315–28.
32. "Thatched Palace."
33. Horace Allison, "English Cottage Types in America," *Country Life in America* 20, no. 11 (October 1, 1911): 39–42.
34. For an introduction to the Tudor Revival house, see Kevin Murphy, *The Tudor Home* (New York: Rizzoli, 2015).
35. On the John E. Aldred estate, Ormston, see "Aldred, John E., Estate," National Register of Historic Places, NR 79001594, listed August 3, 1979, prepared by Terry Winters. See also Oliver, *Bertram Grosvenor Goodhue,* 102–4; Robert MacKay et al., *Long Island Country Houses and Their Architects, 1860–1940* (New York: Society for the Preservation of Long Island Antiquities, in association with W. W. Norton, 1997), 193–97; Romy Wyllie, *Bertram Goodhue: His Life and Residential Architecture* (New York: W. W. Norton, 2007), 62–67, 86–88.
36. Lawrence Sommer, "Kitchi Gammi Club," Society of Architectural Historians: SAH Archipedia, https://sah-archipedia.org/buildings/MN-01-137-0025.
37. For the history of Forest Hills Gardens, see Susan L. Klaus, *A Modern Arcadia: Frederick Law Olmsted Jr. and the Plan for Forest Hills Gardens* (Amherst: University of Massachusetts Press, in association with Library of American Landscape History, 2002).
38. These were the goals stated in 1908 by Robert de Forest of the Russell Sage Foundation, quoted by Klaus, *Modern Arcadia,* 31.
39. On Atterbury, see Peter Pennoyer and Anne Walker, *The Architecture of Grosvenor Atterbury* (New York: W. W. Norton, 2009).

40. *Year Book of the Architectural League of New York and Catalogue of the Twenty-Sixth Annual Exhibition* (New York: Architectural League of New York, 1911), n.p.
41. From "The Sage Foundation Property at Forest Hills Gardens, Forest Hills, Long Island," in Samuel Howe, *American Country Houses of Today* (New York: Architectural Book Publishing, 1915), 412.
42. Klaus, *Modern Arcadia,* 127, and illustration on 122.
43. On the Roycroft campus, see "Roycroft Campus," National Register of Historic Places, NR 74001236, listed November 8, 1974, prepared by C. E. Brooke, revised form prepared by Carolyn Pitts, July 1985; Jack Quinan, "Elbert Hubbard's Roycroft," in *Head, Heart, and Hand: Elbert Hubbard and the Roycrofters,* ed. Marie Via and Marjorie Searl (Rochester, NY: University of Rochester Press, 1994), 1–19; and Robert Rust and Kitty Turgeon, *The Roycroft Campus* (Charleston, SC: Arcadia, 2013). On Hubbard and the artisans he attracted, see Brandon K. Ruud, "'To Promote and to Extend the Principles Established by Morris': Elbert Hubbard, Gustav Stickley, and the Redefinition of American Arts and Crafts," in *Apostles of Beauty: Arts and Crafts from Britain to Chicago,* exh. cat., ed. Judith A. Barter (Chicago: Art Institute of Chicago, 2009), 83–118.
44. *East Aurora (NY) Advertiser,* January 20, 1898.
45. Rust and Turgeon, *Roycroft Campus,* 71.
46. Buffalo's most impressive Tudor houses include the John J. Albright mansion (1904), designed by E. B. Green, and the Annie Lang Miller House (1929), designed by Duane Lyman. The Albright House has been demolished.
47. Today the Unitarian Universalist Church of Buffalo. For illustrations, see "Unitarian Church, Buffalo, N.Y.," *Brickbuilder* 18, no. 1 (January 1909): 7.
48. For Edward Austin Kent, see Ellicott R. Colson, "Edward A. Kent, FAIA," *Bulletin of the American Institute of Architects* 13, no. 1 (April 1912): 46–47. For William Winthrop Kent, see *Catalogue of the Delta Kappa Epsilon Fraternity* (New York: Delta Kappa Epsilon Council, 1910), 497.
49. "Our Illustrations," *Inland Architect and News Record* 48, no. 5 (December 1906): 60.
50. Jack Quinan, *Frank Lloyd Wright's Martin House: Architecture as Portraiture* (New York: Princeton Architectural Press, 2004).
51. Frank Lloyd Wright, "In the Cause of Architecture," *Architectural Record* 23, no. 3 (March 1908): 163. The Martin House is illustrated on pages 198–207.
52. David A. Hanks, *The Decorative Designs of Frank Lloyd Wright,* with new preface (1979; repr., Mineola, NY: Dover, 1999). See also Eric Jackson-Forsberg, ed., *Frank Lloyd Wright: Art Glass of the Martin House Complex* (Petaluma, CA: Pomegranate, 2009).
53. The other three founders of the Rochester Arts and Crafts Society were M. Louise Stowell, John E. Dumont, and Thillman P. J. Fabry. On the founding of the Rochester Arts and Crafts Society and Ellis, see Eileen Manning Michels, *Reconfiguring Harvey Ellis* (Minneapolis: Beaver's Pond, 2004).
54. *Rochester Arts and Crafts Society: Exhibition Catalogue* (Rochester, NY: Rochester Arts and Crafts Society, May 24, 1897), Memorial Art Gallery of the University of Rochester Archives, Rochester, New York.
55. Claude Bragdon, "Harvey Ellis: A Portrait Sketch," *Architectural Review* (Boston) 15, no. 12 (December 1908): 176.
56. Bragdon, "Harvey Ellis," 175.
57. On Ellis's life, see Michels, *Reconfiguring Harvey Ellis.*
58. On Bragdon's life and theoretical views about design, see Jonathan Massey, *Crystal and Arabesque: Claude Bragdon, Ornament, and Modern Architecture* (Pittsburgh: University of Pittsburgh Press, 2009). See also Eugenia Victoria Ellis and Andrea G. Reithmayr, eds., *Claude Bragdon and the Beautiful Necessity,* exh. cat. (Rochester, NY: RIT Cary Graphic Arts, 2010).
59. From the essay by R. W. E. [Ralph Waldo Emerson], "Beauty," in *The Conduct of Life* (Boston: Ticknor and Fields, 1860), 266.
60. See Claude Bragdon, "An Architect's House," *Good Housekeeping,* May 1904, 484–88.
61. For attribution of the andirons design to Bragdon, see "May Bragdon Diaries," Rare Books, Special Collections, and Preservation, Rush Rhees Library, University of Rochester, New York, photo dated October 16, 1903.
62. Claude Bragdon, *Projective Ornament* (Rochester, NY: Manas, 1915).
63. For an overview of Stickley's career, see David Cathers, *Gustav Stickley* (London: Phaidon, 2003). See also Ruud, "'To Promote and to Extend,'" 94–105.
64. "Henry Wilkinson Buried," *New York Times,* December 9, 1931, 25.
65. The *Boston Directory* (Boston: George Adams, 1891), 1393, lists Wilkinson's office at 122 Ames Building, next door to Shepley, Rutan, and Coolidge, listed at 121 Ames Building. In the 1892 *Boston Directory* (Boston: George Adams, 1892), 1437, Wilkinson lists himself as "removed to New York City."
66. *Boston Architectural Club Exhibition* (Boston: Boston Society of Architects and Boston Architectural Club, 1891), 19, lists "Henry W. Wilkinson" as a member.
67. See "Stickley, Gustav, House," National Register of Historic Places, NR 84002820, listed August 23, 1984, prepared by John F. Harwood. See also Samuel Howe, "A Visit to the House of Mr. Stickley," *The Craftsman* 3, no. 3 (December 1902): 161–69.
68. Howe, "Visit to the House of Mr. Stickley," 161.
69. Cleota Reed, "Gustav Stickley and Irene Sargent: United Crafts and *The Craftsman,*" *The Courier* 30 (1995): 35–50 (published by Syracuse University Library Associates).
70. See Ray Stubblebine, *Stickley's Craftsman Homes: Plans, Drawings, Photographs* (Layton, UT: Gibbs Smith, 2002). See also Beverly Brandt, "The Paradox of The Craftsman Home," in *Gustav Stickley and the American Arts and Crafts Movement,* exh. cat., by Kevin W. Tucker et al. (Dallas: Dallas Museum of Art, 2010), 66–79.
71. Edward Hale Brush, "A Garden City for the Man of Moderate Means," *The Craftsman* 19, no. 5 (February 1911): 445–51; Bertram Goodhue, "The Home of the Future," *The Craftsman* 29, no. 5 (February 1916): 449–55, 543–44; H. T. Lindeberg, "The Home of the Future," *The Craftsman* 29, no. 6 (March 1916): 602–13, 675–77.
72. On Four Winds and Adelaide Alsop Robineau, see Louise Shrimpton, "An Art Potter and Her Home," *Good Housekeeping,* January 1910, 57–63; and Grace Wickham Curran, "An American Potter, Her Home and Studio," *American Homes and Gardens,* September 1910, 364–66.
73. For biographical sketches of Katharine Cotheal Budd, see Gary Lawrance and Anne Surchin, *Houses of the Hamptons, 1880–1930* (New York: Acanthus, 2007), 322; and Sarah Allaback, *The First Women Architects* (Urbana: University of Illinois Press, 2008), 57.
74. Shrimpton, "Art Potter and Her Home," 63.
75. Curran, "American Potter," 365.
76. On various topics relating to Byrdcliffe, see Nancy E. Green, ed., *Byrdcliffe: An American Arts and Crafts Colony,* exh. cat. (Ithaca, NY: Herbert F. Johnson Museum of Art, Cornell University, 2004), esp. Tom Wolf, "Byrdcliffe's History" (16–35). See also "Byrdcliffe Historic District," National Register of Historic Places, NR 79001643, listed May 7, 1979, prepared by L. Corwin Sharp.

77. On the influence of Ruskin, see Cheryl Robertson, "Nature and Artifice in the Architecture of Byrdcliffe," in Green, *Byrdcliffe,* 120–59.
78. Architectural drawings for Byrdcliffe's buildings are in Col. 209, "Byrdcliffe (Art Colony) records," Winterthur Library, Henry Francis du Pont Winterthur Museum, Winterthur, Delaware.
79. Discussed and illustrated in Robertson, "Nature and Artifice," 120–25.
80. Poultney Bigelow, "The Byrdcliffe Colony of Arts and Crafts," *American Homes and Gardens,* October 1909, 393.

CHAPTER 3. VISIONARIES IN THE MID-ATLANTIC

1. "Joy Wheeler Dow, 1860–1937," *Thistle* 7, no. 1 (October 1982): 3–6 (newsletter of Millburn-Short Hills Historical Society); Sandy Brown Hamingson, "Joy Wheeler Dow," *Encyclopedia of New Jersey,* ed. Maxine N. Lurie and Marc Mappen (New Brunswick, NJ: Rutgers University Press, 2004), 216.
2. Joy Wheeler Dow, *American Renaissance: A Review of Domestic Architecture* (New York: William T. Comstock, 1904), 95.
3. Dow, *American Renaissance,* 42.
4. Dow, *American Renaissance,* 38.
5. Dow, *American Renaissance,* 151.
6. Joy Wheeler Dow, "The Sparrow House and the Rabbit House," *American Architect* 115, no. 2259 (April 9, 1919): 505–10. See also "Rabbit House," entry 95, in T Square Club and Philadelphia Chapter of the American Institute of Architects, *The Sixteenth Annual Architectural Exhibition,* exh. cat. (Philadelphia: Pennsylvania Academy of the Fine Arts, 1910).
7. Kornwolf, *M. H. Baillie Scott,* 435–36, 546–47. See also "House at Short Hills, N.J., by Baillie Scott," in *"The Studio" Year Book of Decorative Art* (London: The Studio, 1914): frontispiece; "The Close: Residence of Henry Binsse, Esq., at Short Hills, N.J.," *Country Life* (America) 39, no. 4 (February 1921): 68–69. Harold Tatton (1879–1965) was supervising architect while he was working for McKim, Mead & White in New York City.
8. See "Short Hills Park Historic District," National Register of Historic Places, NR 80002482, listed September 18, 1980, prepared by David Gibson and Associates.
9. Kornwolf, *M. H. Baillie Scott,* 312–13.
10. The most thorough study of Craftsman Farms is Mark Alan Hewitt, *Gustav Stickley's Craftsman Farms: The Quest for an Arts and Crafts Utopia* (Syracuse: Syracuse University Press, 2001).
11. Hewitt, *Gustav Stickley's Craftsman Farms,* 121–24.
12. Hewitt, *Gustav Stickley's Craftsman Farms,* 9–10.
13. "Distinguishing Features of Craftsman Houses," *Craftsman* 23, no. 6 (March 1913): 727.
14. "Distinguishing Features."
15. "Distinguishing Features," 728.
16. Turpin C. Bannister, ed., *The Architect at Mid-Century: Evolution and Achievement,* vol. 1 (New York: Reinhold, 1954), 96–99. Bannister provides opening years for the first architecture programs in the United States, beginning with MIT (1868); University of Illinois (1870); Cornell (1871); Syracuse (1873); and University of Pennsylvania (1874). By 1898 there were nine schools, including Columbia, Armour Institute of Technology (now Illinois Institute of Technology), and Harvard.
17. "Society Biographies: The Arts and Crafts Guild of Philadelphia," *Handicraft* 4, no. 2 (May 1911): 63–65.
18. For an early history, see "Philadelphia T-Square Club," *Inland Architect and News Record* 30, no. 2 (September 1897): 16–17.
19. *Catalogue of the T Square Club Architectural Exhibition, 1896–97,* exh. cat. (Philadelphia: T Square Club, 1897).
20. See *Exhibition by the Boston Architectural Club,* exh. cat. (Boston: Boston Architectural Club, 1897).
21. *Catalogue of the T Square Club Architectural Exhibition, 1896–97,* 48.
22. *Catalogue of the Annual Architectural Exhibition, 1899–1900,* exh. cat. (Philadelphia: T Square Club), 18, 22.
23. *Catalogue of the Thirteenth Annual Exhibition of Architecture and the Allied Arts, 1906–07,* exh. cat. (Philadelphia: T Square Club, 1907).
24. For a short modern biography of Eyre, see Hewitt, *Architect and the American Country House,* 272. Hewitt discusses Eyre's contribution to the Tudor Revival. See also Alfred Morton Githens, "Wilson Eyre, Jr., His Work," in *Architectural Annual,* ed. Albert Kelsey (Philadelphia: Architectural Annual for the American Institute of Architects, 1900), 121–84; Julian Millard, "The Work of Wilson Eyre," *Architectural Record* 14, no. 4 (October 1903): 279–320; John Harbeson, "Wilson Eyre," *AIA Journal* 5, no. 3 (March 1946): 129–35.
25. Wisteria, the Charles A. Newhall House, is included in "Chestnut Hill Historic District, Philadelphia," National Register of Historic Places, NR 85001334, listed June 20, 1985, prepared by Jefferson M. Moak. The Newhall House is included in George William Sheldon's *Artistic Country Seats: Types of Recent American Villa and Cottage Architecture* (New York: Appleton, 1886–87), plate 23. The house and plan are discussed and illustrated in Scully, *Shingle Style,* 121 and figs. 95 (garden elevation) and 96.
26. The Newhall House was illustrated without commentary in *Architecture* 2, no. 9 (September 15, 1900): 327.
27. *Architecture* 2, no. 9 (September 15, 1900): 345.
28. Wilson Eyre, "A House Expressing Domesticity," *Country Life in America* 24, no. 1 (May 1913): 35.
29. Edward Teitelman, "Wilson Eyre in Camden: The Henry Genet Taylor House and Office," *Winterthur Portfolio* 15, no. 3 (Autumn 1980): 229–55.
30. Kornwolf discusses Eyre frequently in the context of English Arts and Crafts architects. He calls Eyre "a forerunner of the Arts and Crafts in American architecture"; Kornwolf, *M. H. Baillie Scott,* 350.
31. Wilson Eyre, "The Development of American Dwelling Architecture during the Last Thirty Years," *Architectural Review,* n.s., 5, no. 11 (November 1917): 241.
32. Eyre, "American Dwelling Architecture," 243.
33. For biographical information on Price and a study of his career, see George E. Thomas, *William L. Price: Arts and Crafts to Modern Design* (New York: Princeton Architectural Press, 2000).
34. Thomas, *William L. Price,* 70. See also "Overbrook Farms," National Register of Historic Places, NR 85000690, listed March 21, 1985, prepared by Edith L. Willoughby et al.
35. On the Overbrook house, see Thomas, *William L. Price,* 70–71, 266–69, 349.
36. Thomas, *William L. Price,* 70.
37. Thomas, *William L. Price,* 50, 70–72.
38. Artisans were identified by owners of the house when it was listed for sale in 2019.
39. On Mellor and Meigs, see Harold D. Eberlein, "Examples of the Work of Mellor and Meigs," *Architectural Record* 39, no. 3 (March 1916): 212–46; and Hewitt, *Architect and the American Country House,* 198–206.
40. The Caspar Wistar Morris House is discussed by Eberlein, "Mellor and Meigs," 242, 246; Kornwolf, *M. H. Baillie Scott,* 353; and Hewitt, *Architect and the American Country House,* 203–6. See also "House for Caspar W. Morris, Esq., Haverford, Pa.," *Catalogue of the Twenty-Third Annual Architectural Exhibition,* exh. cat. (Philadelphia: Philadelphia Chapter of the AIA and T Square Club, 1917), 63.

41. Eberlein, "Mellor and Meigs," 242.
42. Eberlein, "Mellor and Meigs," 246.
43. "The T-Square Club of Philadelphia," in Kelsey, *Architectural Annual,* 283.
44. Millard, "Work of Wilson Eyre," 313–14; George B. Tatum, *Penn's Great Town: 250 Years of Philadelphia Architecture Illustrated in Prints and Drawings* (Philadelphia: University of Pennsylvania Press, 1961), 120 and fig. 128.
45. Tatum, *Penn's Great Town,* fig. 128.
46. Sheldon, *Artistic Country Seats,* plate 22.
47. See Millard, "Work of Wilson Eyre," 317–18, for the Leidy House, and pages 318–20 for the Jayne House.
48. Frank Miles Day, "Cogslea: The Home of Four Artists. A Modern Home and Studios Built on the Ruins of an Old Pennsylvania Farmhouse and Barn," *Country Life in America* 18, no. 3 (July 1910): 329–32. Photographs of the house, studio building, and gardens appear in *American Country Houses of Today* (New York: Architectural Book Publishing, 1912), illustrations 62–67. See also Bailey Van Hook, *Violet Oakley: An Artist's Life* (Newark: University of Delaware Press, 2016), 125–28.
49. H. C. W. [Herbert C. Wise], "Frank Miles Day," *Brickbuilder* 24, no. 12 (December 1915): 316.
50. Frank Miles Day, preface to *American Country Houses of Today* (1912), ii.
51. Frank Miles Day, "The Restoration of Congress Hall, Philadelphia," *Yearbook of the Twentieth Annual Architectural Exhibition,* exh. cat. (Philadelphia: Philadelphia Chapter of American Institute of Architects and T Square Club, 1914), 98–102.
52. The studio is illustrated in Day, "Cogslea," 332.
53. On Oakley's commissions to paint murals for the Pennsylvania capitol, see Van Hook, *Violet Oakley.* See also Patricia Likos Ricci, "Violet Oakley: American Renaissance Woman," *Pennsylvania Magazine of History and Biography* 126, no. 2 (April 2002): 217–48.
54. Van Hook, *Violet Oakley,* 196–98.
55. On Arden, see Thomas, *William L. Price,* 81–83.
56. On Rose Valley, see Thomas, *William L. Price,* 83–113, 355. See also "Rose Valley Historic District," National Register of Historic Places, NR 10000470, listed July 19, 2010, prepared by George E. Thomas.
57. Will Price, "The Relation of Arts and Crafts to Architecture," *The Artsman* 1, no. 11 (August 1904): 407–14.
58. Price, "Relation of Arts and Crafts," 408.
59. Price, "Relation of Arts and Crafts," 411.
60. Cleota Reed, *Henry Chapman Mercer and the Moravian Pottery and Tile Works* (Philadelphia: University of Pennsylvania Press, 1987).
61. One of Mercer's Harvard classmates was Arthur Astor Carey, second president of the Society of Arts and Crafts, Boston.
62. For more on Mercer and his relationship with the Society of Arts and Crafts, Boston, see Meister, *Architecture and the Arts and Crafts Movement.* The architect H. Langford Warren was among the first architects to specify Moravian tile, installed in the chancel of the New Church Theological School chapel (1899–1901), in Cambridge, Massachussetts; see Meister, *Architecture and the Arts and Crafts Movement,* 112.
63. On the pottery complex, see Reed, *Henry Chapman Mercer,* 49–57. See also Historic American Engineering Record, *Moravian Pottery and Tile Works* (Doylestown, PA: n.p., 1968), HAER PA, 9-DOYLT,V,8-; and "Moravian Pottery and Tile Works," National Register of Historic Places, NR 72001098, listed June 1, 1972, prepared by Pennsylvania Register of Historic Sites and Landmarks.
64. Linda F. Dyke describes how Mercer built similar concrete vaults at his home, Fonthill, in "Henry Mercer's Fonthill: An Arts and Crafts House in the 'Red House' Tradition," *Arts and Craft Quarterly* 7, no. 2 (August 1994): 16.
65. Reed, *Henry Chapman Mercer,* 72–74.
66. E. Bruce Glenn, *Bryn Athyn Cathedral: The Building of a Church* (Bryn Athyn, PA: Bryn Athyn Church of the New Jerusalem, 1971). See also Shelley K. Nickles, "The Bryn Athyn Cathedral Project: Craft, Community, and Faith," in Denker, *Substance of Style,* 397–414.
67. Glenn, *Bryn Athyn Cathedral,* relates his history from Raymond Pitcairn's perspective.
68. For Cram's version of the saga of building the cathedral, see Ralph Adams Cram, "A Note on Bryn Athyn Church," *American Architect* 113, no. 2214 (May 29, 1918): 709–12.
69. Cram, *My Life in Architecture,* 248.
70. Cram, "Note on Bryn Athyn Church," 712.
71. Cram, *My Life in Architecture,* 249.
72. Cram, *My Life in Architecture,* 249.
73. See George E. Thomas and David B. Brownlee, *Building America's First University* (Philadelphia: University of Pennsylvania Press, 2000), 90–91. Thomas writes that when C. R. Ashbee visited the Philadelphia area in 1900, he commented on the "Anglomania" of the region (91).
74. Montgomery Schuyler, "The Architecture of American Colleges. V. University of Pennsylvania, Girard, Haverford, Lehigh and Bryn Mawr Colleges," *Architectural Record* 28, no. 3 (September 1910): 182–212.
75. On Cope and Stewardson's Quadrangle Dormitories, see Thomas and Brownlee, *Building America's First University,* esp. 235–38.
76. "Grotesque Designs on Sculpted Bosses," *Monumental News* 12, no. 11 (November 1900): 619. Cope is the source who identifies the people who did the work.
77. Schuyler, "Architecture of American Colleges," 194.
78. Schuyler, "Architecture of American Colleges," 195.
79. Ralph Adams Cram, "The Work of Cope and Stewardson," *Architectural Record* 16, no. 5 (November 1904): 411.
80. Cram, "Work of Cope and Stewardson," 415.
81. The Carnegie Library and Music Hall were designed by Longfellow, Alden, and Harlow (1892–95); Alden and Harlow, as an independent firm, oversaw the museum (1899–1907). Cram designed the Calvary Episcopal Church (1906–7); Holy Rosary Church (1928); and East Liberty Presbyterian Church (1931–35). Goodhue designed the First Baptist Church (1910).
82. On Scheibler and his career, see Martin Aurand, *The Progressive Architecture of Frederick G. Scheibler, Jr.* (Pittsburgh: University of Pittsburgh Press, 1994).
83. Aurand, *Progressive Architecture,* 28–38.
84. For reliable overviews, see Franklin Toker, *Pittsburgh: An Urban Portrait* (University Park: Pennsylvania State University Press, 1986), 83–87; and Toker, *Buildings of Pittsburgh* (Chicago: Society of Architectural Historians and Center for American Places, 2007), 48–50. See also Anke Koeth, "Gothic with an American Accent: The Cathedral of Learning," in *Skyscraper Gothic: Medieval Style and Modernist Buildings,* ed. Kevin D. Murphy and Lisa Reilly (Charlottesville: University of Virginia Press, 2017), 157–82.
85. Charles Z. Klauder and Herbert C. Wise, *College Architecture in America—and Its Part in the Development of the Campus* (New York: Charles Scribner's Sons, 1929).
86. Albert M. Tannler, *Charles J. Connick: His Education and His Windows in and near Pittsburgh* (Pittsburgh: Pittsburgh History and Landmarks Foundation, 2008), 106–28.

CHAPTER 4. THE NEW SOUTH

1. See "Pinehurst Historic District," National Historic Landmark, NR 73001361, listed June 19, 1996, prepared by Davyd Foard Hood and Laura A. W. Phillips.

2. Early accounts of Pinehurst include B. A. Goodridge, "A New England Village in Southern Pines," *New England Magazine,* n.s., 15, no. 3 (November 1896): 321–36; and Harry Redan, "Pinehurst of Today," *New England Magazine,* n.s., 25, no. 2 (October 1901): 256–64.
3. Martha Lyon, "Pinehurst Village: Pinehurst, North Carolina," in *Warren H. Manning: Landscape Architect and Environmental Planner,* ed. Robin Karson, Jane Roy Brown, and Sarah Allaback (Amherst, MA: Library of American Landscape History; Athens: University of Georgia Press, 2017), 240–47.
4. Goodridge, "New England Village," 330.
5. Bertrand E. Taylor, "A Southern Village among the Pines," *Indoors and Out* 1, no. 4 (January 1906): 167–73.
6. Taylor was a charter member of the Boston Architectural Club and a member of the Boston Society of Architects. He is listed as a Craftsman member in *Annual Report of the Society of Arts and Crafts* (Boston: Society of Arts and Crafts, 1908) and *Annual Report of the Society of Arts and Crafts* (Boston: Society of Arts and Crafts, 1909).
7. "The Carolina: Its Welcome to the Twentieth Century," *Pinehurst Outlook* 4, no. 9 (January 4, 1901): 1.
8. Taylor, "Southern Village," 167, illustrates the cabin.
9. For observations about racial treatment at Pinehurst, see Richard J. Moss, *Eden in the Pines: A History of Pinehurst Village* (Pinehurst, NC: privately printed, 2014), esp. 20–21, 32, 72.
10. The best history of the Grove Park Inn is Bruce E. Johnson, *Built for the Ages: A History of the Grove Park Inn* (Asheville, NC: Grove Park Inn Resort and Spa, 2004). See also "Grove Park Inn," National Register of Historic Places, NR 73001295, listed April 3, 1973, prepared by Survey and Planning Unit Staff, NC Department of Archives and History.
11. A biography of G. W. McKibbin has been written by Kenneth H. Thomas, Jr., for *North Carolina Architects and Builders* (Raleigh, NC: NC State University Libraries, 2013), n.p.
12. On the Biltmore Industries, see Johnson, *Built for the Ages,* 55–59. See also "Biltmore Industries, Inc.," National Register of Historic Places, NR 80002802, listed February 1, 1980, prepared by Susanne Brendel-Pandich and Michael Southern.
13. Robert C. Broward, *The Architecture of Henry John Klutho: The Prairie School in Jacksonville* (Jacksonville: University of North Florida Press, 1983).
14. Broward, *Architecture of Henry John Klutho,* 52.
15. Broward, *Architecture of Henry John Klutho,* 125–52. See also Ennis Davis and Sarah Gojekian, *Cohen Brothers: The Big Store* (Charleston, SC: History Press, 2012), esp. 17–42.
16. "St. James Building," National Register of Historic Places, NR 76000594, listed May 3, 1976, prepared by Diane D. Greer. After a long decline, the building was restored and repurposed as Jacksonville City Hall in 1997.
17. Klutho's designs of ornament for the St. James Building are illustrated in a promotional brochure, *Conkling-Armstrong Terra Cotta Co.* (Philadelphia: Conkling-Armstrong Terra Cotta Company, 1914), plate 51. Examples of ornament designed by Philadelphia architect Frank Miles Day, cast by Conkling-Armstrong, also appear. Klutho's St. James Building, its ornament, and other projects by Klutho are illustrated in *Western Architect* 20, no. 6 (June 1914): n.p.
18. Broward, *Architecture of Henry John Klutho,* 85–94. "Klutho, Henry John, House," National Register of Historic Places, NR 78000939, listed December 19, 1978, prepared by Dan G. Deibler.
19. Kenneth Treister and David Price, *Bok Tower Gardens: America's Taj Mahal* (New York: Skira Rizzoli, 2013). See also "Mountain Lake Sanctuary and Singing Tower," National Historic Landmark, NR 72000350, listed April 19, 1993, prepared by Rebecca Spain Schwarz.
20. Treister and Price, *Bok Tower Gardens,* 53.
21. For profiles of the artisans, see Treister and Price, *Bok Tower Gardens,* 74–78.
22. Treister and Price refer to Negro Day as one of several "educational gatherings"; Treister and Price, *Bok Tower Gardens,* 108. See also the notice for Negro Day when carillonneur Anton Brees played at the Bok Singing Tower: *Sarasota Herald Tribune,* April 28, 1946, 4. It should be added that in the context of the era, sponsoring such a day was an enlightened gesture. Special thanks to Steven G. Noll and Lu Vickers for their insights on this aspect of segregation history.
23. Sarah J. Boykin and Susan M. Hunter, *Southern Homes and Plan Books: The Architectural Legacy of Leila Ross Wilburn* (Athens: University of Georgia Press, 2018). See also Jan Jennings, "Leila Ross Wilburn: Plan Book Architect," *Woman's Art Journal* 10, no. 1 (Spring–Summer 1989): 10–16; Willa Granger, "Ordering Arts and Crafts: Leila Ross Wilburn's Plan-Book Bungalows," in Penick and Long, *Rise of Everyday Design,* 173–77.
24. Leila Ross Wilburn, *Southern Homes and Bungalows* (Atlanta: n.p., 1914), 3.
25. Wilburn, *Southern Homes and Bungalows,* 3.
26. Leila Ross Wilburn, *Brick and Colonial Homes* (Atlanta: n.p., n.d); Boykin and Hunter, *Southern Homes and Plan Books,* 16, provide the 1921 publication date.
27. Wilburn, *Brick and Colonial Homes,* 39, identified as "No. 97." Boykin and Hunter, *Southern Homes and Plan Books,* 74–76, illustrate and discuss this house, but they don't date it or identify the original owner.
28. Michael W. Fazio, "A Lasting Impression: The Overstreet Legacy in Architecture," in *Overstreet and Overstreet: A Legacy in Architecture,* exh. cat. (Jackson: Mississippi Museum of Art, 1993).
29. "Belhaven Historic District," National Register of Historic Places, NR 12000920, listed December 19, 2012, prepared by David Preziosi. For the Overstreet House, see no. 305 (a).
30. The 1914 date for completion of the house was provided by Overstreet's granddaughter Theresa Younce.
31. "Rhodes Park Historic District," National Register of Historic Places, NR 82002043, listed April 15, 1982, prepared by Alice M. Bowsher.
32. "George H. Miller, Housing Designer," *New York Times,* May 18, 1943. On Miller, see also Marjorie L. White, *Altamont: A Portion of Red Mountain and Its Park* (Birmingham, AL: Birmingham Historical Society, 2020), 5, 9.
33. Miller is quoted by Ellen Cooper Erdreich, "Birmingham Craftsman: An Introduction," *Journal of the Birmingham Historical Society* 8, no. 1 (December 1983): 20.
34. Erdreich, "Birmingham Craftsman," 6–28, discusses Welton throughout her article.
35. Illustrations of "Two Designs for Churches," by William L. Welton, Lynn, Massachusetts, in *American Architect and Building News* 46, no. 984 (November 3, 1894): n.p.
36. "Bungalow for Mrs. W. L. Welton," Birmingham, Alabama, by Warren and Welton, Birmingham, in *American Architect and Building News* 95, no. 1746 (June 9, 1909): 188–89 and illustration.
37. Erdreich, "Birmingham Craftsman," 14.
38. Julie L. Sloan, "William A. Hazel: America's First Known Black Stained-Glass Artist," *Nineteenth Century* 43, no. 2 (Fall 2023): 10–19; Louise Daniel Hutchinson, "William Augustus Hazel, 1854–1929," in *African American Architects: A Biographical Dictionary, 1865–1945,* ed. Dreck Spurlock

Wilson (New York: Routledge, 2004), 195–97.

39. Very little has been written about the Willcox Trade Buildings. See Ellen Weiss, *Robert R. Taylor and Tuskegee: An African American Architect Designs for Booker T. Washington* (Montgomery, AL: New South, 2012), 73, 112, 181.
40. For an overview of the architecture of the campus, see Commonwealth Heritage Group [Laura L. Knott], "Historic Resource Study: Tuskegee Institute National Historic Site," Atlanta, Cultural Resources Division, Southeast Region, National Park Service, June 2019.
41. Weiss, *Robert R. Taylor and Tuskegee,* 181, reports that four of the five trade buildings were constructed with brick that was purchased.
42. Information on the Pottery Building runs through more broadly written histories of the pottery enterprise. See especially Sally Main, "Conscious Freedom: The Newcomb Pottery Enterprise," in *The Arts and Crafts of the Newcomb Pottery,* exh. cat., ed. David H. Conradsen (New York: Skira Rizzoli, 2013), 39–67; Jessie Poesch, "The Art Program at Newcomb College and the Newcomb Potter, 1886–1940," in *Newcomb College, 1886–2006: Higher Education for Women in New Orleans,* ed. Susan Tucker and Beth Willinger (Baton Rouge: Louisiana State University Press, 2012), 164–79; and Poesch, *Newcomb Pottery: An Enterprise for Southern Women, 1895–1940,* exh. cat. (Exton, PA: Schiffer, 1984).
43. Wilson Eyre also designed the Sophie Newcomb Memorial College Chapel (1894–95). Both the chapel and art building have been demolished.
44. "N.O. Architect Taken by Death," obituary for Rathbone DeBuys, *New Orleans Times-Picayune,* June 28, 1960.
45. Oliver Coleman, "Notes and Comments," *House Beautiful,* July 1902, 110. See also the illustration and plans, "Pottery Building, Newcomb College," New Orleans, by Rathbone E. du Buys [*sic*], in *American Architect* 96, no. 1759 (September 8, 1909): n.p.
46. DeBuys quoted in Coleman, "Notes and Comments," 110.
47. "N.O. Architect Taken by Death."
48. "Great Southern Lumber Company. Bogalusa, Louisiana." Map of Bogalusa, Louisiana (c. 1911), "Bickham, H. D." Martin Shepard Office Records, Southeastern Architectural Archive, Collections Division, Tulane University Archives, New Orleans.

CHAPTER 5. BIG SHOULDERS IN CHICAGO

1. On Chicago and the Arts and Crafts movement, see Judith A. Barter and Monica Obniski, "Chicago: A Bridge to the Future," in Barter, *Apostles of Beauty,* 151–88.
2. Florence Boos, "The First Morris Society: Chicago, 1903–1905," *Journal of the William Morris Society* 21, no. 1 (Winter 2014): 35–48.
3. "The Chicago Arts and Crafts Society, Formed at Hull-House" (Chicago: Hull-House, 1898), in *Catalogue of the Eleventh Annual Exhibition of the Chicago Architectural Club* (Chicago: Art Institute of Chicago, 1898), 119–21. Founding architects also included Myron Hunt and Dwight Perkins.
4. "Chicago Arts and Crafts Society."
5. "Chicago Arts and Crafts Society," 118.
6. On the Industrial Art League and Oscar Lovell Triggs, see Barter and Obniski, "Chicago: A Bridge to the Future," 156–58.
7. Boos, "First Morris Society," 36–37.
8. H. Allen Brooks, "Chicago Architecture: Its Debt to the Arts and Crafts," *Journal of the Society of Architectural Historians* 30, no. 4 (December 1971): 312–17.
9. The influence of the Abingdon Abbey photo is discussed at length by Thomas C. Hubka, "H. H. Richardson's Glessner House: A Garden in the Machine," *Winterthur Portfolio* 24, no. 4 (Winter 1989): 209–29. See also Mary Alice Malloy, "Richardson's Web: A Client's Assessment of the Architect's Home and Studio," *Journal of the Society of Architectural Historians* 54, no. 1 (March 1995): 9; James F. O'Gorman, *Living Architecture: A Biography of H. H. Richardson* (New York: Simon and Schuster, 1997), 151.
10. William Tyre, "Mr. and Mrs. John J. Glessner Request the Pleasure . . . Dining with the Glessners in Gilded Age Chicago," *Nineteenth Century* 40, no. 2 (Fall 2020): 13–21.
11. A silver dish made by Frances Glessner is illustrated by Barter and Obniski, "Chicago: A Bridge to the Future," 160.
12. Allen B. Pond, "The Settlement House," *Brickbuilder* 11, no. 9 (September 1902): 178–85.
13. Jane Addams, *Twenty Years at Hull-House* (New York: Macmillan, 1910), 149.
14. Addams, *Twenty Years at Hull-House,* 151.
15. Addams, *Twenty Years at Hull-House,* 375.
16. Addams, *Twenty Years at Hull-House,* 376.
17. Guy Szuberla, "Three Chicago Settlements: Their Architectural Form and Social Meaning," *Journal of the Illinois State Historical Society* 70, no. 2 (May 1977): 114–29.
18. Fiske Kimball, "The Social Center: Philanthropic Enterprises," *Architectural Record* 45, no. 6 (June 1919): 528.
19. Kimball, "Social Center," 527.
20. On Shaw's Ragdale, see Virginia A. Greene, *The Architecture of Howard Van Doren Shaw* (Chicago: Chicago Review, 1998), 12–19, 60–61; and Stuart Cohen, *Inventing the New American House: Howard Van Doren Shaw, Architect* (New York: Monacelli, 2015), 33–41.
21. Greene, *Howard Van Doren Shaw,* 2–6.
22. Greene, *Howard Van Doren Shaw,* 15.
23. Irving K. Pond, "Howard Van Doren Shaw," *Pencil Points* 7, no. 6 (June 1926): 369.
24. James F. O'Gorman, *Three American Architects: Richardson, Sullivan, and Wright, 1865–1915* (Chicago: University of Chicago Press, 1991), 69–92; Lauren W. Weingarden, "Naturalized Naturalism: A Ruskinian Discourse on the Search for an American Style of Architecture," *Winterthur Portfolio* 24, no. 1 (Spring 1989): 43–68.
25. Richard Nickel and Aaron Siskind, with John Vinci and Ward Miller, *The Complete Architecture of Adler and Sullivan* (Chicago: Richard Nickel Committee, 2010), 303–23, 364, 384, 403, 412, 434.
26. "The New Schlesinger and Mayer Building, Chicago," *Brickbuilder* 12, no. 5 (May 1903): 101.
27. See O'Gorman, *Three American Architects;* Weingarden, "Naturalized Naturalism."
28. *The Industrial Art League* (Chicago: Industrial Art League, [1902]).
29. The quotation is a close rewording of what Morris said in his 1884 lecture "Art and Socialism," delivered in London and issued as a pamphlet.
30. Louis H. Sullivan, "What Is Architecture? A Study of the American People," *The Craftsman* 10, nos. 2–4 (May, June, and July 1906): 143–49, 352–58, 507–13.
31. Sullivan, "What Is Architecture?," 143, in a note from the editor.
32. Sullivan, "What Is Architecture?," 353.
33. Sullivan, "What Is Architecture?," 357.
34. Sullivan, "What Is Architecture?," 511.
35. Sullivan, "What Is Architecture?," 513.
36. Claude Bragdon, foreword to Louis H. Sullivan, *The Autobiography of an Idea* (New York: American Institute of Architects, 1924), n.p.
37. O'Gorman, *Three American Architects,* esp. 113–32; H. Allen Brooks, *The Prairie School: Frank Lloyd Wright and His Contemporaries* (Toronto: University of Toronto Press, 1972), 14–26, 78–87.
38. On Wright and the Arts and Crafts movement in Chicago, see Joseph M. Siry,

"Frank Lloyd Wright's 'The Art and Craft of the Machine': Text and Context," in *The Education of the Architect,* ed. Martha Pollak (Cambridge, MA: MIT Press, 1997), 3–36; and Cheryl Robertson, "Progressive Chicago: Frank Lloyd Wright and the Prairie School," in Livingstone and Parry, *International Arts and Crafts,* 164–81.

39. Frank Lloyd Wright, "A Home in a Prairie Town," *Ladies' Home Journal,* February 1901, 17.
40. Frank Lloyd Wright, "The Art and Craft of the Machine," *Catalogue of the Fourteenth Annual Exhibition of the Chicago Architectural Club* (Chicago: Chicago Architectural Club, 1901), n.p.
41. Donald Hoffmann, *Frank Lloyd Wright's Dana House* (Mineola, NY: Dover, 1996).
42. For a discussion and illustrations of the house, including its "conventionalized" decoration, see Wright, "In the Cause of Architecture," 155–221.
43. O'Gorman, *Three American Architects,* 127–30.
44. Cheryl Robertson, *Frank Lloyd Wright and George Mann Niedecken: Prairie School Collaborators,* exh. cat. (Milwaukee: Milwaukee Art Museum; Lexington, MA: Museum of Our National Heritage, 1999).
45. Brooks, *Prairie School,* 78–87.
46. Hoffmann, *Dana House,* 54.
47. Kornwolf, *M. H. Baillie Scott,* 117–18.
48. For information on Spencer, see Paul Kruty, "Wright, Spencer, and the Casement Window," *Winterthur Portfolio* 30, nos. 2/3 (Summer/Autumn 1995): 103–27; and Kruty, "Planning the Suburban House: Robert Spencer's Advice to Clients," *Nineteenth Century* 36, no. 1 (Spring 2016): 14–23.
49. Brooks, *Prairie School,* 195.
50. Kornwolf, *M. H. Baillie Scott,* 171, 371–77.
51. The Grepe House is discussed in Kruty, "Wright, Spencer," 107.
52. Brooks, *Prairie School,* 37–42.
53. Robert C. Spencer, Jr., "The Work of Frank Lloyd Wright," *Architectural Review* 7, no. 6 (June 1900): 62.
54. Brooks, *Prairie School,* 97–98. See also Douglas Kaarre, "Edward and Caroline McCready House," Historic Landmark Nomination Report, Oak Park, Illinois: Oak Park Historic Preservation Commission, designated March 15, 2010.
55. See Paul Kruty, "Walter Burley Griffin: An Architect of America's Middle West," in *Walter Burley Griffin in America,* by Mati Maldre and Paul Kruty (Urbana: University of Illinois Press, 1996), 15–36.
56. Kruty, "Walter Burley Griffin," 19–20; Brooks, *Prairie School,* 72–76. See also "William H. Emery Jr. House," National Register of Historic Places, NR 04000421, listed May 12, 2004, prepared by Linda S. Von Dreele.
57. Robert C. Spencer, Jr., "Planning the House: Inside Finish," *House Beautiful,* July 1907, 31–32, 45. Additional photographs of the Emery House were published, without commentary, in "Recent Suburban Houses," *Architectural Record* 23, no. 6 (June 1908): 443, 486–87, 496, 499.
58. "Some Houses by Walter Burley Griffin," *Architectural Record* 28, no. 4 (October 1910): 307. The article is unsigned and may have been written by editor Harry W. Desmond.
59. Kruty, "Walter Burley Griffin," 18; Brooks, *Prairie School,* 79–80.
60. Hoffmann, *Dana House,* 81–85. The terra-cotta was cast by the company of William D. Gates (85n1). See also Alice T. Friedman, "Girl Talk: Feminism and Domestic Architecture at Frank Lloyd Wright's Oak Park Studio," in *Marion Mahony Reconsidered,* exh. cat., ed. David Van Zanten (Chicago: University of Chicago Press, 2011), 40.
61. Brooks, *Prairie School,* 86.
62. Kruty, "Walter Burley Griffin," 26, 178; Brooks, *Prairie School,* 149–53, 157–61.
63. The Adolph Mueller House was illustrated in Peter B. Wight, "Country House Architecture of the Middle West," *Architectural Record* 40, no. 4 (October 1916): 299–300. Credit for the design is given to "Von Holst and Fyfe, Architects, Marion M. Griffin, Associate," reflecting the contractual relationship.
64. Robertson, *Wright and Niedecken,* 39, 48, 107–8.
65. Robertson, *Wright and Niedecken,* 107–8.
66. See Mary Corbin Sies, "George W. Maher's Planning and Architecture in Kenilworth, Illinois: An Inquiry into the Ideology of Arts and Crafts Design," in Denker, *Substance of Style,* 415–45.
67. On Maher, see Sies, "George W. Maher," 424–26; Brooks, *Prairie School,* 33–34.
68. George W. Maher, "Truth in Design," *Inland Architect and News Record* 35, no. 1 (February 1900): 4.
69. George W. Maher, "The Western Spirit," *Inland Architect and News Record* 47, no. 3 (April 1906): 38.
70. Sies, "George W. Maher," 428–29.
71. See "Kenilworth Club," National Register of Historic Places, NR 79000832, listed March 21, 1979, prepared by Philip L. Pomerance. The hall was illustrated in *Inland Architect and News Record* 50, no. 4 (October 1907): n.p. See also Sies, "George W. Maher," 430–32; Brooks, *Prairie School,* 108–10.
72. For a comprehensive study, see Joseph M. Siry, *Unity Temple: Frank Lloyd Wright and Architecture for Liberal Religion* (Cambridge: Cambridge University Press, 1996). See also Neil Levine, *The Architecture of Frank Lloyd Wright* (Princeton, NJ: Princeton University Press, 1996), 40–46.
73. Siry, *Unity Temple,* 108.
74. C. R. Ashbee, "Man and the Machine: The Soul of Architecture, II," *House Beautiful,* July 1910, 56.
75. Ashbee, "Man and the Machine," 56.
76. Brooks, *Prairie School,* 82, writes that at Wright's studio, working drawings, specifications, and oversight of construction were handled by Barry Byrne. Siry, *Unity Temple,* 186, also mentions Byrne's role.
77. Siry, *Unity Temple,* 130, 150–54.
78. Siry, *Unity Temple,* 166–68, 187–88.
79. Oliver, *Bertram Grosvenor Goodhue,* 137–42.
80. Jean F. Block, *The Uses of Gothic: Planning and Building the Campus of the University of Chicago, 1892–1932,* exh. cat. (Chicago: University of Chicago Library, 1983), 152–61. See also Jean Guarino, *Rockefeller Memorial Chapel* (Chicago: Commission on Chicago Landmarks, 2004).
81. Block, *Uses of Gothic,* 156–57.
82. Rockefeller's directive is quoted in Block, *Uses of Gothic,* 250n1.
83. Guarino, *Rockefeller Memorial Chapel,* 11.
84. Construction was managed by Goodhue's associates, Mayers, Murray and Phillip.

CHAPTER 6. CROSSING THE HEARTLAND

1. See Helen Plumb, "The Pewabic Pottery," *Art and Progress* 2, no. 3 (January 1911): 63–67. See also "Pewabic Pottery," National Register of Historic Places, NR 71000430, listed September 3, 1971, prepared by Jim Schutze; "Pewabic Pottery," National Historic Landmark designation, listed December 4, 1991, prepared by Jill S. Topolski. For a comprehensive history, see Thomas W. Brunk, *Pewabic Pottery: The American Arts and Crafts Movement Expressed in Clay* (East Lansing: Michigan State University Press, 2021).
2. Marion L. Holden, "The Pewabic Pottery," *American Magazine of Art* 17, no. 1 (January 1926): 22.
3. Holden, "Pewabic Pottery," 22; also reported by Plumb, "Pewabic Pottery," 64.
4. Holden, "Pewabic Pottery," 26, wrote that the only duplication in the shop involved the tile stamp, "which is run by hand."

5. "Arts and Crafts Exhibit," *Bulletin of the Detroit Museum of Art* 1, no. 4 (October 1904): 4. In 1919 the museum became the Detroit Institute of Arts.
6. See *Arts and Crafts in Detroit, 1906–1976: The Movement, the Society, the School,* exh. cat. (Detroit: Detroit Institute of Arts, 1976), including Joy Hakanson Colby, "The Detroit Society of Arts and Crafts 1906–1976: An Introduction" (21–35). The Detroit Society of Arts and Crafts has evolved into the College for Creative Studies, Detroit.
7. See "Building of Arts and Crafts Society of Detroit, Michigan," *American Architect* 111, no. 2145 (January 31, 1917): 78–80, where its design is attributed to Smith, Hinchman, and Grylls and William B. Stratton. The building, which has been demolished, is illustrated with an exterior view by Thomas Holleman, "Arts and Crafts Architecture in Detroit," in *Arts and Crafts in Detroit,* 40. It also appears in Kathryn Bishop Eckert, *Buildings of Michigan,* rev. ed. (Charlottesville: University of Virginia Press, with the Society of Architectural Historians, 2012), 30.
8. On the architecture of Cranbrook and Cranbrook House, see Kathryn Bishop Eckert, *Cranbrook* (New York: Princeton Architectural Press, 2001), esp. 24–29.
9. This relationship was observed by Meister in *Architecture and the Arts and Crafts Movement,* 172n61.
10. Meister, *Architecture and the Arts and Crafts Movement,* 41–44, on the Scripps mortuary chapel.
11. Betsey Warren Davis, *The Warren, Jackson, and Allied Families: Being the Ancestry of Jesse Warren and Betsey Jackson* (Philadelphia: J. B. Lippincott, 1903), 18, 30, 41. Harriet (Messinger) Scripps and H. Langford Warren also were related through marriage to Denman W. Ross of Cambridge, Massachusetts. Like Warren, Ross was a founder of the Society of Arts and Crafts, Boston. See Davis, *Warren, Jackson, and Allied Families,* 34.
12. Warren visited James and Harriet Scripps in Detroit from October 23 through October 27, 1885, as recorded in diary entries by their daughter Ellen Scripps, later Ellen (Scripps) Booth. The entries were shared with me by Leslie Edwards, archivist, Cranbrook Archives and Cultural Properties, Bloomfield Hills, Michigan.
13. Ellen M. Dodington writes that Booth joined the Boston society in 1897 in *Cranbrook and the British Arts and Crafts Movement: George Booth's Legacy,* exh. booklet (Bloomfield Hills, MI: Cranbrook Art Museum, 2003), n.p.
14. *Catalogue of the Architectural Exhibition, Boston Architectural Club and Boston Society of Architects* (Boston: Boston Architectural Club and Boston Society of Architects, 1899), nos. 301 and 302.
15. "Arts and Crafts Exhibit." Kahn was also a member of the committee.
16. Eckert, *Cranbrook,* esp. 54–66.
17. Robert Judson Clark et al., *Design in America: The Cranbrook Vision, 1925–1950,* exh. cat. (Detroit: Detroit Institute of Arts, 1983).
18. Thomas A. Arbaugh, *Grosse Pointe Memorial Church, 1865–1990, Its History, Its Life* (Grosse Pointe Farms, MI: Grosse Pointe Memorial Church, 1991). Additional information appears in "Grosse Pointe Memorial Church," National Register of Historic Places, NR 93001351, listed December 6, 1993, prepared by Deborah M. Goldstein.
19. Lewis W. Simpson, an architect from Hunter's office, later said he handled the church design after Hunter developed the initial plans. See Goldstein, "Grosse Pointe Memorial Church."
20. Eckert, *Cranbrook,* 172; "Scarab Club," National Register of Historic Places, NR 79001176, listed November 20, 1979, prepared by Leslie J. Vollmert.
21. "Sukert to Design New Scarab Club Building," *Detroit Free Press,* January 30, 1927.
22. For a photograph of Colby and the modeled medallion before firing as well as a caption, see *Detroit Free Press,* February 13, 1928.
23. The Clarke Historical Library at Central Michigan University, Mount Pleasant, Michigan, owns a collection of catalogues of houses that the Aladdin Company sold.
24. See the cover of the 1908 catalogue, "Aladdin Knocked-Down Houses" (Bay City, MI).
25. See the spring 1909 catalogue, "Aladdin Houses" (Bay City, MI), 13–14.
26. See a 1914 catalogue, "Aladdin Houses: The New Home" (Bay City, MI), 32.
27. For the Ponds, see Brooks, *Prairie School,* 30; for Irving Pond, see R. Randall Vosbeck, *A Legacy of Leadership: The Presidents of the American Institute of Architects, 1857–2007* (Washington, DC: American Institute of Architects, 2008), 42–43.
28. Howard H. Peckham, *The Making of the University of Michigan, 1817–1992,* rev. and ed. by Margaret L. Steneck and Nicholas H. Steneck (Ann Arbor: University of Michigan, 1994), 120–36.
29. The purpose of a student union was to "minister broadly to the social and communal life of the college," wrote Irving K. Pond in "The College Union," *Architectural Forum* 54, no. 6 (June 1931): 771.
30. Klauder and Wise, *College Architecture in America,* 247, 243–60 (on student union buildings).
31. The University of Michigan's enrollment was surpassed only by Columbia and Chicago; Peckham, *Making of the University of Michigan,* 127.
32. Plans for the Michigan Union appear in Klauder and Wise, *College Architecture in America,* 252.
33. Irving Pond's tile designs are held by Bentley Historical Library, University of Michigan. See "Polychrome Ornament-Michigan Union," Pond Family Papers, HS 15486.
34. Michael Thomas Murphy was a member of the Art Workers' Guild, London, from 1895 to 1912. Prior to his work at Michigan, he carved the sculpture on Rosenwald Hall, University of Chicago, by Holabird and Roche, completed in 1915. He is listed as an exhibitor in *Catalogue of the Thirty-First Annual Exhibition of American Oil Paintings and Sculpture* (Chicago: Art Institute of Chicago, November 7, 1918–January 1, 1919), no. 225, with an address at 4 E. Ohio Street, Chicago.
35. Photographs of the Purdue Memorial Union appear in *Architectural Forum* 54, no. 6 (June 1931): 713–16.
36. Minutes of the Purdue University Board of Trustees, October 19–20, 1937, 852, Purdue University Archives and Special Collections, West Lafayette, Indiana.
37. Minutes of the Purdue University Board of Trustees, January 19, 1938, 106, Purdue University Archives and Special Collections, West Lafayette, Indiana.
38. The sculptor for the union at Michigan State was Samuel A. Cashwan. The commissions for sculpture for Kansas University and the Michigan League Building, University of Michigan, went to Nellie Verne Walker.
39. The window was donated by Alice Earl Stuart and dedicated to James A. Smart, Purdue president from 1883 to 1900.
40. Connick served as president of the Society of Arts and Crafts, Boston, from 1935 to 1939.
41. On the Arts and Crafts movement in Indianapolis, see *Traces of Indiana and Midwestern History* 6, no. 1 (Winter 1994), an issue devoted in its entirety to the topic, edited by Robert M. Taylor, Jr., and Barry Shifman.
42. Robert M. Taylor, Jr., and Barry Shifman, "Utility Embellished by Skilled Hands: The Arts and Crafts Movement in Indianapolis," in *Traces of Indiana,* 6.

43. Robert M. Taylor, Jr., "'Some Special Object': The Arts and Crafts Society of Indianapolis," in *Traces of Indiana*, 26.
44. Florence N. Levy, ed., *American Art Annual, 1907–1908*, vol. 6 (New York: American Federation of Arts, 1908), 173.
45. "Two Houses by Robert Spencer Jr.," *Architectural Record* 19, no. 4 (April 1906): 295–305. Labeled only as "The Adams House," the full name of the client was identified for me through research by Sharon Butsch Freeland of Indianapolis. The house has been demolished. It is illustrated and briefly discussed by Brooks, *Prairie School*, 60–61.
46. See "Women Rally Forces for Final Struggle: 'Equal Representation' Is Slogan for the Art Association Election Tonight," *Indianapolis News*, April 7, 1908. Rebecca Adams joined the agitators seeking equal representation in the Art Association. This article was shared with me by Sharon Butsch Freeland.
47. Robert C. Spencer, Jr., "Planning the House: Windows," *House Beautiful*, March 1906, 25; Spencer, "Planning the House: The Fireplace," *House Beautiful*, November 1905, 29.
48. For these periodicals, see notes 45 and 47.
49. "North Meridian Street Historic District," National Register of Historic Places, NR 86002695, listed September 22, 1986, prepared by Eric Utz and Suzanne Rollins.
50. Records of Rubush and Hunter are archived at the William Henry Smith Memorial Library, Indiana Historical Society, Indianapolis. The Scott Wadley House is now the Governor's Residence for the state of Indiana.
51. Marsha Weisiger, *Buildings of Wisconsin* (Charlottesville: University of Virginia Press, 2016), 37–38, 456–57. See also Cora Tuttle House, Madison, Dane County, in Wisconsin Architecture and History Inventory, Wisconsin Historical Society, Madison, WI, ref. no. 29115, surveyed 1989 and 2019.
52. See "Wingra Park Historic District," National Register of Historic Places, NR 99001257, listed October 14, 1999, prepared by Elizabeth L. Miller.
53. "Wingra Park Historic District."
54. On the original Taliesin house, studio, and farm buildings, see Ron McCrea, *Building Taliesin: Frank Lloyd Wright's Home of Love and Loss* (Madison: Wisconsin Historical Society, 2012). McCrea includes many illustrations of photographs of the house that came to light in 2002, 2005, and 2011. See also Kathryn Smith, *Frank Lloyd Wright's Taliesin and Taliesin West* (New York: Harry N. Abrams, 1997), 47–55. James F. O'Gorman places Taliesin in the history of American architecture in *Three American Architects*, 148–54.
55. McCrea, *Building Taliesin*, 175, writes that John Reese, editor of the *Dodgeville (WI) Chronicle*, visited Taliesin in December 1911 and described the house as a "bungalow."
56. Taliesin was published in "The Studio-Home of Frank Lloyd Wright," *Architectural Record* 33, no. 1 (January 1913): 45–54; and "Taliesin, the Home of Frank Lloyd Wright and a Study of the Owner," *Western Architect* 19, no. 2 (February 1913): 16–19, and plates with elevations, sections, a plan, and photographs.
57. Marcia G. Anderson, "Art for Life's Sake: The Handicraft Guild of Minneapolis," in *Minnesota 1900: Art and Life on the Upper Mississippi, 1890–1915*, ed. Michael Conforti (Newark: University of Delaware Press, 1994), 122–50. See also Marcia Gail Anderson, "The Handicraft Guild of Minneapolis: A Model of the Arts and Crafts Movement," in Denker, *Substance of Style*, 213–28.
58. On the leased locations of the Handicraft Guild and the construction of their building, see Anderson, "Art for Life's Sake," 128–30.
59. Illustrations of the Handicraft Guild Building appear in *Western Architect* 16, no. 1 (July 1910): n.p.
60. For example, see William C. Whitney's Elbert L. Carpenter House (1906), Minneapolis, which is derived from Bulfinch's first Harrison Gray Otis House (1795), Boston.
61. An addition to the secondary entrance has altered Whitney's original design.
62. Anderson, "Art for Life's Sake," 129.
63. On Mary Emma Roberts and an illustration of a fireplace in her house, see "Appendix I: Biographies of Prominent Members of the Handicraft Guild of Minneapolis," in Conforti, *Minnesota 1900*, 164–65. See also Sue Leaf, "A Tale of Two Siblings," *Minnesota History* 63, no. 6 (Summer 2013): 236–45.
64. "Edwin H. Hewitt House," National Register of Historic Places, NR 78001539, listed April 6, 1978, prepared by Charles W. Nelson and Susan Zeik. See also the entry for Edwin Hawley Hewitt, AIA Historical Directory of American Architects, updated by Nancy Hadley, August 2, 2010. Hewitt became a Fellow of the American Institute of Architects in 1916.
65. Conforti, "Appendix I: Biographies," in *Minnesota 1900*, 164.
66. On Batchelder and the Handicraft Guild of Minneapolis, see Anderson, "Art for Life's Sake," 130–33.
67. On the *Western Architect* and its coverage of architecture in the Midwest, see Brooks, *Prairie School*, 197–99.
68. On Purcell, Feick, and Elmslie, see Jennifer Komar Olivarez, "The Purcell-Cutts House: A Modern Home for the Twentieth and Twenty-First Centuries," in *Progressive Design and the Midwest: The Purcell-Cutts House and the Prairie School Collection at the Minneapolis Institute of Arts*, by Jennifer Komar Olivarez et al. (Minneapolis: Minneapolis Institute of Arts, 2000), esp. 23–26. See also David Gebhard, *Purcell and Elmslie: Prairie Progressive Architects*, ed. Patricia Gebhard (Salt Lake City: Gibbs Smith, 2006), 46–65; Brooks, *Prairie School*, 131.
69. Mark Hammons, "Purcell and Elmslie, Architects," in Conforti, *Minnesota 1900*, 244–47; Olivarez, "Purcell-Cutts House," 28–31; Gebhard, *Purcell and Elmslie*, 106–7; Brooks, *Prairie School*, 191–92.
70. The Powers House is illustrated with plates in "Statics and Dynamics of Architecture," *Western Architect* 19, no. 1 (January 1913): n.p.
71. Olivarez, "Purcell-Cutts House," esp. 32–63; Gebhard, *Purcell and Elmslie*, 111–15; Brooks, *Prairie School*, 212–19.
72. Quoted by Olivarez, "Purcell-Cutts House," 19.
73. Gebhard, *Purcell and Elmslie*, 133–39; Brooks, *Prairie School*, 296–301. See also "Woodbury County Court House, Sioux City, Iowa," *Western Architect* 30, no. 2 (February 1921): 13–20 and plates.
74. *Timeline* 2, no. 15 (Spring 2018): n.p. (the newsletter of the Sioux City Public Museum), accompanying the 2018 exhibition titled *Modernism's Messengers: The Art of Alfonso and Margaret Iannelli*.
75. William Gray Purcell and George G. Elmslie, "The American Renaissance?," *Craftsman* 21, no. 4 (January 1912): 435.
76. For a scholarly overview of Kimball's career, see David Lynn Batie, "Thomas Rogers Kimball (1890–1912): Nebraska Architect," *Nebraska History* 60 (1979): 321–56. See also Joan M. Fogarty, *Thomas Rogers Kimball: Nebraska Architect* (Omaha: n.p., 2019); and the biographical entry in Vosbeck, *Legacy of Leadership*, 52–53.
77. Batie, "Thomas Rogers Kimball," 334.
78. See Meister, *Arts and Crafts Architecture*, esp. 115–53.
79. In addition to Steele, Kimball asked Josiah Dow Sandham to join the practice. The firm

was reorganized as Kimball, Steele, and Sandham.

80. "Mary Rogers Kimball House," National Register of Historic Places, NR 96000765, listed July 19, 1996, prepared by Stacey C. Pilgrim. See also Fogarty, *Thomas Rogers Kimball,* 1–5, 117–18, especially for biographical information on Mary Rogers Kimball.
81. Meister, *Architecture and the Arts and Crafts Movement,* 36–39. Kimball also would have been familiar with Warren's well-publicized Troy (New York) Orphan Asylum (1891), a large building with crow-stepped gables (47–49).
82. Julius K. Hunter, *Westmoreland and Portland Places: The History and Architecture of America's Premier Private Streets, 1888–1988* (Columbia: University of Missouri Press, 1988); Charles C. Savage, *Architecture of the Private Streets of St. Louis: The Architects and the Houses They Designed* (Columbia: University of Missouri Press, 1988). See also "Portland and Westmoreland Places," National Register of Historic Places, NR 74002276, listed February 12, 1974, prepared by Stephen J. Raiche.
83. "Chas. A. Stix," obituary, *Jewish Voice,* St. Louis, September 8, 1916. In addition to the house for the Stixes, at 26 Portland Place, Mauran designed a Tudor Revival house at 10 Portland Place.
84. For example, see the *St. Louis Social Register, 1913,* vol. 27 (New York: Social Register Association, 1913). Mauran and his wife are also listed.
85. See the biographical entry for Mauran in Vosbeck, *Legacy of Leadership,* 49–51.
86. "Judge Louis R. Gates House," National Register of Historic Places, NR 80001477, listed December 1, 1980, prepared by Julie A. Wortman and Dale Nimz; "Hanover Heights Neighborhood Historic District," NR 90000776, listed May 17, 1990, prepared by Martha Hagedorn-Krass.
87. Doran L. Cart, "A Kansas City Architect: Clarence Erasmus Shepard," *Historic Kansas City Foundation Gazette* 11, no. 4 (July–August 1987): 4–5.
88. "St. John AME Church," National Register of Historic Places, NR 80002449, listed May 29, 1980, prepared by Robert Peters.
89. The contract was announced in *American Contractor* 43 (December 2, 1922): 56D. The Rev. W. C. Williams, minister of the church, represented the congregation.
90. Peters, "St. John AME Church."

CHAPTER 7. MOUNTAIN STATES AND RUSTIC LIVING

1. Anne Farrar Hyde, *An American Vision: Far Western Landscape and National Culture, 1820–1920* (New York: New York University Press, 1990).
2. Hyde, *American Vision,* 259.
3. "Pahaska Tepee," National Register of Historic Places, NR 73001938, listed March 20, 1973, prepared by Ned Frost. For an early description of the lodge, see *Ranch Life in the Buffalo Bill Country* (Chicago: Chicago, Burlington, and Quincy Railroad Company, [c. 1932]).
4. Joanita Monteith, "Pahaska Tepee: The Gem of the Rockies," *Points West: Quarterly Journal of the Buffalo Bill Historical Center* (Winter 1998): 18–20.
5. On vernacular mountain cabins, see Jon T. Kilpinen, "The Front-Gabled Log Cabin and the Role of the Great Plains in the Formation of the Mountain West's Built Landscape," *Great Plains Quarterly* 15, no. 1 (Winter 1995): 19–31.
6. "Anderson Lodge," National Register of Historic Places, NR 87001548, listed September 14, 1987, prepared by Judy A. Rose.
7. On Yellowstone National Park, see Hyde, *American Vision,* 245–68. On the paradoxes relating to its conservation and commodification through tourism, see Chris J. Magoc, *Yellowstone: The Creation and Selling of an American Landscape, 1870–1903* (Albuquerque: University of New Mexico Press, 1999).
8. Rudyard Kipling, *From Sea to Sea: Letters of Travel,* pt. 2 (1899; repr., New York: Doubleday, Page, 1914), 67.
9. Kipling, *From Sea to Sea,* 70.
10. Hyde, *American Vision,* 245–55. See also Karen Wildung Reinhart, "Old Faithful Inn: Centennial of a Beloved Landmark," *Yellowstone Science* 12, no. 2 (Spring 2004): 5–22.
11. On Robert C. Reamer, see Ruth Quinn, "Overcoming Obscurity: The Yellowstone Architecture of Robert C. Reamer," *Yellowstone Science* 12, no. 2 (Spring 2004): 23–40. See also David Leavengood, "A Sense of Shelter: Robert C. Reamer in Yellowstone National Park," *Pacific Historical Review* 54, no. 4 (November 1985): 495–513.
12. Old Faithful Inn was featured in "A Rustic Yellowstone Hostelry, Yellowstone National Park," *Western Architect* 3, no. 10 (October 1904): 4–6.
13. Christine Barnes, *Great Lodges of the National Parks* (Bend, OR: W. W. West, 2002), 14–25.
14. Quinn, "Overcoming Obscurity," 24, writes that while in Chicago, Reamer designed furniture.
15. Reinhart, "Old Faithful Inn," 11–12.
16. Reinhart, "Old Faithful Inn," 10.
17. Elizabeth Clair Flood, *Old-Time Dude Ranches Out West* (Salt Lake City: Gibbs Smith, 1995), esp. 8–15.
18. *Ranch Life,* 7, 15.
19. *Ranch Life,* 20, 21, 23. See also "Elephant Head Lodge," National Register of Historic Places, NR 03001107, listed October 30, 2003, prepared by Jeannie Cook and Joanita Monteith; "Elephant Head Lodge," *American Resorts,* May 1929, 21–23. The *American Resorts* article was shared with me by the co-owner of the lodge, Debbie Millard.
20. The permit was located by Cook and Monteith and cited in "Elephant Head Lodge."
21. "Elephant Head Lodge" (*American Resorts*), 21.
22. Cook and Monteith, "Elephant Head Lodge."
23. Thurston indicates her objectives in the description of the lodge in *Ranch Life* and in "Elephant Head Lodge" (*American Resorts*).
24. See the photo in Park County Archives, Cody, Wyoming, labeled "Harry & Josephine Goodman (Josie) Thurston & their grandchildren," cat. no. P01-41-01.
25. "Elephant Head Lodge" (*American Resorts*), 21.
26. "Lorraine Lodge," National Register of Historic Places, NR 84000858, listed January 18, 1984, prepared by Susan Becker and Kathryn Johnston.
27. Thomas J. Noel and Barbara S. Norgren, *Denver: The City Beautiful and Its Architects, 1893–1941* (Denver: Historic Denver, 1987), 123–24.
28. Quoted in Noel and Norgren, *Denver,* 123.
29. "Boettcher Mansion Architectural Drawings," Record Series 241, Document Center, Jefferson County, Golden, Colorado.
30. Reproductions of the settle benches and light fixtures have been installed at the mansion.
31. See biographical entries by Rutherford W. Witthus in Noel and Norgren, *Denver,* 199–200 (on William Ellsworth Fisher) and 198–99 (on Arthur Addison Fisher).
32. Witthus in Noel and Norgren, *Denver,* 199.
33. Noel and Norgren, *Denver,* 124.
34. For biographical information on Artus and Anne Van Briggle, see R. Laurie Simmons and Thomas H. Simmons, "Artus and Anne Van Briggle and Colorado College," in *A Colorado College Reader: Selected Writings on the History of Colorado College,* ed. Robert D. Loevy (Colorado Springs: Colorado College, 2013), 112–30.

35. "Van Briggle Pottery Company," National Register of Historic Places, NR 09000249, listed April 29, 2009, prepared by R. Laurie Simmons and Thomas H. Simmons.

36. *Exhibition of the Society of Arts and Crafts,* exh. cat. (Boston: Society of Arts and Crafts, 1907), in "Papers of the Society of Arts and Crafts, Boston," Archives of American Art, Smithsonian Institution, microfilm reel 320, frame 88.

37. Clara Anne McKenna, ed., *A Golden Legacy: Winfield Scott Stratton and the Myron Stratton Home, 1848–1998* (Colorado Springs: Myron Stratton Home, 1998).

38. Meister, "From Architecture to Occupational Therapy," 3–7. On Barton, see also Meister, *Arts and Crafts Architecture,* 16–18.

39. George Edward Barton, "Port Sunlight: A Model English Village," *Architectural Review* 6, no. 5 (May 1899): 62–66.

40. George Edward Barton, *An Analysis of the Conditions Influencing the Building of the Myron Stratton Home and Recommendations for Its Foundation and Development* (Colorado Springs: Myron Stratton Home, 1911). See also Clara Anne McKenna, "Winfield Scott Stratton: Prospector, Entrepreneur, Humanitarian," in McKenna, *Golden Legacy,* 9, 10.

41. Karl Ross, "The Foundation: Making the Dream a Reality," in McKenna, *Golden Legacy,* 13.

42. Meister, "From Architecture to Occupational Therapy," 5.

43. Maurice B. Biscoe practiced in the partnership of Warren, Smith, and Biscoe from 1900 until 1905 when he left Boston for Denver. See Meister, *Architecture and the Arts and Crafts Movement,* 103. The Boston firm of Andrews, Jaques, and Rantoul also received multiple commissions for projects in Denver and Colorado Springs, and two partners, Robert Day Andrews and Herbert Jaques, were members of the Society of Arts and Crafts.

44. "Norlin Quadrangle Historic District," National Register of Historic Places, NR 80000879, listed March 27, 1980, prepared by John D. Smith. See also Thomas J. Noel, *Buildings of Colorado* (New York: Oxford University Press, 1997), 177–78.

45. Klauder and Wise, *College Architecture in America,* 3. Wise, a Philadelphia architect, worked in his later years with Klauder.

46. Klauder and Wise, *College Architecture in America,* 4.

47. Klauder and Wise, *College Architecture in America,* 17.

48. The Liberal Arts Building is illustrated in Klauder and Wise, *College Architecture in America,* 47. See also Noel, *Buildings of Colorado,* 179. Wings were added later.

49. Klauder and Wise, *College Architecture in America,* 294.

CHAPTER 8. TEXAS AND THE SOUTHWEST

1. On the Rice campus, see Stephen Fox, *Rice University* (New York: Princeton Architectural Press, 2001); and James C. Morehead, Jr., *A Walking Tour of Rice University,* rev. ed. (Houston: Rice University Press, 1990).

2. Cram's work at Rice is discussed in the context of his career by Shand-Tucci, *Ralph Adams Cram,* 106–18.

3. Cram, *My Life in Architecture,* 124–25.

4. Cram, *My Life in Architecture,* 125.

5. Oliver, *Bertram Grosvenor Goodhue,* 106–8.

6. On Lovett Hall, the administration building, see Fox, *Rice University,* 28–37; and Morehead, *Walking Tour of Rice University,* 3–19. See also Franz Winkler, "The Administration Building of the Rice Institute, Houston, Texas," *Brickbuilder* 21, no. 12 (December 1912): 321–24; "Rice Institute," *Western Architect* 19, no. 2 (February 1913): 20–23.

7. Winkler, "Administration Building," 324, recognizes Richardson's example.

8. Fox, *Rice University,* 35.

9. Both Lassig and Dietsch are credited in "Rice Institute."

10. Fox, *Rice University,* 35.

11. Lloyd C. Engelbrecht and June-Marie F. Engelbrecht, *Henry C. Trost: Architect of the Southwest* (El Paso: El Paso Public Library Association, 1981), 39–47. See also Troy Ainsworth, "Henry C. Trost: Architect of 'Arid America,'" *Journal of Big Bend Studies* 21 (2009): 83; "Henry C. Trost House," National Register of Historic Places, NR 76002024, listed July 12, 1976, prepared by Joe R. Williams and Michael Yancey.

12. Engelbrecht and Engelbrecht, *Henry C. Trost,* 3–8.

13. The Chicago Architectural Sketch Club, renamed the Chicago Architectural Club, elected Trost to membership in November 1888; Engelbrecht and Engelbrecht, *Henry C. Trost,* 9, 9–16 (on Trost in Chicago).

14. The Trost House retains its original decoration and some furniture, preserved by later owners.

15. Mitchell and Halbach made the art glass for casement windows in the Tullius M. Wingo House (1907), El Paso, designed by Trost, as reported in the *El Paso Herald,* August 14, 1935, according to Jon Eckberg of the El Paso Historical Society.

16. Chris Wilson, *The Myth of Santa Fe: Creating a Modern Regional Tradition* (Albuquerque: University of New Mexico Press, 1997), 121–25, 236–37; Harry Moul and Linda Tigges, "The Santa Fe City Plan: A 'City Beautiful' and City Planning Document," *New Mexico Historical Review* 71, no. 2 (April 1996): 135–55; Nicholas C. Markovich, "Santa Fe Renaissance: City Planning and Stylistic Preservation, 1912," in *Pueblo Style and Regional Architecture,* ed. Nicholas C. Markovich, Wolfgang F. E. Preiser, and Fred G. Sturm (New York: Van Nostrand Reinhold, 1990), 197–212.

17. Corinne P. Sze, "The Harry Howard Dorman House, 707 Old Santa Fe Trail," *Bulletin of the Historic Santa Fe Foundation* 28, no. 1 (November 2001): 1–22. See also "Dorman Dies; Services Set Here Monday," *Santa Fe New Mexican,* October 30, 1960.

18. "The Ancient City and the New Santa Fe," *Albuquerque Morning Journal,* March 4, 1912, quoted by Markovich, "Santa Fe Renaissance," 197.

19. "Proceedings of the City Council," *Santa Fe New Mexican,* December 24, 1912. The final plan was signed by Dorman, Cutting, Morley, Sam Cartwright, James Seligman, and Marcelino Garcia. Special thanks to Kathleen Dull, librarian, New Mexico History Museum, for her assistance.

20. Wilson, *Myth of Santa Fe,* 120, 123–25.

21. Wilson, *Myth of Santa Fe,* 138–40.

22. Wilson, Moul and Tigges, Markovich, and Sze discuss these men as well as other Planning Board members. See esp. Sze, "Harry Howard Dorman House," 2–3, 7–8, 13–16.

23. Robert W. Larson and Carole B. Larson, *Ernest L. Blumenschein: The Life of an American Artist* (Norman: University of Oklahoma Press, 2013), 205–10; "Ernest L. Blumenschein House," National Register of Historic Places, NR 66000495, listed October 15, 1966, revised form prepared by Richard Greenwood, June 30, 1975.

24. On the Taos Society of Artists, see Larson and Larson, *Ernest L. Blumenschein, passim.* See also Arrell Morgan Gibson, *The Santa Fe and Taos Colonies: Age of the Muses, 1900–1942* (Norman: University of Oklahoma Press, 1983), 24–38, 149.

25. Quoted by Gibson, *Santa Fe and Taos Colonies,* 149.

26. Larson and Larson, *Ernest L. Blumenschein,* 210. See also James Moore, "Ernest Blumenschein's Long Journey with Star Road," *American Art* 9, no. 3 (Autumn 1995): 6–27.

27. Kate Wingert-Playdon, *John Gaw Meem at Acoma: The Restoration of San Esteban del Rey Mission* (Albuquerque: University of New Mexico Press, 2012).
28. The committee was incorporated in 1932 as the Society for the Preservation of New Mexico Mission Churches; Wingert-Playdon, *John Gaw Meem at Acoma,* 244.
29. Bainbridge Bunting, *John Gaw Meem: Southwestern Architect* (Albuquerque: University of New Mexico Press, 1983), 3–21.
30. Quoted in Wingert-Playdon, *John Gaw Meem at Acoma,* 95.
31. Wingert-Playdon, *John Gaw Meem at Acoma,* 90.
32. Gibson, *Santa Fe and Taos Colonies,* 163–75. The society was renamed the Spanish Colonial Arts Society.
33. Gibson, *Santa Fe and Taos Colonies,* 71.
34. Pedro J. [de] Lemos, "Marvelous Acoma and Its Craftsmen," *El Palacio* 24, nos. 13–14 (March 31–April 7, 1928): 234–44.
35. On Meem's ornament, see Anne Taylor, *Southwestern Ornamentation and Design: The Architecture of John Gaw Meem* (Santa Fe: Sunstone, 1989).
36. On Meem's work at the University of New Mexico, see Bunting, *John Gaw Meem,* 86–106.
37. Audra Bellmore, "The University of New Mexico's Zimmerman Library: A New Deal Landmark Articulates the Ideals of the PWA," *New Mexico Historical Review* 88, no. 2 (Spring 2013): 123–63.
38. Bellmore, "Zimmerman Library," 157, quotes Meem's statement from a paper he delivered at a banquet in May 1953.
39. Artisans are discussed by Bellmore, "Zimmerman Library," 143–47.
40. "Architectural Survey of Fuller Lodge Historic District," County of Los Alamos, New Mexico, March 1, 2013, prepared by Beverly Spears of Spears Architects; Bunting, *John Gaw Meem,* 40–41.
41. "Riordan Estate," National Register of Historic Places, NR 79000416, listed February 28, 1979, prepared by Thomas S. Rothweiler and Marjorie H. Wilson. See also Robert Winter, *Craftsman Style* (New York: Harry N. Abrams, 2004), 50–57.
42. Charles F. Whittlesey designed and built his family house (1902–3) in Albuquerque, now owned by the Albuquerque Press Club.
43. Barnes, *Great Lodges of the National Parks,* 100–109.
44. Winter, *Craftsman Style,* 56, adds that Harvey Ellis designed the United Crafts furniture during the period when he worked for Stickley.
45. The contributors to the design of Hopi House are identified by Fred Shaw, "The Genuine Genesis of Hopi House," *The Ol' Pioneer* 30, no. 2 (Spring 2019): 10–16 (magazine of the Grand Canyon Historical Society). Shaw establishes that Mary Colter was not the architect, and he supports his article with extensive references to newspapers and archival sources.
46. Shaw, "Genuine Genesis of Hopi House," 10. Shaw illustrates the perspective drawing and elevations, located in the Santa Fe Railway Collection of the Grand Canyon Museum Collection, National Park Service, Grand Canyon Village, Arizona.
47. On Colter's role at Hopi House, Shaw refutes what has been written in earlier publications and makes a convincing case for Colter's limited involvement. See Shaw, "Genuine Genesis of Hopi House," 13–15. On Colter's Arts and Crafts interests, see Linda C. Reeder, "Architect Mary E. J. Colter and the Arts and Crafts Movement," *Journal of the Southwest* 61, no. 3 (Autumn 2019): 613–39. On Hopi House, see Arnold Berke, *Mary Colter: Architect of the Southwest* (New York: Princeton Architectural Press, 2002), 64–70; and Virginia L. Grattan, *Mary Colter: Builder upon the Red Earth,* rev. ed. (Grand Canyon, AZ: Grand Canyon Natural History Association, 1992), 13–19.
48. "California Atchison, Topeka, and Santa Fe Railroad Station," National Register of Historic Places, NR 82002188, listed July 15, 1982, prepared by Judy Wright; David Gebhard and Robert Winter, *An Architectural Guidebook to Los Angeles,* rev. ed. (Salt Lake City: Gibbs Smith, 2003), 427.
49. On early examples of the Pueblo Revival, including buildings by Whittlesey, see David Gebhard, "The Myth and Power of Place: Hispanic Revivalism in the American Southwest," in Markovich, Preiser, and Sturm, *Pueblo Style and Regional Architecture,* 143–58.
50. Berke, *Mary Colter,* 52, writes that Minnie Harvey Huckel, a daughter of Fred Harvey, introduced the idea for the company's Indian Department and suggested appointing Herman Schweizer as its manager.
51. "Arizona Inn," National Register of Historic Places, NR 88000240, listed April 5, 1988, prepared by Jean H. Cox; Will Conroy, *Tucson's Arizona Inn: A History* (Tucson: n.p., 2013).
52. "Tucson Leaders of Today. M. H. Starkweather," *(Tucson) Arizona Daily Star,* April 8, 1948.
53. "The Arizona Inn," Historic American Landscapes Survey, HALS No. AZ-9, July 23, 2013, prepared by Gina Chorover, Jennifer Levstik, and Helen Erickson.
54. Gladding, McBean also supplied roof tile, noted in an ad placed by "J. Knox Corbett," *Tucson Daily Citizen,* December 18, 1930. The fountain now serves as a base for a sculpture by Anne Varick Lauder, *Orbi Fera* (1982).

CHAPTER 9. PIONEER SPIRIT IN THE PACIFIC NORTHWEST

1. On the organizations in the Pacific Northwest relating to the Arts and Crafts movement, see Lawrence Kreisman and Glenn Mason, *The Arts and Crafts Movement in the Pacific Northwest* (Portland, OR: Timber, 2007), 62–95.
2. Kreisman and Mason, *Arts and Crafts Movement,* 66, 80–81, 94–95.
3. "The Portland Architectural Club's First Exhibit," *Architect and Engineer* 11, no. 3 (January 1908): 51.
4. "Portland Architectural Club's First Exhibit," 51–53. See also Kreisman and Mason, *Arts and Crafts Movement,* 93–94.
5. On the Arts and Crafts Society of Portland, including the significant role of Julia Hoffman, see Kreisman and Mason, *Arts and Crafts Movement,* 66–75.
6. Kreisman and Mason, *Arts and Crafts Movement,* 18, 73.
7. Jeffrey Karl Ochsner, "Introduction: A Historical Overview of Architecture in Seattle," in *Shaping Seattle Architecture: A Historical Guide to the Architects,* 2nd ed., ed. Jeffrey Karl Ochsner (Seattle: University of Washington Press, 2014), 7–8. He writes that unlike Seattle, Portland and San Francisco were served as early as 1890 by architects trained at the École des Beaux-Arts. English revival styles remained popular in Seattle through the 1920s (13).
8. On the Stimsons' First Hill house, see Lawrence Kreisman, *The Stimson Legacy: Architecture in the Urban West* (Seattle: Willows, 1992), 57–76; and Henry C. Matthews, *Kirtland Cutter: Architect in the Land of Promise,* rev. ed. (Seattle: University of Washington Press, 2007), 141–47. The house is known today as the Stimson-Green Mansion and in 2001 became a property of the Washington Trust for Historic Preservation. On Cutter, see Matthews, *Kirtland Cutter;* Henry Matthews, "Kirtland Kelsey Cutter," in Ochsner, *Shaping Seattle Architecture,* 108–13. Cutter also is discussed throughout Kreisman and Mason, *Arts and Crafts Movement.*
9. Kreisman, *Stimson Legacy,* 60.
10. Kreisman, *Stimson Legacy,* 67, 73, 74.

11. Capitol Hill Tudor Revival houses are discussed and documented in "Harvard-Belmont Historic District," National Register of Historic Places, NR 82004237, listed May 13, 1982, prepared by the Office of Urban Conservation, Seattle.
12. Matthews, *Kirtland Cutter,* 196–97; "Harvard-Belmont Historic District," no. 4. Matthews, *Kirtland Cutter,* 196, writes that Karl Nuese, Cutter's chief designer, was responsible for the project.
13. See Thomas Veith, "Arthur L. Loveless," in Ochsner, *Shaping Seattle Architecture,* 180–85.
14. The John A. Porter House is illustrated by Veith, "Arthur L. Loveless," 182.
15. Arthur L. Loveless, "A Northwest Architecture. A Symposium . . . By Five Seattle Architects," *Town Crier* 28, no. 50 (December 16, 1933): 14.
16. An illustration of the original studio, captioned as "Office of Arthur L. Loveless," appeared in "Seattle Honor Awards, Washington State Chapter, A.I.A.," *American Architect* 133, no. 2538 (February 5, 1928): 188. The design was honored by the chapter in a category for "Mercantile Buildings."
17. The mixed-use Studio Building is now known as the Loveless Building. Plans, elevations, and illustrations appear in "Studio Building, Seattle, Washington," *American Architect* 143, no. 2620 (November 1933): 49–54. The project is credited to Arthur L. Loveless, architect; Lester P. Fey, associate; and O. E. Holmdahl, landscape architect.
18. Jess M. Giessel and Grant Hildebrand, "Andrew Willatsen," in Ochsner, *Shaping Seattle Architecture,* 204–9; Michael Houser, "Andrew P. Willatzen," Architect and Builder Biographies, Department of Archaeology and Historic Preservation, State of Washington, Olympia, April 2019. A native of Germany, Willatsen changed the spelling of his last name from Willatzen around 1918. See Giessel and Hildebrand, "Andrew Willatsen," 204.
19. Houser writes that Willatsen worked for Spencer and Powers and Pond and Pond.
20. On the Matzen House, see Giessel and Hildebrand, "Andrew Willatsen," 205. Kreisman and Mason, *Arts and Crafts Movement,* discuss the Matzen House (135–36), as well as Willatsen's involvement with designs for interiors and furnishings (217–19).
21. Grant Hildebrand, "Ellsworth Storey," in Ochsner, *Shaping Seattle Architecture,* 132–37; Kreisman and Mason, *Arts and Crafts Movement,* 133–34. The one extensive study of Storey and his architecture is Christine Carr, "The Seattle Houses of Ellsworth Storey: Frames and Patterns" (M.Arch. thesis, University of Washington, 1994).
22. Victor Steinbrueck, "Seattle's Storey Cottages," *Pacific Architect and Builder* 66 (June 1960): 22; Hildebrand, "Andrew Willatsen," 132.
23. Kreisman and Mason, *Arts and Crafts Movement,* 36–37; illustrated in Hildebrand, "Andrew Willatsen," 132–33.
24. Kreisman and Mason, *Arts and Crafts Movement,* 116; Hildebrand, "Andrew Willatsen," 134.
25. Steinbrueck, "Seattle's Storey Cottages," 21–24; "Ellsworth Storey Cottages Historic District," National Register of Historic Places, NR 76001891, listed July 6, 1976, prepared by Elisabeth Walton Potter; Carr, "Seattle Houses of Ellsworth Storey," fig. 1 (a front elevation drawing of a cottage) and 41, 50, 98, 137, 150.
26. Steinbrueck, "Seattle's Storey Cottages," 22, illustrates a cottage plan.
27. Steinbrueck, "Seattle's Storey Cottages," 24.
28. Steinbrueck, "Seattle's Storey Cottages," 24.
29. See Janet Ore, "Jud Yoho, 'The Bungalow Craftsman,' and the Development of Seattle Suburbs," *Perspectives in Vernacular Architecture* 6 (1997): 231–43; Erin Doherty, "Jud Yoho and the Craftsman Bungalow Company: Assessing the Value of the Common House" (M.Arch. thesis, University of Washington, 1997). See also Kreisman and Mason, *Arts and Crafts Movement,* 156–57, 159–65; Dennis Alan Andersen and Katheryn Hills Krafft, "Plan Books, Pattern Books, Periodicals," in Ochsner, *Shaping Seattle Architecture,* 98–99.
30. Ore, "Jud Yoho," 234–36.
31. On Paradise Inn, see Barnes, *Great Lodges of the National Parks,* 49–57; and "Paradise Inn," National Register of Historic Places, NR 87001336, listed May 28, 1987, prepared by Laura Soullière Harrison. Kreisman and Mason, *Arts and Crafts Movement,* 186–87, discuss it in the context of the Arts and Crafts movement.
32. Sarah Allaback, "Anything but Natural: The Rustic Furniture Movement and Mount Rainier National Park," *Columbia: The Magazine of Northwest History* 13, no. 3 (Fall 1999): 8–14.
33. Barnes, *Great Lodges of the National Parks,* 53.
34. Michael Shellenbarger, "Ellis F. Lawrence (1879–1946): A Brief Biography," in *Harmony in Diversity: The Architecture and Teaching of Ellis F. Lawrence,* ed. Shellenbarger (Eugene, OR: Museum of Art and the Historic Preservation Program, School of Architecture and the Allied Arts, University of Oregon, 1989), 8–24. On Lawrence as an Arts and Crafts architect, see Kimberly K. Lakin, "Ellis F. Lawrence: Residential Design," in Shellenbarger, *Harmony in Diversity,* 30–35. Kreisman and Mason, *Arts and Crafts Movement,* 21, 93–95, 149, 158, also associate him with the movement.
35. Meister, *Arts and Crafts Architecture,* 12–14.
36. Shellenbarger, "Ellis F. Lawrence," 12.
37. Shellenbarger, "Ellis F. Lawrence," 11.
38. Shellenbarger, "Ellis F. Lawrence," 14–15; Leland M. Roth, "Ellis F. Lawrence: The Architect and His Times," in Shellenbarger, *Harmony in Diversity,* 63.
39. The change of name between 1916 and 1917 is documented in the school's "Announcements," and in "The General Academic Catalogs," Special Collections and University Archives, University of Oregon, Eugene.
40. Meister, *Architecture and the Arts and Crafts Movement,* 84–101.
41. Lawrence's architectural history courses are listed in the school's "Announcement" and "The General Academic Catalogs" from 1914 and onward.
42. On the development of Irvington, a streetcar suburb of Portland, see "Irvington Historic District," National Register of Historic Places, NR 10000850, listed October 22, 2010, prepared by Kirk Ranzetta and Heather Scotten, assisted by Mary Piper and Jim Heuer.
43. Esther Kelly Watson, *Westminster Presbyterian Church, 1889–1979* (Portland, OR: Irwin Hodson, 1980), 25.
44. Watson, *Westminster Presbyterian Church,* 30–31; Kreisman and Mason, *Arts and Crafts Movement,* 79.
45. "Westminster Presbyterian Church," *American Architect* 114, no. 2221 (July 17, 1918): plate 17.
46. "Notable Examples of Architecture, Landscape Architecture and Sculpture in Portland, Oregon," *Architect and Engineer of California* 56, no. 3 (March 1919): 64–66.
47. "Notable Examples of Architecture," 65.
48. C. Howard Walker, "The Review of Recent Architectural Magazines," *Architectural Review,* n.s., 8 (o.s., 25), no. 6 (June 1919): 171.
49. On Walker's role as jury critic, see Brandt, *Craftsman and the Critic,* 167–77.
50. Lakin, "Ellis F. Lawrence," 25–42.
51. Shellenbarger, "Ellis F. Lawrence," 11; Lakin, "Ellis F. Lawrence," 32–35; Kreisman and Mason, *Arts and Crafts Movement,* 149–50.
52. Shellenbarger, "Ellis F. Lawrence," 11, writes that the Lawrence House "may be the earliest Arts and Crafts style house in Oregon."

53. "T. A. Livesley House," National Register of Historic Places, NR 90000684, listed April 26, 1990, prepared by Nahani A. Stricker. In 1988 Oregon acquired the house for use as the governor's mansion, and it was named Mahonia Hall.
54. Ann Brewster Clarke, *Wade Hampton Pipes: Arts and Crafts Architect in Portland, Oregon* (Portland, OR: Binford and Mort, 1986); Kreisman and Mason, *Arts and Crafts Movement,* 147–48, 214–15.
55. "Maurice Crumpacker House," National Register of Historic Places, NR 92001378, listed October 23, 1992, prepared by John M. Tess and Richard Ritz. See also Clarke, *Wade Hampton Pipes,* 20.
56. Clarke, *Wade Hampton Pipes,* 26, citing E. Kimbark MacColl, *The Growth of a City: Power and Politics in Portland, Oregon, 1915–1950* (Portland, OR: Georgian, 1979), 87.

CHAPTER 10. CALIFORNIA

1. On the Arts and Crafts movement in California, see Kenneth R. Trapp, ed., *The Arts and Crafts Movement in California: Living the Good Life,* exh. cat. (Oakland, CA: Abbeville, 1993). On California architects associated with the movement, see Robert Winter, ed., *Toward a Simpler Way of Life: The Arts and Crafts Architects of California* (Berkeley: University of California Press, 1997).
2. On Polk's early years, see Richard Longstreth, *On the Edge of the World: Four Architects in San Francisco at the Turn of the Century* (1983; repr., Berkeley: University of California Press, 1998), 51–56, 89–96.
3. Longstreth, *On the Edge of the World,* 92.
4. Leslie M. Freudenheim, *Building with Nature: Inspiration for the Arts and Crafts Home* (Salt Lake City: Gibbs Smith, 2005), 69–71. See also Longstreth, *On the Edge of the World,* 232–34.
5. Freudenheim, *Building with Nature,* 70–71. Exhibitions took place in January and May 1896. See also "San Francisco Guild of Arts and Crafts Poster" (1896), lithograph, by Arthur Mathews and Lucia Mathews, Oakland Museum of California, A94.107.
6. Meister, *Arts and Crafts Architecture,* 53.
7. Longstreth, *On the Edge of the World,* 117–24; Freudenheim, *Building with Nature,* 28–31. See also "Russian Hill/Vallejo Street Crest Historic District," National Register of Historic Places, NR 87002289, listed January 22, 1988, prepared by Anne Bloomfield.
8. On Coxhead's training, see Longstreth, *On the Edge of the World,* 41–51.
9. Freudenheim, *Building with Nature,* 69.
10. Longstreth, *On the Edge of the World,* 129–31; Freudenheim, *Building with Nature,* 83, 85–87.
11. "Julian Waybur House," National Register of Historic Places, NR 11000143, listed March 28, 2011, prepared by Johanna Street. See also Longstreth, *On the Edge of the World,* 394n26; Freudenheim, *Building with Nature,* 157.
12. On the Church of the New Jerusalem, now known as the Swedenborgian Church, see Freudenheim, *Building with Nature,* 33–68. See also "Swedenborgian Church," National Register of Historic Places, NR 04001154, listed August 18, 2004, prepared by Bridget Maley and Jody R. Stock.
13. Freudenheim, *Building with Nature,* 37.
14. Scholars have disagreed about whether A. C. Schweinfurth played a role as a designer of the church while working in Brown's office. Freudenheim makes a convincing case that he had little to do with the design, whereas Maybeck appears to have been actively involved; Freudenheim, *Building with Nature,* 53–61.
15. Discussed in Maley and Stock, "Swedenborgian Church." See also John Beach, "The Bay Area Tradition, 1890–1918," in *Bay Area Houses,* ed. Sally Woodbridge (Salt Lake City: Gibbs-Smith, 1988), 23–98.
16. Freudenheim, *Building with Nature,* 62–68.
17. Charles Keeler, "Municipal Art in American Cities: San Francisco," *The Craftsman* 8, no. 5 (August 1905): 592.
18. On Maybeck's early years, see Sally B. Woodbridge, *Bernard Maybeck: Visionary Architect* (New York: Abbeville, 1992), 15–27. On Maybeck and the Keeler House, see Freudenheim, *Building with Nature,* 89–100; Woodbridge, *Bernard Maybeck,* 30–32; and Longstreth, *On the Edge of the World,* 316–25.
19. A sleeping porch designed in this way seemed to be the first example in Berkeley. See Cheryl Robertson, "The Resort to the Rustic: Simple Living and the California Bungalow," in Trapp, *Arts and Crafts Movement in California,* 93, citing George Wharton James, "Charles Keeler: Scientist and Poet," *National Magazine* 35 (November 1911): 47. See also Woodbridge, *Bernard Maybeck,* 30, for an illustration of the house and open porch.
20. The term "living room library" was used by Keeler. See Freudenheim, *Building with Nature,* 95, quoting Keeler in a manuscript titled "Friends Bearing Torches" (p. 230), Bancroft Library, University of California, Berkeley.
21. Freudenheim, *Building with Nature,* 91, 93.
22. Charles Keeler, *The Simple Home* (San Francisco: Paul Elder, 1904).
23. Maybeck said Richardson's Trinity Church, Boston, was his favorite church in America; Woodbridge, *Bernard Maybeck,* 91.
24. Leland M. Roth, *Shingle Styles: Innovation and Tradition in American Architecture, 1874 to 1982* (New York: Norfleet, 1999), 140–43. See also Freudenheim, *Building with Nature,* 110–16; Longstreth, *On the Edge of the World,* 294–95.
25. Although obituaries for Schweinfurth and modern publications about him have stated that his birth year was 1864, Daniella Thompson of the Berkeley Architectural Heritage Association has determined that the architect was born in 1863. Documentation includes Schweinfurth's passport application of May 27, 1898, and the 1900 federal census. For a short biography of the architect, see Longstreth, *On the Edge of the World,* 56–60.
26. The Saratoga Foothill Club is discussed and illustrated in Victoria Kastner, *Julia Morgan: An Intimate Biography of the Trailblazing Architect* (San Francisco: Chronicle, 2021), 117–19; Mark Anthony Wilson, *Julia Morgan: Architect of Beauty,* rev. ed. (Layton, UT: Gibbs Smith, 2012), 42; and Sara Holmes Boutelle, *Julia Morgan, Architect* (New York: Abbeville, 1988), 122–23. See also "Saratoga Foothill Club," National Register of Historic Places, NR 05000069, listed February 27, 2005, prepared by Beth Wyman.
27. Longstreth, *On the Edge of the World,* 338–39.
28. On the First Church of Christ, Scientist, Berkeley, see Woodbridge, *Bernard Maybeck,* 89–98; Edward R. Bosley, *First Church of Christ, Scientist, Berkeley: Bernard Maybeck* (London: Phaidon, 1994); and William H. Jordy, *American Buildings and Their Architects: Progressive and Academic Ideals at the Turn of the Twentieth Century* (Garden City, NY: Doubleday, 1972), 275–313.
29. Woodbridge, *Bernard Maybeck,* 98.
30. On Maybeck identifying the influence of Viollet-le-Duc on his work, see Jordy, *American Buildings,* 280.
31. Woodbridge, *Bernard Maybeck,* 89.
32. Woodbridge, *Bernard Maybeck,* 89.
33. On Saint-Jean de Montmartre, see Richard Etlin, "Fin de Siècle," in *Architecture: The Critics' Choice,* ed. Dan Cruickshank (New York: Watson-Guptil, 2000), 216.
34. De Baudot was a disciple of Viollet-le-Duc, which is significant given that Maybeck also was keenly interested in him. Furthermore,

between 1897 and 1898, Maybeck returned to Paris and was living there when Saint-Jean de Montmartre was under construction.

35. This observation is made by Francis S. Onderdonk, *The Ferro-Concrete Style* (New York: Architectural Book Publishing, 1928), 134. He credits de Baudot with setting an example at Saint-Jean de Montmartre with its concrete tracery.
36. On the Spanish Revival in the Bay Area, see Longstreth, *On the Edge of the World,* 258–73, 289–91. See also Karen J. Weitze, "Utopian Place-Making: The Built Environment in Arts and Crafts California," in Trapp, *Arts and Crafts Movement in California,* 57–58.
37. Henry Merritt, "Old California Missions," *Architectural News,* November 1890, 7–9, and December 1890, 14–16.
38. Weitze, "Utopian Place-Making," 58; Longstreth, *On the Edge of the World,* 263–66.
39. Keeler, "Municipal Art," 592.
40. Keeler, "Municipal Art," 597.
41. Keeler, "Municipal Art," 597.
42. Beach, "Bay Area Tradition," 80–82; Longstreth, *On the Edge of the World,* 289–91.
43. "Mission Dolores, San Francisco," National Register of Historic Places, NR 72000251, listed March 16, 1972, prepared by Ralph A. Mead.
44. Claire Mowbray Golding and Wyatt Wade, "Why Pedro de Lemos Still Matters," *School Arts* 114 (April 2015): 27–31.
45. "Pedro de Lemos House," National Register of Historic Places, NR 80000863, listed January 10, 1980, prepared by Paula Boghosian and John Beach.
46. On the building of El Alisal, see Jane Apostol, *El Alisal: Where History Lingers* (Los Angeles: Historical Society of Southern California, 1994), 41–71; and Turbesé Lummis Fiske and Keith Lummis, *Charles F. Lummis: The Man and His West* (Norman: University of Oklahoma, 1975), 97–99. See also "Lummis House," National Register of Historic Places, NR 71000148, listed May 6, 1971, prepared by Allen W. Welts.
47. For an unvarnished biography of Lummis, see Mark Thompson, *American Character: The Curious Life of Charles Fletcher Lummis and the Rediscovery of the Southwest* (New York: Arcade, 2001).
48. Dudley C. Gordon, "Charles F. Lummis: Pioneer American Folklorist," *Western Folklore* 28, no. 3 (July 1969): 177.
49. Gordon, "Charles F. Lummis."
50. Gordon, "Charles F. Lummis," 180.
51. Apostol, *El Alisal,* 53.
52. Robert Winter, *The California Bungalow* (Los Angeles: Hennessey and Ingalls, 1980); Robertson, "Resort to the Rustic," 89–107. See also John Mack Faragher, "Bungalow and Ranch House: The Architectural Backwash of California," *Western Historical Quarterly* 32, no. 2 (Summer 2001): 149–73.
53. For example, Los Angeles architect Henry L. Wilson published a collection of bungalows in 1907 that went through multiple editions. See Henry L. Wilson, *The Bungalow Book,* 5th ed. (Chicago: Henry L. Wilson, 1910). See also Charles E. White, Jr., *The Bungalow Book* (New York: Macmillan, 1923).
54. Robert C. Spencer, Jr., "Building a House of Moderate Cost—A Bungalow Suggestion," *Architectural Record* 32, no. 1 (July 1912): 38.
55. On the Gamble House, see Edward R. Bosley, *Greene and Greene* (London: Phaidon, 2000), 115–26; Bosley, *Gamble House: Greene and Greene* (London, Phaidon, 1992); and Jordy, *American Buildings,* 217–45.
56. Jordy, *American Buildings,* 227.
57. Maureen Meister, "Two Arts and Crafts Houses: Paradigms in Pasadena and Boston," *Magazine Antiques* 172, no. 3 (September 2007): 117.
58. Meister, "Two Arts and Crafts Houses," 112–19.
59. Robert Winter, *Batchelder Tilemaker* (Los Angeles: Balcony, 1999).
60. Marie Frank, *Denman Ross and American Design Theory* (Hanover, NH: University Press of New England, 2011), esp. 225–28.
61. Ernest A. Batchelder, *The Principles of Design* (Chicago: Island Printer, 1904); Batchelder, *Design in Theory and Practice* (New York: Macmillan, 1910).
62. Winter, *Batchelder Tilemaker,* 32, 25, identifies Donaldson as the metalworker.
63. Karen J. Weitze, "Sumner P. Hunt," in Winter, *Toward a Simpler Way of Life,* 184; Weitze, "Arthur B. Benton," in Winter, *Toward a Simpler Way of Life,* 192.
64. Thomas S. Hines, *Irving Gill and the Architecture of Reform: A Study in Modernist Architectural Culture* (New York: Monacelli, 2000), 77. Gill was working at the time with William S. Hebbard in the San Diego partnership of Hebbard and Gill.
65. Joseph R. Knowland, "The Missions of California," *Architect and Engineer of California* 12, no. 3 (April 1908): 35.
66. Knowland, "Missions of California," 48.
67. Charles A. Sepulveda, "Hallucinations of the Spanish Imaginary and the Idealized Hotel California," *California History* 99, no. 3 (Fall 2022): 4, 7–8 (on the interpretation of the missions by the Landmarks Club). See also Phoebe S. Kropp, *California Vieja: Culture and Memory in a Modern American Place* (Berkeley: University of California, 2006), 47–102.
68. Sally Bullard Thornton, "Hazel Wood Waterman," in Winter, *Toward a Simpler Way of Life,* 221–23. See also Hines, *Irving Gill,* 78–79.
69. Thornton, "Hazel Wood Waterman," 221.
70. Christine Palmer, "The Old Adobe Buildings of Santa Barbara," *Noticias: Quarterly Magazine of the Santa Barbara Historical Society* 48, no. 1 (Spring 2002): 8–10. The house was built for José de la Guerra between 1818 and 1828. On Underhill, see David Gebhard, "Francis T. Underhill," in Winter, *Toward a Simpler Way of Life,* 103–10.
71. The role of Craig's widow, Mary McLaughlin Craig, in completing El Paseo appears to have been minimal; however, soon after losing her husband, she embarked on a career as an architectural designer. See Pamela Skewes-Cox, "Architecture and Society," in *Spanish Colonial Style: Santa Barbara and the Architecture of James Osborne Craig and Mary McLaughlin Craig,* by Skewes-Cox and Robert Sweeney (New York: Rizzoli, 2015), 228.
72. On El Paseo, see Robert Sweeney, "Architecture," in Skewes-Cox and Sweeney, *Spanish Colonial Style,* 70–90. See also "El Paseo and Casa de la Guerra," National Register of Historic Places, NR 77000346, listed February 2, 1977, prepared by John C. Woodward.
73. Harris Allen, "Street in Spain," *Pacific Coast Architect* 27, no. 3 (March 1925): 23–39. The article was extensively illustrated.
74. Sweeney, "Architecture," 86–89, provides illustrations that make a convincing comparison between a photograph taken in Cuernavaca, Mexico, published in 1915, and the De La Guerra Street entrance to El Paseo. He also makes a strong case that a convent in Pátzcuaro, Mexico, inspired Craig (89).
75. A small Japanese community lived nearby. See Sweeney, "Architecture," 88, citing Rebecca Wamsley, "A History of the Chinese in Santa Barbara," Manuscript Division, Department of Special Collections, University of California, Santa Barbara; Linda Bentz, "From Canton to Canon Perdido: Chinese Fishermen of Santa Barbara," *Noticias: Quarterly Magazine of the Santa Barbara Historical Society* 44, no. 3 (Autumn 1998): 77–99.

76. For a comprehensive study of Gill and his career, see Hines, *Irving Gill.*
77. Jordy identifies these Arts and Crafts interests in comparing Gill's Dodge House with the Greenes' Gamble House; Jordy, *American Buildings,* 247. See also Hines, *Irving Gill,* 74–75; Irving J. Gill, "The Home of the Future. The New Architecture of the West: Small Homes for a Great Country," *The Craftsman* 30, no. 2 (May 1916): 140–51, 220.
78. Hines, *Irving Gill,* 173–74.
79. On the life of Ellen Browning Scripps, see Molly McClain, *Ellen Browning Scripps: New Money and American Philanthropy* (Lincoln, NE: University of Nebraska, 2017). McClain discusses the building of the La Jolla Woman's Club (141).
80. The "tilt-slab" construction method was patented in 1908 by engineer Robert Aiken for the building of U.S. Army barracks in Panama. See Hines, *Irving Gill,* 124–25.
81. Oliver, *Bertram Grosvenor Goodhue,* 86–87. The project was for the pro-cathedral of La Santisima Trinidad, designed by Goodhue in 1905. It was published as Holy Trinity Church, by the firm of Cram, Goodhue, and Ferguson: *American Architect and Building News* 91, no. 1636 (May 4, 1907): n.p.
82. For a short biography of Hunt, see Stuart Cohen, *Frank L. Wright and the Architects of Steinway Hall: A Study in Collaboration* (Novato, CA: ORO, 2021), 250–63.
83. On Goodhue, see Meister, *Arts and Crafts Architecture,* 10. On Hunt, see Cohen, *Frank L. Wright,* 253.
84. Members of the newly founded Chicago Arts and Crafts Society are listed in "The Chicago Arts and Crafts Society, Formed at Hull-House," in *Catalogue of the Eleventh Annual Exhibition of the Chicago Architectural Club* (Chicago: Art Institute of Chicago, 1898), 119–21
85. Myron Hunt, "First Congregational Church, Riverside, Cal.," *American Architect* 105, no. 2005 (May 27, 1914): 267–68, 271. See also "First Congregational Church of Riverside," National Register of Historic Places, NR 97000297, listed April 3, 1997, prepared by Janet Tearnen and Lauren Weiss Bricker.
86. Hunt, "First Congregational Church," 271.
87. Dwight James Baum, "An Eastern Architect's Impressions of Recent Work in Southern California," *Architecture* 38, no. 1 (July 1918): 178–79.
88. Baum, "Eastern Architect's Impressions," 179.
89. Baum, "Eastern Architect's Impressions," 177.
90. Iris H. W. Engstrand, "Inspired by Mexico: Architect Bertram Goodhue Introduces Spanish Colonial Revival into Balboa Park," *Journal of San Diego History* 58, nos. 1 and 2 (Winter/Spring 2012): 57–70; Kropp, *California Vieja,* 103–56.
91. Oliver, *Bertram Grosvenor Goodhue,* 109–19.
92. After his first trip, Goodhue wrote and illustrated a short book, *Mexican Memories: The Record of a Slight Sojourn Below the Yellow Rio Grande* (New York: George M. Allen, 1892). After a return trip, he prepared plans for Sylvester Baxter's *Spanish-Colonial Architecture in Mexico* (Boston: J. B. Millet, 1901).
93. "California Quadrangle," NR 74000548, listed May 17, 1974, prepared by James A. Lester; Richard W. Amero, "The Making of the Panama-California Exposition, 1909–1915," *Journal of San Diego History* 36, no. 1 (Winter 1990): 1–47.
94. Amero, "Making of the Panama-California Exposition," 24, nn89 and 90, on the Piccirillis. In 1911 Theron H. Tracy founded Tracy Ornamental Brick and Tile Company, which was taken over by Tracy Brick and Art Stone. On Tracy, see William Ellsworth Smythe, *San Diego and Imperial Counties, California,* vol. 2 (Chicago: S.J. Clarke, 1913), 494–98. I thank David Marshall of Heritage Architecture and Planning, San Diego, preservation architects for the California Building, who told me that all sculpture and ornament is cast stone, not carved stone.
95. Marc Appleton, Stephen Gee, and Bret Parsons, *Paul R. Williams: Master Architects of Southern California, 1920–1940* (Santa Barbara: Tailwater, 2020), 15–51.
96. Karen E. Hudson, *Paul R. Williams, Architect: A Legacy of Style* (New York: Rizzoli, 1993), 50–51. See also Appleton, Gee, and Parsons, *Paul R. Williams,* 25.
97. Karen E. Hudson, *Paul R. Williams: Classic Hollywood Style* (New York: Rizzoli, 2021), 14–23, 42–49.
98. Appleton, Gee, and Parsons, *Paul R. Williams,* 54–55.
99. Patricia Gebhard, *George Washington Smith: Architect of the Spanish Colonial Revival* (Salt Lake City: Gibbs Smith, 2005); Hewitt, *Architect and the American Country House,* 207–21.
100. Robert Sweeney, *Casa del Herrero: The Romance of Spanish Colonial* (New York: Rizzoli, in association with the Casa del Herrero Foundation, 2009); Jean Smith Goodrich, "Casa del Herrero," *Noticias: Quarterly Magazine of the Santa Barbara Historical Society* 41, no. 2 (Summer 1995): 21–43; "Steedman Estate," National Register of Historic Places, NR 87000002, listed January 29, 1987, prepared by Alexandra C. Cole. See also Patricia Gebhard, *George Washington Smith,* 76–81; Hewitt, *Architect and the American Country House,* 212–18.
101. Sweeney, *Casa del Herrero,* 27, 159n12. The St. Louis house was built around 1910.
102. A. Lawrence Kocher, "The Country House: Are We Developing an American Style?," *Architectural Record* 60, no. 5 (November 1926): 390.
103. Sweeney, *Casa del Herrero,* 35–38.
104. Sweeney, *Casa del Herrero,* 39–42; Goodrich, "Casa del Herrero," 39.
105. Sweeney, *Casa del Herrero,* 76; Goodrich, "Casa del Herrero," 40.

CONCLUSION

1. "We Don't Want Mission Architecture for the Fair," *Architect and Engineer of California* 26, no. 1 (August 1911): 103.
2. "Exchange Building of Pacific Telephone and Telegraph Company, Chinatown, San Francisco, California," *Architect and Engineer of California* 26, no. 1 (August 1911): frontis. The building dates from 1909 and has been attributed to architect "M. Fisher" in "San Francisco Chinese American Historic Context Statement, Draft 1," San Francisco Planning Department, June 2021, p. D-38.
3. Don Hibbard, Glenn Mason, and Karen Weitze, *Hart Wood: Architectural Regionalism in Hawaii* (Honolulu: University of Hawaii Press, 2010).
4. "Sheldon Jackson School," National Register of Historic Places, NR 72000193, listed February 23, 1972, prepared by Alice E. Postell; "Sheldon Jackson School," National Historic Landmark, designated August 7, 2001, prepared by Janet C. Clemens et al.
5. Thomas S. Marvel, *Antonin Nechodoma, Architect, 1877–1928: The Prairie School in the Caribbean* (Gainesville: University of Florida Press, 1994).
6. "Castillo de Serralles," National Register of Historic Places, NR 800004494, listed November 3, 1980, prepared by Luis Muñoz Polanco. A group of Puerto Rican women also were involved with the Arts and Crafts movement, sending handmade lace to Boston for exhibition in 1907. See entries of the Puerto Rico Lace Industry, Ponce, in *Exhibition of the Society of Arts and Crafts, Copley Hall* (Boston: Society of Arts and Crafts, 1907), 82. The tea cloths were designed by Mrs. Zoilo Cintron and made by "women of the Island."

Index

Note: Page numbers in *italic* type indicate illustrations.

Illustration Credits

Provided by National Trust Images, © all rights reserved, photograph by Andrew Butler (**fig. 0.1**); provided by RIBA Collections, photograph by Martin Charles (**fig. 0.2**); provided by Trinity Church in the City of Boston, photograph by Anton Grassl (**fig. 1.1**); Moraine Farm Archive, The Trustees of Reservations, Archives and Research Center (**fig. 1.2**); H. Langford Warren and Edward Everett Hale, *Picturesque and Architectural New England* (Boston: D. H. Hurd, 1889) (**fig. 1.3**); photograph by David Feigenbaum (**figs. 1.4–1.20, 2.17, 3.9–3.13**); photograph by Peter Feigenbaum (**figs. 2.1–2.4, 2.7, 2.8**); "A Thatched Palace: An Estate at Pocantico Hills," *Architectural Record* 28, no. 5 (November 1910), provided by Boston Athenaeum (**fig. 2.5**); photograph by Corey William Schneider, New York Adventure Club (**fig. 2.6**); photograph by Amanda Falkowski, Roycroft Campus Corporation (**figs. 2.9, 2.10**); photograph by Anna Wager (**fig. 2.11**); photograph by Matthew Digati (**fig. 2.12**); provided by Frank Lloyd Wright's Martin House, photograph by Noah Kalina (**fig. 2.13**); provided by the Department of Rare Books, Special Collections, and Preservation, River Campus Libraries, University of Rochester (**fig. 2.14**); provided by Gustav Stickley House Foundation, photograph by David Rudd (**fig. 2.15**); photograph by Samuel D. Gruber (**fig. 2.16**); photograph by Eric Hado (**fig. 3.1**); provided by The Maggee Miggins Group at Compass Real Estate, photograph by Front Door Photography (**fig. 3.2**); provided by the Stickley Museum at Craftsman Farms, photograph by Jonathan Clancy (**fig. 3.3**); provided by John Toates Architecture and Design, photograph by Andrew Frasz (**fig. 3.4**); photograph by Smallbones, from Wikimedia Commons (**figs. 3.5, 3.7**); provided by the Athenaeum of Philadelphia (**fig. 3.6**); provided by Architectural Archives, Weitzman School of Design, University of Pennsylvania (**fig. 3.8**); photograph by Meg Rohtla, Bryn Athyn Cathedral Director (**fig. 3.14**); provided by the University of Pennsylvania (**fig. 3.15**); photograph by Kathy Kruger (**fig. 3.16**); photograph by Tarah Toker (**fig. 3.17**); photograph by Matthew Shuck (**fig. 3.18**); provided by the University of Pittsburgh, photograph by Tom Altany,

Pitt Photography (**fig. 3.19**); author's collection (**figs. 4.1, 5.2**); photograph by Warren LeMay, CC BY-SA 2.0, https://creativecommons.org/licenses/by-sa/2.0/, from FLICKR (**figs. 4.2, 5.4**); photograph by Kevin O'Toole, © all rights reserved (**fig. 4.3**); photograph by Carol Pyles, CC BY 2.0, https://creativecommons.org/licenses/by/2.0/, from FLICKR (**fig. 4.4**); provided by Atlanta Fine Homes, Sotheby's International Realty, photograph by Henry R. Hibbert (**fig. 4.5**); photograph by Jennifer Baughn, © all rights reserved (**fig. 4.6**); photograph by Samantha Moats/Bham Now, https://bhamnow.com/2019/08/13/11-birmingham-neighborhood-parks-to-visit-when-you-need-to-get-ooo-out-of-office/ (**fig. 4.7**); photograph by Raymond Moore (**fig. 4.8**); provided by the Historic New Orleans Collection, 1974.25.41.318 (**fig. 4.9**); photograph by James Caulfield for Glessner House (**fig. 5.1**); provided by Ragdale Foundation, photograph by Martha Machuca (**fig. 5.3**); photograph courtesy of the Dana-Thomas House Foundation, Doug Carr, photographer (**figs. 5.5, 5.6**); photograph by Jim Steinhart on TravelPhotoBase.com (**fig. 5.7**); photograph by Teemu008, CC BY-SA 2.0, https://creativecommons.org/licenses/by-sa/2.0/, from FLICKR (**fig. 5.8**); photograph by Randy von Liski (**fig. 5.9**); provided by Kenilworth Park District (**fig. 5.10**); photograph by Matthew Fujibayashi (**fig. 5.11**); photograph by Cole Camplese, CC BY 2.0, https://creativecommons.org/licenses/by/2.0/, from FLICKR (**fig. 5.12**); provided by Pewabic Pottery, photograph by Amanda Rogers (**fig. 6.1**); provided by Cranbrook House and Gardens, photograph by Eric Franchy (**figs. 6.2, 6.3**); photograph by P. D. Rearick, © Cranbrook Center for Collections and Research (**fig. 6.4**); photograph by John D. Buckwalter (**fig. 6.5**); Library of Congress, Prints and Photographs Division, photograph by Carol M. Highsmith (reproduction number, LC-DIG-highsm-60401) (**fig. 6.6**); photograph by J. Adrian Wylie, © 2018 (**fig. 6.7**); photograph by Bob Bohmer (**fig. 6.8**); photograph by fwbradha, all rights reserved, from FLICKR (**fig. 6.9**); "Two Houses by Robert Spencer Jr.," *Architectural Record* 19, no. 4 (April 1906), provided by Boston Athenaeum (**fig. 6.10**); photograph by Harry Carmichael (**fig. 6.11**); provided by the Governor's Office, State of Indiana, photograph by Marianne Molony (**fig. 6.12**); photograph by Michael Bridgeman (**fig. 6.13**); used by permission, Utah Historical Society (**fig. 6.14**); provided by Minnesota Historical Society (**fig. 6.15**); photograph by Keith Nelson (**fig. 6.16**); provided by David Heide Studio, photograph by Michael Crull (**fig. 6.17**); photograph by Charles Walbridge (**fig. 6.18**); photograph by Tom McLaughlin (**fig. 6.19**); photograph by Ammodramus, https://creativecommons.org/publicdomain/zero/1.0/, from Wikimedia Commons (**fig. 6.20**); provided by Missouri Historical Society, photograph by W. C. Persons (**fig. 6.21**); photograph by Rick McNees (**fig. 6.22**); photograph by Janice Goodlow (**fig. 6.23**); photograph by Acroterion, CC BY-SA 4.0, https://creativecommons.org/licenses/by-sa/4.0/, from Wikimedia Commons (**fig. 7.1**); National Park Service, photograph by Jim Peaco, from FLICKR (**figs. 7.2, 7.3**); provided by the Park County Archives (**fig. 7.4**); photograph by Jeffrey Beall, CC BY-SA 2.0, https://creativecommons.org/licenses/by-sa/2.0/, from FLICKR (**fig. 7.5**); photograph by Leonard J. Infranca, from FLICKR (**fig. 7.6**); provided by Myron Stratton Home, photograph by Brenda Gussin (**fig. 7.7**); University of Colorado, Boulder, from FLICKR (**fig. 7.8**); photograph by Thomas Noble (**fig. 8.1**); photograph by Bill Falk (**fig. 8.2**); photograph by Rogelio Rivero Cagigas, CC BY-SA 3.0, https://creativecommons.org/licenses/by-sa/3.0/, from Wikimedia Commons (**fig. 8.3**); provided by Palace of the Governors Photo Archives (New Mexico History Museum/Department of Cultural Affairs), negative number 023103 (**fig. 8.4**); photograph by Tim Stewart, from FLICKR (**fig. 8.5**); photograph by Jamie Zucek, from FLICKR (**fig. 8.6**); photograph by Sodapopsupercop, CC BY-SA 4.0, https://creativecommons.org/licenses/by-sa/4.0/, from Wikimedia Commons (**fig. 8.7**); provided by Arizona State Parks and Trails (**fig. 8.8**); Grand Canyon National Park 0545-0026, CC BY 2.0, https://creativecommons.org/licenses/by/2.0/, photograph by Michael Quinn, from FLICKR (**fig. 8.9**); provided by Arizona Inn (**fig. 8.10**); photograph by Nathan Tain, CC BY-SA 4.0, https://creativecommons.org/licenses/by-sa/4.0/, from Wikimedia Commons (**fig. 9.1**); photograph by Joe Mabel, CC BY-SA 4.0, https://creativecommons.org/licenses/by-sa/4.0/, from Wikimedia Commons (**fig. 9.2**); photograph by Jon Roanhaus (**fig. 9.3**); photograph by Joe Mabel, CC BY-SA 3.0, https://creativecommons.org/licenses/by-sa/3.0/, from Wikimedia Commons (**figs. 9.4, 9.5**); National Park Service, photograph by S. Redman, from FLICKR (**fig. 9.6**); from Historical Marker Database, photograph by Cosmos Mariner (**fig. 9.7**); photograph by Mark E. McClure, from FLICKR (**fig. 9.8**); provided by Oregon Department of Administrative Services, photograph by Linda L. Morrell (1957–2023), from FLICKR (**fig. 9.9**); photograph by Steve Morgan, CC BY-SA 3.0, https://creativecommons.org/licenses/by-sa/3.0/, from Wikimedia Commons (**fig. 9.10**); Library of Congress, Prints and Photographs Division, HABS, reproduction number HABS CA-2217 (**fig. 10.1**); photograph by Alvis E. Hendley (**fig. 10.2**); provided by San Francisco Swedenborgian Church, photograph by Dana Owens (**fig. 10.3**); provided by the Environmental Design Archives, University of California, Berkeley, from the Kenneth Cardwell Collection (**fig. 10.4**); photograph by Matthew X. Kiernan/New York Big Apple Images (**fig. 10.5**); photograph by Maria Guldner (**fig. 10.6**); photograph by Mike O'Brien (**fig. 10.7**); provided by California Office of Historic Preservation, photograph by Paula Boghosian (**fig. 10.8**); provided by City of Los Angeles Department of Recreation and Parks, photograph by JuanCarlos Chan (**fig. 10.9**); photograph by Cullen328, CC BY-SA 3.0, https://creativecommons.org/licenses/by-sa/3.0/, from Wikimedia Commons (**fig. 10.10**); provided by the Gamble House, © Alexander Vertikoff | Vertikoff Archive (**fig. 10.11**); photograph by Carl von Bibra, from Wikimedia Commons (**fig. 10.12**); photograph by Dan Soderberg (**fig. 10.13**); photograph by Lutfi Hussein, from FLICKR (**fig. 10.14**); provided by La Jolla Woman's Club, photograph by Erin Miller (**fig. 10.15**); from Historical Marker Database, photograph by Craig Baker (**fig. 10.16**); provided by the Museum of Us, photograph by Alexander Adams (**fig. 10.17**); photograph by Michael Locke, from FLICKR (**fig. 10.18**); photograph by Michelle Chiang (**fig. 10.19**); photograph by Winifredo Torres, CC BY-SA 2.0, https://creativecommons.org/licenses/by-sa/2.0/, from FLICKR (**fig. 11.1**).